THE VISUAL IDENTITY OF THE BOOK

Chandos Information Professional Series

THE VISUAL IDENTITY OF THE BOOK

FROM THE RENAISSANCE TO THE DIGITAL AGE

Christina Banou

Chandos Publishing is an imprint of Elsevier
50 Hampshire Street, 5th Floor, Cambridge, MA 02139, United States
125 London Wall, London EC2Y 5AS, United Kingdom

Copyright © 2025 Christina Banou. Published by Elsevier Ltd. All rights are reserved, including those for text and data mining, AI training, and similar technologies.

For accessibility purposes, images in electronic versions of this book are accompanied by alt text descriptions provided by Elsevier. For more information, see https://www.elsevier.com/about/accessibility.

Publisher's note: Elsevier takes a neutral position with respect to territorial disputes or jurisdictional claims in its published content, including in maps and institutional affiliations.

No part of this publication may be reproduced or transmitted in any form or by any means, electronic or mechanical, including photocopying, recording, or any information storage and retrieval system, without permission in writing from the publisher. Details on how to seek permission, further information about the Publisher's permissions policies and our arrangements with organizations such as the Copyright Clearance Center and the Copyright Licensing Agency, can be found at our website: www.elsevier.com/permissions.

This book and the individual contributions contained in it are protected under copyright by the Publisher (other than as may be noted herein).

Notices

Knowledge and best practice in this field are constantly changing. As new research and experience broaden our understanding, changes in research methods, professional practices, or medical treatment may become necessary.

Practitioners and researchers must always rely on their own experience and knowledge in evaluating and using any information, methods, compounds, or experiments described herein. In using such information or methods they should be mindful of their own safety and the safety of others, including parties for whom they have a professional responsibility.

To the fullest extent of the law, neither the Publisher nor the authors, contributors, or editors, assume any liability for any injury and/or damage to persons or property as a matter of products liability, negligence or otherwise, or from any use or operation of any methods, products, instructions, or ideas contained in the material herein.

ISBN: 978-0-443-19167-1

For information on all Chandos Publishing publications
visit our website at https://www.elsevier.com/books-and-journals

Publisher: Glyn Jones
Editorial Project Manager: Ashi Jain
Production Project Manager: Maria Bernard
Cover Designer: Matthew Limbert

Typeset by MPS Limited, Chennai, India

Dedication

To Petros and Mary, for their love and patience,
And For Time shared and Time to come

Contents

Foreword	ix
Preface and Acknowledgments	xi

1. Introduction: The visual identity of the book — 1

1.1 The visual evolution and information mechanisms of the book	1
1.2 Redefining the book: Quests and questions	4
1.3 Understanding the publishing industry: A history of innovations and challenges	10
1.4 The aesthetic capital of the publishing industry	13
1.5 The structure of the book	15

2. Through the page: The evolution of the visual identity — 21

2.1 The "horseless carriage" period: The early printed books	21
2.2 The visual order of the page	34
2.3 Information mechanisms of the book: Parts of the book	87
2.4 The democratization of taste and visual expectations	106
2.5 Establishing everyday book culture from Aldus Manutius to Allen Lane	112
2.6 Conclusions of the chapter: Defining the page, maturing the book	118

3. Converged aesthetics: Personalized publishing services — 121

3.1 Converged aesthetics: The evolution of "luxury" copies and deluxe editions	121
3.2 The systemization of deluxe and limited editions from the Renaissance to nowadays	133
3.3 The post-luxury copy: Customized copies, personalized publishing services and reader engagement	140
3.4 The uses of the book	154

4. Conclusions: Challenges and opportunities — 159

4.1 Reframing the world: Visual structures, strategies, and uses of the book	159
4.2 Constant challenges for the book and the publishing industry. Future research	176

Bibliography	183
Appendix 1: Illustrations	191
Appendix 2: List of illustrations	217
Index of names	219
Index of terms	221

Foreword

The survival of the book continues to surprise some, given the wealth of competition from other media. Yet there are many people for whom the printed book remains a haven, a welcome respite from our laptops and phones, offering immersive, long-form reading. The arrival of ebooks spurred publishers to make print books beautiful again, with high production and design values. Those who read in paperback may also purchase special hardback editions of their favorite books, at a premium price, to be displayed on BookTok or their home bookshelves. TV and film adaptations of novels lead to a rise in sales for the original texts.

Christina Banou's book gives the reader a fascinating view of the visual identity of the book and how it has developed over the centuries. Her stimulating analysis deconstructs the page to understand its set of verbal and visual clues. The reader is taken from running heads in the 17th century and the use of manicules by Laurence Sterne in *Tristram Shandy* to the mass-produced paperback we are familiar with today.

She encourages the reader to make links between the present and the past of the book. For example, the success of colored books recalls early printed books in which the reader was encouraged to add their own color to the woodcut borders. The sprayed edges on the special editions of bestselling works by fantasy authors take us back to the 17th century when fore edges were decorated with pictures.

The title page found in printed books was not there in manuscript books. It began as a blank page to protect the first page of the printed text and later was enriched with information to feed the expectations and taste of readers. When starting an ebook, often the reader is led to begin at the first page of the main text, rather than begin with the title pages. This brings us full circle back to the time of the manuscript book. Also in ebooks, there is a function so that you can see the passages highlighted by other readers. The habit of commenting in the margins of the page again goes back to the era of the manuscript book.

A key player in the story of the visual identity of the book is the Venetian printer Aldus Manutius. Christina Banou writes that Aldus Manutius transformed his business from a printing to a publishing activity with a variety of innovations. He was the first to curate a publishing list, he produced smaller, portable books, and he added his printer's mark of the anchor and the dolphin to his title pages. Manutius deserves to be celebrated and Roberto Calasso in *The Art of the Publisher* writes "If I told you in no uncertain terms that in my view a good publisher today ought simply to try to do what Manutius did in Venice a year before the start of the sixteenth century, you might think that I'm joking – but I'm not." (page 8)

Christina Banou offers inspiring thoughts about the book and its future. She believes that the transition made from the manuscript to the printed book sheds light on ongoing trends, such as the coexistence and convergence of media; it also offers insights into the future of the book and the introduction of new features. Further she argues that books will continue to thrive since their value and role rely not simply on their content but also on their visual identity and visual meanings.

Angus Phillips
Oxford International Centre for Publishing

Preface and Acknowledgments

A life in books

For those of us who were born at the beginning of the 1970s, the printed book was the known, familiar, beloved, and trusted medium for all the uses that the book and an information medium is supposed and expected to have (reading, access to information, communication, information sharing, collection, entertainment, and so on). Alongside the newspapers, the printed book framed and reframed the world in words and images, in text and pictures. Then, information and communication technologies and the advent of the Internet transformed the page and the book, altering the structure and features of the publishing industry. Other forms of the book, such as the ebook and the audio book, and new types of publications coexisted and coexist with the printed book which obviously has not disappeared. Undeniably, this transition took place rapidly from one technology to another, from one form of the book to others, from one traditional medium to complex opportunities and challenges. People nowadays in their 50s experienced this transition from the certainty of the printed material to the digital explosion. Visual communication and information changed too. Those changes are complex and significant in a lifetime. We were often exploring the new opportunities, while boundaries were widened.

It is true that the printed book was not abolished from the radio, the TV, the telephone, the cinema, and the Internet. Young people still read multipaged and multivolumed books alongside short forms, where they combine printed with electronic, digital, and audio books. Children explore the world via picture or silent books, via cloth books or activity books. At the beginning of each of my semester courses in Publishing, I ask my undergraduate students (born approximately 20 years ago), if they have paid for listening to music—no one did, and a few of them even seem to be surprised or wondering about it. To my next question, it turns out—hopefully—that they all have bought books in every form (mainly printed but also ebooks and chapters/papers in pdf as well as audio books). They also offer books as gifts; and they have been given books as gifts during their childhood and teens. They know that the Academic Library—through the consortium of academic libraries in Greece called HEALINK—provides access to large STM publishers. So I ask them to think during our courses and to discuss at the end of the semester the reasons that explain why the publishing companies not only have survived in our rapidly changing society but flourish.

When the last lines of this book were written in the Summer of 2024, the word "epilogue" reminded me that this research and work went back in time and was actually developed for years and decades. I realized that a strong interest for the evolution of the printed book as a material visual object and device, as well as for the much challenging period of the transition from the manuscript to the printed book has often been a cornerstone of my research. More specifically, the incunables and the hybrid books (hand illuminated copies), which I studied at the Marciana Library and at other libraries at the turn of the century, recalled the transitions and coexistence of different media nowadays. Even though, the story of my interest probably goes back in time at the books I had read for which I still remember every cover and dust jacket. Actually, the books in our personal library narrate and often deconstruct the story of our itineraries, desires, and quests. Like notebooks or personal storage devices, our books enlighten and recall our moments in time, constituting—like the pieces of a puzzle—the story of our life. A life in books.

As the book was about to complete, I was also reminded of the things I had not included or not investigated in depth as well as of issues, details, aspects, and ideas for new research. Actually, every end of the book presupposes the beginning of a new one for which I wish to find the time, my time in books.

Acknowledgments

Obviously, writing this book was no less than an adventure. I am grateful to Professor Angus Phillips, Oxford International Centre for Publishing Studies, Oxford Brookes University, for his collaboration and for writing the Foreword as well as for his excellent hospitality at the Oxford Brookes University in the Spring of 2024. I would like to cordially thank my Publisher Glyn Jones for his collaboration and encouragement. My students offer always another point of view and I thank them for this—I am never bored. I also have to thank the librarians and the Director of the Academic Library of the Ionian University, N. Anastasiou, and the Director of the Central Public Library of Corfu,

Christos Koulouridis, for their librarian support. The Steve Hare's Penguin Collection of almost 9000 books at the Library of the Oxford Brookes University was more than a surprise to me; I have to thank Professor Jane Potter, Oxford Brookes University, for indicating this and Mrs. Annabel Valentine, Archivist at the Library, for guiding me. I have dedicated this book to my family, and I also thank my husband and daughter for their patience since my life in books means a home and time in books.

Christina Banou

CHAPTER

1

Introduction: The visual identity of the book

1.1 The visual evolution and information mechanisms of the book

A literary civilization can be recognized by the way its books are presented.
Roberto Calasso (2015: 80).

The history of the book and of the publishing industry is a history of challenges, initiatives, surprises, collaborations and innovations, as well as of needs, expectations, quests, and desires. It is also a history not only and not always of discoveries but often of rediscovering, reconsidering, redeveloping, reusing, reshaping, reengaging, and reimagining (Banou, 2017). "Publishers have long been on the frontlines of change. They pioneered the first industrial technology, the printing press, the crucible of standardized mass production that defines the modern condition" (Phillips and Bhaskar, 2019: 2). These frontlines of change can be mostly observed in our hybrid era in which challenges and opportunities are many and complex due to a number of reasons that we will explore; in that framework, the printed coexists and is combined with other forms of the book.

This book will try to investigate the gradual and often complex evolution of the visual identity of the book since the invention of printing so as to understand and interpret diachronic and current issues of the publishing industry as well as to explore publishing strategies and policies. Taking as starting point that the evolution and history of the book is at the same time the history and evolution of the publishing industry, we will focus on the role of the publisher in our attempt to define the visual identity of the book; we will also consider parameters such as the kind of text, the reading audience, the printing and illustration techniques, the

The Visual Identity of the Book
DOI: https://doi.org/10.1016/B978-0-443-19167-1.00001-2
Copyright © 2025 Christina Banou. Published by Elsevier Ltd. All rights reserved, including those for text and data mining, AI training, and similar technologies.

1

book market, the art of the era. The transition from the manuscript to the printed book, the creation of the visual order of the page and of the information mechanisms of the book, the combination of tradition with innovation, enlighten issues and trends for the uses of the book, for the establishment of an everyday book culture, as well as for readers' needs and visual expectations.

In that context, the printed book is investigated as a visual–information device that can be at the same time a memory device, a notebook, an object of desire and a personal device. Additionally, customized copies and personalized publishing services during the Renaissance shed light to hybrid forms of the book and to issues of taste, power, communication whereas they enlighten the book as a symbol. We will also discuss the impact of technology, of printing and illustration techniques, of customer and collection behavior, of promotion methods, publishing strategies and policies as well as of changes in the publishing value chain. Thus, we will focus on the typology and the materiality of the book through the centuries, the construction and "deconstruction" of the page, consumption issues and the reception of the text, discussing the aesthetic capital of the book in a broader framework of expectations, needs, strategies formed in specific social, cultural, economic conditions.

This book goes back to the invention of printing by Gutenberg in the middle of the 15th century as to approach the visual evolution of the printed book. The book and the page, as established and known for centuries, were gradually matured and developed during the first centuries of printing constituting an indispensable part of our civilization. It is thus noteworthy to describe and recognize the impact of the manuscript book on the printed one as well as the gradual and challenging evolution of the typology of the printed book as a visual medium and information tool. It is also exciting to highlight on the one hand the relationship and convergence between the old and the new forms of the book and, on the other, the ways by which the first publishers/printers exploited and explored the new opportunities in complex environments. During the first centuries of printing, hybrid (hand-illustrated and decorated) books—as discussed in the third chapter—enlighten not only the coexistence and convergence of different media but also issues of taste and prestige, the uses of the book and the development of the publishing value chain. Apart from the publisher, the role of other stakeholders, such as the editor, bookseller, corrector, artist, cutter, miniaturist, binder, type designer, was under development.

In that framework, the printed book was gradually gaining its visual autonomy from the manuscript precedent in terms of continuing and innovating, of exploring and exploiting both the used and the new. Undoubtedly, this hybrid period of transition, coexistence, collaborations, convergence, innovations, experimentation, conflicts, and discussions reminds much of our period of rapid and significant changes, of convergence of media, of new technologies, and "new" forms of the book. Thus, in this book we will go back in time so as to explore and analyze issues and trends that not only developed the visual identity of the book but at the same time established cultures of the book; in this wy, we can interpret current issues. These cultures of the book are still recognizable maintaining till today a certainty of the book which—although under reconstruction and constant redevelopments—is the bedrock of communication as well as of the industry. It is interesting to look how these certainties and issues—based on psychological, technological, cultural, historic, and social features—still define book publishing and the book per se.

The term "visual identity of the book" will be used; decades ago, probably we would have used the term "typographic identity." But new information and communication technologies have offered to us other forms of the book defining a hybrid era of new trends, concepts and challenges which bring about significant changes in all the publishing chain. In that context, convergence of media is one of the main features. The printed book coexists with the ebook, the audio book, the digital publication, and other forms of the book as described by Thompson (2021: 68–102) while new publishing and business models provide new opportunities (Phillips, 2014). It is though significant to recognize that the printed book coexists with other forms of the book in accordance, among other parameters, on the kind of text and the audience. Moreover, specific kind of books, such as coloring books will be highlighted. Additionally, limited—deluxe—collectable editions are still produced, demanded, offered, promoted, offering thus another point of view for the publishing activity. Furthermore, personalized publishing services and customized copies will also be investigated from the Renaissance to nowadays discussing as well the impact of new information technologies and new publishing models. The role of social media and of the upgraded role of the reader will be looked at. Obviously, in that "new publishing world," the publishing value chain is constantly altered, widened, and enriched.

It is though more than interesting that in an era of open access, of new business and publishing models (such as crowdfunding and self-publishing), the book publishing industry and the publishing companies flourish. This can be attributed on the dipole: on the one hand, publishers invest on what they have always invested, thus on authors and good texts/content, on innovation, on the recognizable visual identity, on the added value that their services give to the content; on the other hand, they invest on new services that go beyond the book per se and focus on their relationship with the readers, on recommendation and information sharing, as well as on new promotion and marketing strategies in which reader engagement may take a central role. Clark and

Phillips have stated that: "In a world of abundance, the publishers offer a vital service in selecting authors and developing their content to meet readers' needs. They manage the author's brands and focus readers on the books they have selected. That service is worth paying for when time is scarce. To attempt another definition: the publishing process may be described as managing the scarcity of good authors and content to drive profitability" (Clark and Phillips, 2014: 21).

During the last years, the upgraded role of the reader and of the reading communities constitutes a significant parameter; in this book reader participation and engagement will be enlightened since the invention of printing so as to discuss not only their history and evolution but also their features and potential strategies in regard to the visual identity. In that framework, reader creativity will be introduced in this book as an aspect of the book industry and as a publishing strategy nowadays. We have to bear in mind that one of the main attempts of the publishing companies nowadays is to communicate directly with their reading audience building a trust relationship with their readers who are no longer just customers or readers but also members of a community who can communicate, intervene, review, recommend, give feedback, participate, and interact. Additionally, the upgraded role of online reading communities redevelops publishing policies and promotion strategies, so we will look at their impact on the visual identity of the book. The development of an everyday book culture is also discussed in this book. Thus the printed book will be investigated as a visual, viable, material object, as a commodity, a personal device, an information and communication medium, a personal-domestic object, from the Renaissance to nowadays; this visual identity nowadays goes beyond the physical appearance of the book due to "new," other forms of the book which are intangible.

1.2 Redefining the book: Quests and questions

Redefining the book as known for centuries is one of the main features nowadays. In that context, questions are raised on the nature, function, typology and use of the book. In regard to the nature of the printed book, we all think that we know the answer. The printed book has been a certainty that defined our civilization as an information medium and a visual object. These certainties were though redefined during the last decades due to new information technologies, the internet, the social media, other forms of the book, communication networks that brought about changes in the nature of the book and in the industry. These structural changes have established a new order, culture, reality, everyday life, and concept of the world in which access to information, convergence of media, communication prevail.

From this point of view, the study of the invention of printing and of the gradual development of the printed book till Renaissance can enlighten all types of transitions and can also explain our changing and challenging era. Thus, the study of the development of the visual identity of the book will be used in this book in order to discuss current trends and issues as well as to introduce strategies and to support theories. Obviously, this is a privileged point of view; the transition from the manuscript to the printed book has much in common with the coexistence of the printed book with the other forms of the book nowadays. Furthermore, we will point out to innovations that developed and defined the typology and visual identity of the book, such as the introduction of small-sized editions of Greek and Latin classics by Aldus Manutius in Venice at the beginning of the 16th century. From the friendly, convenient, accessible "libri portatiles" by Aldus Manutius to the Penguins, we can observe a revolution that shaped attitudes, strategies, models, taste, establishing thus communication—reading—consumption—reception aspects.

Undoubtedly, the printed book in Gutenberg's time was a new, innovative medium the typology of which was gradually developed; various and often complex opportunities were discovered and explored by the first printers-publishers. In this way, tradition was formed and the visual identity of the book was establishing and evolving according to the technological challenges, techniques, strategies, taste, needs, expectations of the readers. Financial, cultural, social, educational, scientific, religious conditions had and have always an impact on the publishing activity. The much-discussed "printing revolution," which Eisenstein introduced (1983), seems, from this point of view, to be a permanent revolution (Banou, 2017) as constant changes in the publishing industry take place and redefine the publishing value chain. Works such as the ones by Johns (1998), Barbier (2001), McKitterick (2005), Darnton (2009), Richardson (1999), Chartier (1994, 2014), Smyth (2024), Braida (1999), Levarie (1995), Smith (2000a) enlighten the transition from the manuscript precedent to the printed book and the creations of print culture. In the second chapter of this book, bibliography is provided for the impact of printing, for the transition from the manuscript to the printed book and for the development of the printed book, thus we will not focus on it here.

Undeniably, the book is constantly redefined and redeveloped. Nowadays, the boundaries of the book have been extended and widened due to the parameters named above. In that context, the older definitions of the book seem not to apply any more, failing to outline and express the nature, function and features of the book as both content

6   1. Introduction: The visual identity of the book

and object. Phillips and Kovac (2022) have discussed this point in their work "Is this a book?" considering the ongoing aspects and trends.

The book is defined by UNESCO (1964) as "a non-periodical printed publication of at least 49 pages, exclusive of the cover pages, published in the country and made available to the public."[1] This definition was given in 1964 and obviously does not serve any more the nature and function of the book. Questions are set such as: A book of 46 pages is not a book? What about children's books or silent books or short stories or small books? A book is only printed? What about ebooks or audio books? Coloring books are books? In which ways limited editions reach the reading audience? In Britannica (2014) we read that: "no strict definition satisfactorily covers the variety of publications so identified."[2] The cover is also taken as granted according to the above definition. The first printed books, the incunables, did not have dust jackets and covers; they did not even have title-pages during the first decades of printing and they began with the first page of the text as in the manuscript period. The evolution of the title page from the first decades after the invention of printing (Smith, 2000a; Baldacchini, 2009) brought about significant changes not only in the visual identity of the book but also in its promotion, advertisement, information sharing, copyright declaring, introduction to the text, as we will discuss in the second chapter.

It is though obvious that we are discussing what a book is according to definitions that are mainly based on its typology, nature, and function. Thus, the study of the book as visual object and the evolution of its visual identity since the Renaissance can shed light on the nature, structure, meaning, function, ideology, typology of the book explaining issues of production, design, promotion, marketing, dissemination, reception of text, success of the book and the publishing industry as part of the creative–cultural industries. These may lead to the interpretation and understanding of changes and current challenges.

The book is a mass information medium, the first mass information medium in history. The invention of printing by Gutenberg has been called "printing revolution" by Elizabeth Eisenstein (1983), a term on which thereafter researchers and historians of the book argued. The printed book since its origins revolutionized learning, teaching, knowledge dissemination, communication and information sharing, leading thus to social, economic, educational, scientific and cultural changes. It disseminated knowledge and information in a massive, rapid

---

1   UNESCO (1964), Recommendation concerning the International Standardization of Statistics Relating to Book Production and Periodicals, available at

2   "Book," in Britannica, available online at https://www.britannica.com/topic/book-publication, date of last access 16/3/2023

(in comparison to the manuscript book) and effective manner. The nature and function of the printed book led to its rapid dissemination and to the mass production of books (Febvre-Martin, 1990; Chartier, 2014; Barbier, 2001; Braida, 1999; Martin, 1995: 182−282). As discussed (Banou, 2017), the Gutenberg revolution is still a continuing revolution enriched with new media and widened with new options, strategies and theories. New information technologies have brought about significant changes and trends; it must though be pointed out that these issues and features derive from the past of the publishing industry and have the same diachronic aims: access to knowledge and information, communication, knowledge dissemination, information sharing, collection, convenient reading, friendly books, and aesthetic pleasure. These values and aims form the core of the book publishing activity and industry.

From this point of view, the book had and has to be friendly, accessible, portable, affordable, convenient, nice, and desirable. In all its forms, it is an adaptable, constantly revolutionizing medium that takes into consideration the needs, expectations, desires of the readers-users-customers-members. Its visual identity is part of the publishing policies and strategies of the publishers that aspire to create a recognizable visual−artistic−aesthetic typology. Additionally, the book is a knowledge dissemination medium that transmits knowledge, provides access to information and introduces new ways of communication and dialogue, thus new ways of thinking, reading and writing (Baron, 2009). As a communication medium, the printed book helped people to communicate, discuss, exhibit, solve, share, recommend, study, search, compare, argue, agree and disagree, exchange, experiment; it was the first mass medium of what we currently call "recommendation technologies." Moreover, the printed book had been since its beginning a medium for recognition for authors (Richardson, 1999: 77−104) and all stakeholders such as publishers-printers, editors, illustrators and translators. After the invention of printing, for example, authors discovered that the new form of the book helped them to be recognizable, to establish their fame, to communicate and share ideas, to further collaborate. In that context, the study of the development of the visual identity of the book can provide a framework for understanding and interpreting the publishing value chain, as well as for introducing policies and strategies, and for further exploring and exploiting new opportunities.

Furthermore, the book has been, since its invention, the best advertisement of itself. In an era -in which promotion methods were a few (without the Press and without adequate bookstores which were reduced only to the big cities and towns) and the "word of mouth" was the protagonist- the main promotion method was the book itself as both content and object. The design of the book, the visual order of the page, the development of the parts of the book, the introductions and epilogues, the illustration and decoration, the quality of paper, the printing types were among the features that promoted the new product. The publisher, editor, author could also advertise and recommend to users-readers other books as well as to introduce authors, works, ideas, theories.

In that framework, the printed book led to the democratization of knowledge and of taste; this is a starting point for our research. The information needs went hand to hand with the aesthetic needs even if the latter were not always and obviously declared and understood. The printed book as a material, visual object could be at the same time a (potential) work of art. Thus, it has been a highly desirable object, whether collectable or of everyday use. The printed book is a visual, viable and valuable product of high importance, being part of our culture that expresses the civilization in which it was born, created, produced, distributed, promoted. The book is a mirror of its age and at the same time an "agent of change."

The book has always existed as content and object; Bhaskar (2013) uses the term "content machine" in his work for a theory in publishing. Nowadays, that books may be intangible, the term "visual identity" and not "materiality" is better to be used. The book may be a personal or memory device constituting an extraordinary and authentic diary of our life. It is certainly a symbol of taste, power, fame, prestige, that demonstrates values, taste, social class, power. Hand-illustrated printed books during the incunable period and the first decades of the 16th century, often printed on a better-quality paper or on vellum, exhibit the complex uses of the book and may be considered the precedents of customized copies and personalized publishing services. And definitely, the book is always a commercial product and the publishing industry is part of the creative industries.

Nowadays, the book is redefined and reinvented (Phillips and Kovac, 2022; Phillips and Bhaskar, 2019; Thompson, 2021; Smyth, 2024; Banou, 2017), whereas many competitive to the book media redefine the reading experiences and user-customer behaviors. Publishers have often a privileged point of view. New opportunities and challenges emerge whereas social media redevelop communication, reading and writing, storytelling, information sharing. Convergence of media further extends the boundaries of the book. Communities of readers, the rise of self-publishing, issues of discoverability and visibility, new promotion and marketing methods have also to be studied. For example, discoverability is of high concern in the publishing industry forming one of its values and priorities (Phillips, 2014). Furthermore, as it will be argued in this book, discoverability is highly interrelated with the information seeking behavior of the reading audience and with promotion and marketing issues. Discoverability takes a key role in deciding the strategies. In that context, the book is a hybrid converged medium that connects and combines the past and the present, the printed and the virtual, the traditional and innovative, bringing about "new" points of view and publishing strategies. The first printers/publishers adopted new methods for developing their products, for satisfying the needs and expectations of the readers, for improving their working conditions, for promoting their books. They were adaptable, ready to adopt and use the new techniques and technologies for the production, marketing, dissemination, sales of the book as well as for communication and information. The publishing industry is actually an industry of surprises and discoveries.

In that industry, the evolution and development of the visual identity of the book had been essential. Chartier (2014: 5) writes for the "print culture as a culture of the image" recognizing that "a printed image has characteristics that distinguish it from all others. It is to be viewed close to, not at a distance; it is manipulable, easily cut out, pasted up, or carried on the person; it is always connected with the written word, sharing space on the printed page or located in the same book or tract...the image was often a proposal or a protocol for reading, suggesting to the reader a correct comprehension and a proper meaning of the text."

Nowadays, other forms of the book, convergence of media and interactivity enrich the visual identity of the book. Furthermore, we have to bear in mind that new production, design, distribution and promotion methods alter nature of the book. As Howard (2009) argues, the technologies and techniques define the nature of the book in each era. New media and old media, tradition and innovation, printed and virtual set the framework for our approach. In that context, the role of publishers will be investigated. "Publishers may control every aspect of a physical book's design but, as content providers for electronic distribution, their influence over the appearance of an electronic book and how readers interact with it may be limited by the devices and platforms on which they publish. The design of both the material book and the virtual book therefore need to be considered, because design for publishing involves the creation of both engaging individual artefacts and complex design systems" (Luna, 2019: 311).

Nowadays, the book (in all its forms) and the publishing industry are in a constant turning point that create a multitask framework in which questions are raised such as "Why and how does the book thrive?," "How the book has been transformed?," "What does 'book' mean?," "Which is the future of the publisher?," "Which is the future of the book?," "Will we have printed books?" "How will we read?" etc. But this is not the first time that questions like the above are set. Each time that the technology of the book changed, much discussion was done on the book and the publishing chain whereas fears, evaluations, anxieties, eschatological theories often prevailed. Actually, the evolution of the

10 1. Introduction: The visual identity of the book

book is full of transformations, anxieties and coexistences. As discussed in the second chapter, convergence of media is a diachronic and constant feature of the book and of the publishing industry. What we have also "learnt" is that publishers always thrive whatever the "danger." They always found the way not just to survive but to flourish as they kept and keep on innovating and exploiting the new opportunities for reinventing the book and satisfying the audience's needs and expectations which at the same time they redevelop. This goes back to Gutenberg's time. The development of the page and of the book during the first centuries of printing and the transition from the manuscript to the printed book can provide the framework for interpreting, explaining, and exploiting current changes, challenges, and trends.

1.3 Understanding the publishing industry: A history of innovations and challenges

Trends and features of the publishing industry at the end of the 20th century and the first decades of the 21st century have been studied in a number of works such as Phillips (2014, 2015), Phillips and Bhaskar (2019), Clark and Phillips (2019), Thompson (2010, 2021), Greco et al. (2007), Greco et al. (2013), Striphas (2009), Smyth (2024), Squires (2007), Borsuk (2018), and Baverstock (1993, 2004). At the introduction to the *Oxford Handbook of Publishing*, Phillips and Bhaskar (2019: 4) write: "Publishing is a plural, variegated entity, not just an industry but a set of industries and industries within industries." The publishing industry, one of the creative industries, has managed not just to survive but to explore and exploit the opportunities provided by new information and communication technologies.

By investigating the evolution, function and history of the visual identity of the book, we enlighten the publishing policies and strategies, the role of the stakeholders in the publishing value chain, readers' and consumer behavior; at the same time, issues that are taken into consideration include the reception of the text, the art and literature of the era, social and cultural conditions, educational systems, technological changes. The evolution of the book per se is the bedrock of the publishing industry which seems to be at a constant turning point.

Nowadays, there are many and significant changes and challenges in the publishing industry . Phillips has discussed these ongoing issues in "Turning the Page," where he (2014: xiii–xiv) points out the "big themes" of our era: disintermediation, globalization, convergence, discoverability. These themes characterize the evolution of the book and the publishing industry since the invention of printing by Gutenberg. Thompson (2010) investigated the issues and features of the publishing

The Visual Identity of the Book

industry in an era of tremendous changes focusing on mergers and acquisitions of publishing houses, the rise of the literary agent, structural changes in bookstores and in the promotion of books, the role of the editor; in his recently published monograph "The Book Wars" (2022), Thompson provides an insight explanation of the publishing activity nowadays looking at issues such as self-publishing, audio books, crowdfunding, storytelling, other forms of the book, the role of social media. Bhaskar (2013) proposes a theoretical framework, a theory of publishing while Borsuk (2018) provides an overview of the evolution of the book. Greco et al (2007, 2013) investigate the publishing industry by providing data and looking at specific features. "Inside book publishing" (Clark & Phillips, 2019), now at the sixth edition, provides an insight of the publishing industry through updated data, case studies and discussion on current issues such as online retail, the development of digital products, the design of books, the role of social media in book promotion; the authors highlight the publishing process (product development, design and production, marketing, sales and distribution).

Obviously, publishers seem always to thrive whatever the "dangers" or "threats"; we can even conclude that threats often become challenges and opportunities. Publishers have found the way not just to survive but to flourish as they keep on reinventing the book by exploiting the new opportunities that derive mainly from new information and communication technologies as well as from new publishing and business models. This is a feature that goes back to Gutenberg's time. Among the main features of nowadays publishing industry, we can recognize convergence of media, competition with other media, the upgraded role of the reader and of reading communities, new business models, reader participation—reader engagement, the rise of self-publishing, crowdfunding, personalized publishing services, and customized copies (Thompson, 2021; Phillips, 2014). In that context, the publishing value chain is enriched with new stakeholders such as game designers and multimedia artists whereas traditional roles, such as the publisher's and the bookseller's, are redefined. Furthermore, the publishing value chain has also been characterized as information publishing chain (Banou, 2017) due not only to the impact of information technologies but mainly due to the role of information on the whole publishing chain. As we live in economies of knowledge, information is the main value of our era; thus access to information and its evaluation, information needs and expectations, information seeking behavior are issues of high importance. In that framework, the publishers take a vital role as information providers and evaluators.

The publishing companies nowadays focus on and aim to have direct communication with the reader, to interact and communicate with online communities, to reach new audiences, to get feedback from the readers. In that context, they use and invest on information and communication technologies; they exploit social media, create platforms, enforce scholar and reader networks. Thus, the publishing company informs, recommends, evaluates, adds value to the text and creates communication networks in which the reader can be a privileged member. Reader participation and engagement are encouraged as well. In this way, an everyday culture of the book is developed. Aldus Manutius at the end of the fifteenth and the beginning of the 16th century established an everyday book culture through his portable, friendly, high quality books for which distinguished editors, scholars, artists, and type founders had worked. In the 17th century, the Elzevirs in Netherlands managed to develop the culture and use of the series, the books thus being an accessible, affordable tool and an everyday object.

In our hybrid and much challenging era, new technologies on book production, design, distribution, and promotion make the books and publications friendly and accessible in a number of forms and business models, further developing their visual identity. The printed, electronic, digital, multimedia, audio books coexist and the reader in most cases uses them all; thus, the boundaries of the book are constantly extended and redefined (gamification, audio books are good examples). Additionally, the printed book is also redefined, as in the case of coloring books and silent books. Competition with other media is though not new. At the same time, short forms coexist with multipaged or/and multivolumed books, small publishing companies with conglomerates, globalized with localized book markets, while tradition with innovation go hand in hand.

Additionally, we have to consider that during the last fifteen years the publishing industry went through a plethora of crises (economic recession, pandemic of COVID-19, energy crisis) that forced the publishing companies to further explore and exploit the opportunities provided for better distribution, promotion, marketing of books taking advantage of online communities and networks, as well as of online retail. Furthermore, new customer and reading habits were created whereas the role of reading communities has been upgraded. Going back to time, each crisis led to significant changes that redeveloped the structure of the publishing industry and chain bringing about new roles and establishing new protagonists. The pandemic of Covid-19 had an impact in both large and small publishing industries as well as in small publishing houses and conglomerations.

The publishing industry nowadays seems to be at a constant turning point due to changes to the structure of the industry. In that context, readers have augmented needs and expectations not only for friendly, affordable, accessible and desirable books but also for more interactive and easily to be used books, for updated text and access to content, for customized copies and personalized publishing services, for participating in the publishing activity or even for interacting in the publishing procedure, for communicating and intervening in specific themes. Additionally, they have needs for more and precise information on books and on the publishing industry, for recommendation, information sharing, evaluation. Thus, the publishing companies have taken an upgraded role as information providers, and -through innovation, information, and convergence- exploit ongoing trends and opportunities offering "new" products and another point of view to their readers-users. In that framework, the visual identity of the book is developed in multiplicated ways, on the one hand by recalling and exploiting the visual tradition of the book, which is redefined and often transformed, and on the other by experimenting and exploiting the new opportunities.

1.4 The aesthetic capital of the publishing industry

The book is a visual object the identity of which is defined by the social, artistic, cultural, economic, and educational conditions of the era, by the needs and expectations of the reading audience, the tested and successful forms of the book, the publishing policy and the innovation of the publishers, the book market, the ideological uses of the book. As stated above, the printed book was the first mass medium that led to the democratization of knowledge and of taste. Initially, we will focus on the visual development and maturing of the printed book in the incunable era and during the first centuries of printing. This is a fascinating and exciting period since the book matured and established as known for centuries then.

Furthermore, the book is content and object, text and image, words and pictures; it is a visual, viable and desirable object, tangible and intangible. A book is intended not only to be read but also to be seen, collected, selected, underlined, dedicated, offered, gazed, noted, enjoyed, searched, browsed, painted, showed, exhibited, shared, even personalized. The book is not only a material-tangible object, as it was known for centuries and is still known, but also a book intangible such as the ebook, the virtual publication, the vanilla ebook, the gamified book. Whether on paper or on the screen, the book exhibits its visual identity which does not only embellish or illustrate but is indispensable part of the edition, interrelated with the content, enlightening the themes of the book, guiding the reader, providing visual clues for interpreting the text, promoting and informing, as we will discuss in the second chapter. The parts of the book and the elements of the page, whether visual or verbal or a combination of both, were gradually developed as to serve the needs of the text, of the publisher and of the reader being a visual information tool and a personal device; the reader

14   1. Introduction: The visual identity of the book

can read, note, share, understand, indicate, combine, underline, understand, interpret, discover. Obviously, not only the printed books but also the electronic ones have to be desirable gaining a recognizable visual identity. It is the design, the visual typology of the book that makes the text readable, friendly, convenient, accessible, enjoyable.

McKitterick (2005: 5) writes that "by seeking to understand the purposes of illustration, and the artistic and technical conventions, opportunities and restrictions of illustrative reproduction, we may also reconcile in a more satisfactory way our understanding of different forms of print." This can be extended to different forms of the book. The visual information of the page seems to widen the traditional boundaries of the book; we can thus refer to an extended, converged page that may lead to new reading, visual, customer, and user experiences that establish a culture of books. As we will exhibit, the printed page has always been an extended page, an augmented page.

Among the main concerns and issues that have to be studied in regard to the visual identity of the book we may refer to collaborations between stakeholders, illustration and printing techniques, the significance and addition of color, publishers' strategies and policies, the repetition or imitation or reproductions of illustrations and ornaments, hand-illustration and decoration, rubrication in early printed books, cut-and-paste books, extra illustration, customized/luxury copies, reader engagement and participation, reader creativity, issues of patronage, the uses of the book, the visual expectations of the reading audience, the addition and techniques of printing in color, significance of the color, the visual identity of series. Visual communication has obviously been important since the invention of printing. The author and the printer—publisher, sometimes the editor, the author, and the artist—illustrator of the book, decided on the visual typology of the edition. Apart from the role of the stakeholders, parameters that strongly defined and developed the visual identity of the book may include the influence from the manuscript book or from precedent books, convergence of media, the kind of text and the typographic—publishing—illustrative tradition, the needs and expectations of the reading audience, the available printing and illustration technologies, the art of the period, the publishing policy and promotion methods of the publishers, competition, the working methods of printers—publishers, the imitation and reproduction not only of illustrations and ornaments but also of the visual order of the page, of paratext, and of parts of the book.

The study of the visual identity of the book is interdisciplinary, using terms and methodology from different fields, such as book history, art history, publishing studies, literature, marketing, information science, media studies. This is undeniably a privileged point of view and a framework in which we will investigate the development of the visual identity of the book since the invention of printing alongside with the evolution of publishing strategies, methods, and policies. Additionally, we will look at the maturing of the publishing value chain and of the complex roles of the stakeholders. McKitterick writes that (2005: 8) "literature on the history of illustration is noticeable for its general failure to engage with bibliographical issues as they affect books; and on the other hand the bibliographical study of books still has to engage with the related but different strategies of pictorial or figurative reproduction." Theories and aspects in regard to the study of illustration and of the visual identity of the book have also be discussed (Banou, 2017: 19−24). Darnton in regard to his much discussed and acknowledged model that envisages the communication and publishing process recognizes that "manuscript books and book illustrations will need to be considered elsewhere" (2009: 180−181).

The "aesthetic capital" of the book has been introduced as one of the capitals of the publishing industry (Banou, 2017: 67−70). It is true that the capitals of the publishing industry as described in Thompson (2010: 3−14) do not focus nor express the significant role of the visual identity in defining the book and its functions. The visual identity of the book is obviously related with the symbolic capital (the fame and recognizability of the publishing companies are built on the one hand on the content and on the other on the visual appearance of the book) and the human capital (the publisher, the editor, the artist−graphic designer−engraver−illustrator−multimedia artist− etc. add value to the publishing chain and to the book). Thus, the introduction of the aesthetic capital will be also interchained with the intellectual capital being the two faces of Janus in publishing. In this book, we will take this as one of the starting points that exhibit the significance of the visual identity of the book, whether tangible or intangible. In that framework, the term "converged aesthetics" will be used for the page that goes beyond the typology of the book as established and known since Renaissance.

In the aesthetics publishing chain−circle-circuit, introduced by Banou (2017: 33−38), collaborations are developed and relationships can be altered according to the impact of technology, the art of the era, the publishing and business models, the kind of text and the reading audience as well as to social, economic and cultural conditions. Additionally, new roles are added whereas the old ones are redefined and rediscovered.

1.5 The structure of the book

The second chapter, by far the largest, investigates the development of the visual identity of the book mainly during the first centuries of

16   1. Introduction: The visual identity of the book

printing; in that context, emphasis will be given to the defining and maturing of the printed page and of the book during the incunable period as well as during the 16th and 17th centuries. The chapter will study the development of the typology of the printed page and of the printed book as information tool and device in order to understand and explain the nature and its function as well as the publishing policies and strategies. According to Mak (18), "The page is an expressive space for text, space and image; it is a cultural artefact; it is a technological device. But it is also all of these at once." The elements and parts of the page and of the book as visual. material object will be studied arguing that they are strong visual information devices which defined print culture, reading and consumer behavior, promotion and marketing strategies, publishing policies, communication issues, aesthetic values. The chapter will highlight the relationships, influences, and reasons for the visual evolution of the page and of the book, while it will look at the transition from the manuscript to the printed book as indicative to any transition from older and established to new forms of the book. In that framework, convergence of media will be pointed out.

Furthermore, the second chapter aspires to shed light to the publishers'/printers' strategies, decisions, policies, techniques, aspects and aims, as well as to investigate the development of the publishing value chain, and more specifically the role of the stakeholders such as of the publisher/printer, the editor, the reader, the artist, the author. Thus, the chapter exhibits the printed page and the printed book as strong information and visual medium that enforced reading and consumer behaviors, promoted communication and information sharing, contributed to the reception and interpretation of the text, offered to book marketing and promotion, and further established complex and different uses of the book. Aspects that will be studied include the impact of technologies, the information mechanisms of the book, the role of the reading audience and the shaping of visual expectations, the demand for personalized publishing services and customized copies.

The chapter will argue that printers-publishers developed their strategies, aims and policies in a complex environment and in complex relationships, in the new born publishing chain, by exploring the opportunities of the new medium and the printing-illustration techniques, taking into consideration the readers' taste and expectations. These are to be studied in the wider framework of the art and technology of the era, as well as of social, cultural, scientific, educational, religious, and financial conditions. We will point out that intermediation, communication, collaboration, convergence, participation of various stakeholders, engagement had been among the key points. Moreover, early marketing and promotion strategies as developed by the publishers and set in specific markets will be outlined. It is noteworthy that the publishing value chain was under development and the chapter will look at the roles of various stakeholders, whether "new" or deriving from the manuscript tradition.

Focusing initially on the incunables and the early printed books we will try to explore the development of the visual order of the page till nowadays. Undoubtedly, the incunable period, "the horseless carriage period of the book," according to Mcuhan, and the first centuries of printing constitute an exciting and worth studying period for a number of reasons. There are plenty of studies on the printed book. At the beginning of the second chapter, literature review will be provided on the evolution of the printed book.

Thereafter, we will discuss the visual order and the typology of the page as developed during the incunable period and the 16th century, investigating specifically elements and issues that defined the page, such as pagination and foliation, headlines and running titles, headings, manicules, margins and marginalia, chapter heads, decoration/ornamentation (initials, headpieces, fleurons, tailpieces, and other), manicules, catchwords, signatures. We will also discuss the illustration and decoration (initials, headpieces, tailpieces, fleurons) of the book as to approach the evolution of the printed page as a visual information tool. Printing in gold and red, printing in color, colored prints, as well as volvelles and movable parts will also be looked at. Then, the establishment of the book as material object with specific information mechanisms is discussed with emphasis on parts of the book, both at the front matter and back matter, such as the title page, the colophon, the frontispiece, the portrait of the author, the index. The role of the paratext is thus exhibited. Covers, dust jackets and slipcases that matured in the following centuries, will also be investigated. It has to be noted that printing types, printing machines and paper will not be included.

The discussion of the parts and elements of the book and of the page does not aspire to be exhaustive; specific issues, trends, elements, and aspects are enlightened so as to point out their function and contribution to the development of the visual identity of the book. The chapter focuses on the evolution and establishment of the page and the book as visual and information devises in the described framework and in regard to outlined aims. By deconstructing the page and comment on its elements, we can better discover and explain the role, history and contribution of each part so as to consider the various and complex influences from precedent forms of communication and expression, from reading and consumer habits, from aesthetic— visual preferences and information seeking behavior; we can thus evaluate the role of tradition and innovation, discuss the relation of image and text, as well as the impact of social, educational and cultural conditions. Moreover, the impact of the visual mechanisms of the book in the globalized publishing activity will be outlined.

In that framework, the democratization of taste and the role of visual expectations of the readers are discussed so as to further explain the decisions and strategies of the publishers, to trace the function of specific parts of the book and of the page, to interpret aspects of communication, reader engagement and convergence of media. From this point of view, the book as an everyday object and medium will be enlightened looking at publishers who defined and further established an everyday culture of the book through their strategies, choices, and innovations. Conclusions of the chapter follow on the defining of the page and the maturing of the book.

Undeniably, it is more than fascinating to us nowadays to study the turning point and the changes made to the first printed books as they were developed by coexisting with the manuscript precedent and at the same time by gaining gradually their autonomy and defining their visual identity. This is of value for two obvious reasons: firstly, for understanding and explaining the development of the book as a commodity, a medium and a visual object in regard not only to its precedent but also to the social, cultural, educational, economic and political conditions of its time; secondly for studying, understudying and interpreting issues and aspects of our own era in which convergence of media, other "new" forms of the book, new publishing and business models, information and communication technologies, AI provide further opportunities and challenges and create a new framework for the publishing activity. It was in the incunable era and the 16th century that the printed book was developed to what we, since then, know as a book. From this point of view, the transition from the manuscript to the printed book may explain our hybrid, challenging and turbulent era in which innovation and tradition go hand in hand whereas different forms of the book coexist and influence each other.

Additionally, the study of the visual maturing of the page and of the book may reveal the under development relationships in the publishing chain, the emerging role of the publisher, the rise of the authorship and editorship, as well as changes in the promotion, consumption, collection and reading of books. Although the publisher's point of view may seem to be the bedrock of this chapter and of this book, different roles and stakeholders of the publishing chain will also be looked at (such as editors, illustrators, artists, booksellers, readers).

Undeniably, the printed book is contextualized in its era but, at the same time, it is obvious that the boundaries of the book are further expanded in each era. This is demonstrated nowadays in regard to new forms of the book and the convergence of media. This book argues that, apart from the democratization of knowledge, publishing established the democratization of taste through the development of the visual identity of the book, the creation of the visual order of the page and of the book as object; these led to the cultivation of taste to gradually wider audiences and moreover to the establishment of the culture of the book as visual, information, memory device. Furthermore, the period of transition from the manuscript to the printed book, longer that we think, demonstrates the complex procedures for the page's and the book's creation.

The chapters, as well as the book, do not aspire to be exhaustive in regard to the visual evolution of the page and of the printed book. The study is based on the bibliography and on the research of incunables and printed books.

The third chapter introduces the term "converged aesthetics," which describes not only the "luxury" copies intended for wealthy collectors and patrons but also books created and developed for a wider reading audience that could afford the expense of these books. The reading audience was gradually extended with new "dynamic" groups of readers. In this chapter, "luxury" copies and editions will initially be defined and categorized so as to enlighten on the one hand the needs, expectations and taste of the readers—collectors—users and, on the other, the publishing strategies and decisions in a transition period; thus, the complex relationships in the publishing chain will be discussed. The chapter studies this hybrid kind of the printed book (hand decorated and illustrated printed books, specifically bound and often printed on vellum or on better quality of paper) as to explain current issues and features of nowadays forms of the book, of publishing strategies and of design patterns.

Thereafter, the systemization of deluxe—limited—collectable—exclusive editions will be pointed out since their origins in order not only to trace their evolution but also to discuss their production, design, and promotion nowadays. In that context, commemorative editions, signed copies, and facsimiles will be outlined. Customized unique copies and personalized publishing services will then be discussed. The chapter will focus on customized, unique copies—such as cut-and-paste books, extra illustration and luxury books, which will be presented and discusses. In that framework, reader participation and engagement will be investigated both in the past and nowadays. Thereafter, personalized publishing services nowadays will be presented highlighting issues such as the impact on technologies, the participation of the reader, the uses of these books. Reader engagement and—a step forward—reader creativity will also be investigated.

The term "post-luxury" copy will be introduced and discussed in this chapter so as to describe customized copies, even personalized publishing services nowadays. Taking as starting point the luxury copies during the Renaissance, we will discuss the evolution, transformation, and redevelopment in our Digital era. The origins of reader engagement and participation will be explored; the term "reader creativity" will be introduced and discussed in relation not only to coloring books but to a number of strategies and initiatives nowadays in which the role of the reader-user is upgraded. Then, the uses of the book will be pointed out.

Conclusions of the book in the fourth chapter focus on the book as visual, complex, desirable device. Among the themes synopsized we can observe reader engagement and reader creativity, issues of discoverability and promotion, the customized copy and personalized publishing services, the complex uses of the book, the visual identity in regard to the publishing chain, the role of short forms and multipaged novels, the visual redesign and reintroduction of the classics, the relationship between the printed and other forms of the book, convergence of media, the role of innovation and visual expectations and adventures. At the end, a comment on publishing and democracy highlights the role of readers−users−citizens. Future research closes the chapter.

CHAPTER
2

Through the page: The evolution of the visual identity

2.1 The "horseless carriage" period: The early printed books

By taste I mean not only judgment and a feeling for quality and literary values. Taste should also include a sure sense for the form—format, type area, type face, binding, dust jacket—in which a specific book should be represented.
Kurt Wolff (1991: 9).

The first printed books—incunables were similar to its precedent, the manuscript book (Richardson, 1999: 122−157; Baldacchini, 2009: 11−16; Baldacchini, 2009: 46; McKitterick, 2005; Smyth, 2018; Eisenstein, 1983: 20−23; Smith, 2000b; Werner, 2019: 2−3; Howard, 2009: 59; Dondi, 2010). This was more than expected. The manuscript book was the only known form of the book, widely spread, highly respected, familiar, recognizable, successful and used for centuries. It satisfied the readers' needs and had been an object of desire for collectors and readers whereas authors recognized it as the only medium for the transmission of their works. Neither the first typographers—printers nor the first reading audience (humanist scholars, noblemen, students) initially aimed to experiment on the new medium. Literacy levels were extremely low (Richardson, 1999: 107−121; Chartier, 1994) and the first already existing reading audience had obviously the same expectations and needs from the printed book as from the manuscript one. But this was to change shortly due to several reasons. The reading audience had been gradually widening due to social, religious, cultural, educational, and economic reasons. Authors recognized a new, highly valuable mass medium for transmitting their works as well as for gaining fame and recognition; moreover, this new medium facilitated the communication

---

The Visual Identity of the Book
DOI: https://doi.org/10.1016/B978-0-443-19167-1.00002-4
Copyright © 2025 Christina Banou. Published by Elsevier Ltd. All rights are reserved, including those for text and data mining, AI training, and similar technologies.

21

with readers, other authors and the stakeholders of the publishing chain (Richardson, 1999: 77–104).

The printers–publishers of the era exploited the opportunities provided by the new printing techniques and the under construction book market so as to produce, design and promote a better book forcing thus all stakeholders of the publishing chain to significant changes. A better book obviously meant a friendly, convenient, desirable, readable, afford-able, beautiful, accessible medium, of value in regard to the content and to the book as visual, physical object. Inevitably, the printed book was gradually recognized as a strong and effective information medium and its opportunities were exploited and explored by the printers–publishers, editors, booksellers and readers; sometimes these opportunities were praised in prologues, introductions and dedicatory letters to the printed editions written by editors, authors or printers (Eisenstein, 1983; Richardson, 1999: 49–69). Martin (1995: 227) writes that "no invention has struck people's imagination as much as the invention of printing, nor has any been as glorified by its contemporaries, precisely because it involved things of the mind." In that context, the newborn publishing chain was under development.

2.1.1 Notes on bibliography

There are plenty of studies on the incunables, the first printed books and the development of the book as known for centuries. Sarah Werner (2019) in "Studying Early Printed Books: 1450–1800" provides a frame-work and deep insight information regarding the study of early printed books as material objects, guiding readers to recognize and compare specific features. The author highlights specific elements of the page and of the book arguing that not only at the earliest printed books but "even later printed books worked hand in hand with manuscript prac-tices" (Werner, 2019: 2).

Philip Gaskell in his much-acknowledged work "A New introduction to Bibliography" (1972) recognizes and defines two periods, the hand-press period till 1800 and the machine-press period from the beginning of 19th century, discussing the creation of the book as material object in regard to the printing techniques and technologies with special focus on the British book trade. Richardson in "Printing, Writers and Readers in Renaissance Italy" (1999) focuses on Renaissance Italy during the 15th and 16th centuries, and investigates the impact of printing on readers, authors, publishers, editors whereas he highlights the changes to the printed book per se taking into consideration the social and cultural conditions of the era.

Nicole Howard (2009) in "The Book: The life story of a technology" investigates the role of new technologies and of social conditions in printing, and discusses the shaping and development of the printed book as physical object; the chapter that provides an overview for the incunable book is titled "Infancy" (2009: 27–53), whereas the chapter for the book in the 16th century is titled "Youth" (2009: 55–86) where the author gives a brief description of the parts of the book, of book production and print culture. Dennis Baron in "A Better Pencil: Readers, Writers and the Digital Revolution" (2009) refers to the friendly and developed each time writing medium (a "better pencil") that the user needs, desires, expects and demands for writing and communicating; the author highlights the transformations of the mediums and discusses issues and trends of each era, taking as key point the quest for communication, information sharing and knowledge dissemination. H.J. Martin in "the History and Power of Writing" (1995) titles one of his chapter "The reign of the book", after Gutenberg's invention, approaching thus the stakeholders of the publishing chain and placing the book in the society of the era.

David McKitterick in "Print, Manuscript and the Search for Order, 1450–1830" (2005) looks at the printed book since its invention focusing on the changes that took place and established the typology of the book during a long period (longer than we usually think), till 1830. The author discusses the transition from the manuscript to the printed book as alternative mediums whereas he focuses on the development of the printed book for 350 years after the invention of printing arguing that "the joint existence of manuscript and printed lasted long into the sixteenth century" (2005: 64) and that the fifteenth and sixteenth centuries is a period in which we "frequently find less a revolution than an accommodation" (2005: 3). McKitterick (2018) also studies how and when the printed books became "old" enlightening cultures of collection and the role of the book as physical object discussing the impact of the words "rare" and "rarity" in bookselling, book promotion and collections (2018: 135–146).

Pauline Reid in "Reading by Design" (2019:7) investigates the "visual rhetorics" and the "rhetorical vision" of the English Renaissance Book as a "fragile, fragmented material object" (2019: 1) taking into consideration perceptions by the reading audience, changes in science, philosophy and rhetoric, as well as the materials of daily life such as mirrors and glasses (2019: 17–18). Focusing on almanacs, pedagogical books, emblem books, mirror books etc. during the period from 1481 to 1649, Reid enlightens "how these works set up their visual interactions with readers to both create an experience and interrogate forms of knowledge" arguing that the "early modern print book's visual interface and its readers dynamically engaged with one another" (Reid, 2019: 19 and

24   2. Through the page: The evolution of the visual identity

22). Taking as starting point the editions of "Mirror and Description of the World" by Caxton (first published in 1481) and Steven Hawes's *Pastime of Pleasure*, published in 1509, the author provides specific case studies studying the "ways that early modern books responded to—and constructed—the phenomenological crisis of visual perception" (Reid, 2019: 7). Bonnie Mak (2012), by investigating the 15th-century Latin text *Controversia de nobilitate* by Bonaccursius da Montemagno as a manuscript, a printed work, and a digital edition, enlightens how the (printed) page was developed and "how the page mattered" for the readers and the stakeholders of the publishing activity. The author exhibits how different audiences used and interpreted the book as object (types, images etc.) whereas at the third chapter she focuses on the complex role of paratext and on the way that "these devices have exerted pressure on the treatment of the *Contoversia*" (Mak, 2012: 7). The role of the page in the transmission and preservation of knowledge is thus highlighted.

In "Re-Inventing the Book: Challenges from the Past for the Publishing Industry" (Banou, 2017), common trends and features of the publishing industry since the invention of printing were studied in order to interpret current issues, to propose a methodological framework and to introduce publishing strategies in a changing publishing environment nowadays. The aesthetic capital was introduced as one of the capitals of the publishing industry; furthermore, the publishing chain as developed during the Renaissance and as is changing nowadays was highlighted with emphasis on the aesthetics of the book. It was also argued that the Gutenberg revolution is still continuing in a complex environment as the demand for access to information, the desire for knowledge dissemination and the need for friendly books are diachronic features, common between the past and the present. Issues discussed in the book included convergence of media, reader engagement, aesthetics in publishing, the impact of new information technologies and the redevelopment of past publishing strategies such as preorders. Furthermore, the publishing value chain was discussed as an information publishing chain whereas a methodological approach was suggested.

Apart from the books by Eisenstein (1983), Febvre-Martin (1990), Johns (1998), a number of works focus on the incunable and the printed book of the 16th century demonstrating the evolution in regard not only to the printed techniques and to the book as material object but also to the publishing chain, the reading habits, the promotion and reception of books, the book market, taking into consideration the specific conditions of each era and the technological developments. The collective volume "The Renaissance Computer," edited by Rhodes and Sadway (2000), points out to the printed book as information device, as an early "computer" that helped the reader to manage the abundance of information.

The Visual Identity of the Book

By providing case studies and analyzing the production and design of specific editions, the printed book is thus exhibited as a strong information medium and device, precedent to the computers. Actually, the printed book was the medium that on the one hand led to the abundance of information (by the production of editions) and on the other managed the flood of information. In Ann Blair's "Too much to know. Managing scholarly information before the Modern Age" (2010) the author argues on the abundance of information and on the need for its management, and thus investigates the modules and ways for it. Apart from the impact of early printed reference books, which is discussed at the last chapter, Blair enlightens the motivations and methods of compilers, the reference printed genres (such as dictionaries and florilegia) and their finding devices, such as the list of readings, the alphabetical indexes, the branching diagrams.

Giuseppina Zappella in a number of books and publications investigates the incunable and the old printed book as physical, material object focusing on its creation and development during the incunable period and the next centuries; Zappella in her much detailed work *Il libro antico a stampa* (2004) studies in depth the development and the typology of the early printed book as material object whereas she also investigates significant aspects of the book such as the initials (2013; 1989; 1988b), the printer's devices (1998a), the portrait (1988). Sherman (2005, 2010) sheds light in the annotations and marginal notes so as to discuss the reader's perceptions, attitudes and participation in the shaping and maturing of the book exhibiting at the same time the creation of the book as device and object in the social and cultural conditions.

Margaret Smith in the "The title Page: Its Early Development, 1460−1510" (2000a) extends the boundaries of the incunabulum so as to trace and analyze the evolution of the title-page; she also provided a categorization of the title-pages whereas in other works (such as in 2000b) she has looked at issues regarding the relationship of the printed book with the manuscript precedent. Lorenzo Baldacchini in "Aspettando il frontespizio. Pagine bianche, occhietti e colophon nel libro antici" (2009) also studies the creation and development of the title-page in the early printed books, discussing issues of information and visual embellishment. F. Barberi (1969, 1983) previously had provided a first approach and a categorization for the title-pages in his work.

Before that, Sean Jennett (1951) in "The Making of Books" investigated the book as material object and focused on the parts of the book discussing in detail the design of books from the insight of the publishing industry. He looked at specific parts of the book so as to highlight their typology. Norma Levarie in the "Art and History of Books" (1995, first published in 1968) provided an overview of the book as physical object; she gave a panorama of the development of the art of the book in regard to illustration and decoration, trying to trace the reasons and factors that explain this development. More recently, in "Books. A living History" Martin Lyons (2013) outlines the history and evolution of books since Antiquity pointing out to the book as visual object in regard to the social, cultural, technological and economic conditions. John Boardley in *Typographic First. Adventures in Early Printing* (2019) sheds light to the early printed books looking at issues such as the first fonts, gold printing, color printing and illustrated books.

In "Book parts," edited by Dennis Duncan and Adam Smyth in 2019, each chapter, written by an expert, investigates specific parts of the book or of the page, such as the title-page, the frontispiece, the chapter heads, the running titles, the fleurons, the woodcuts and engravings, providing thus a useful tool and a research approach to the printed book. In "Renaissance paratexts" edited by Smith and Wilson (2011), the chapters exhibit and discuss the role of paratext during the Renaissance, pointing out to specific issues and aspects. These volumes, taking into consideration and as starting point the Genette's much discussed "Paratext: Thresholds of Interpretation" (1997), add to the research on the Renaissance paratexts and on the physical development of the early printed book providing as well case studies.

In "The Book Makers: A History of the Book in 18 Remarkable Lives" (2024) Adam Smyth—through case studies—investigates specific aspects of the printing and publishing procedure and activity from the 16th century to nowadays, discussing methods, strategies and issues, such as extra-illustration or cut-and-paste techniques. As the author writes in "Material texts in Early Modern England" (2018: 7−8) he enlightens in detailed way the "features of early bibliographical culture that have been overlooked, misunderstood or underexamined by critics" and "the relationship between the materiality of the text and the workings of literary imagination." In that framework, the author sheds slight to cut and paste methods as an aspect of hybrid books and convergence of media, a theme that also discusses at the much enjoyable third chapter of the *Book Makers* (Smyth, 2024: 76−105). Furthermore, Smyth studies the errors and corrections in early printed books offering thus another point of view, according to which errors reveal the printing process and activity, as well as the role of the author.

Robert Darnton in the *Forbidden Bestsellers of Pre-revolutionary France* approaches (1996) book culture and specific aspects of the publishing activity and the book market as well as the perception of texts, outlining at the same time the social and cultural impact. Darnton in this book (1996: 182), as also in the much-acknowledged "What Is the History of Books?," first published in 1982 (2009), focuses on the model of the communication−publishing chain/circuit that "provides a way of envisaging the entire communication process" (1996: 180). The author recognizes though that "manuscript books and book illustrations will need to be considered elsewhere" (1996: 180−1). In regard to the aesthetics of the book and the book as visual object, the aesthetic capital was introduced as well as the aesthetic publishing chain (Banou, 2017).

John Feather in "A History of British Publishing" (2006, second edition) investigates publishing and the book trade in Britain with emphasis on the Industrial Age and the 20th century looking at publishing strategies and the book market. Amaranth Borsuk in "The Book" (2018) provides in four chapters a brief description and overview of the book as object, content, idea, interface, from the clay tablets since our era. Bibliography is rich and sheds light to specific issues and case studies.

In the first chapter of this book, bibliography on the publishing industry and publishing studies was outlined in regard to current issues and features of the publishing activity nowadays. As argued, the evolution of the book as visual object can be studied in accordance with the evolution of the publishing industry.

2.1.2 In this chapter

This chapter investigates the gradual and challenging development of the visual identity of the printed book with emphasis on the incunable period and the first centuries of printing. More specifically, we will discuss the development of the book as visual, material object; thus, we will focus initially on the maturing and evolution of specific elements, both verbal and visual, of the printed page and then on the creation of the structure of the book so as to understand and interpret the role of the page and of the book as visual and information devices. We will as well trace the reasons that led to specific decisions and publishing/ printing strategies. In that framework, the role of the publisher, the editor and other stakeholders of the under development publishing chain will be enlightened alongside with the influence of the manuscript book, the reading and consumer habits, the taste of the readers; the transition from the manuscript to the printed book will be analyzed arguing that this transition was at the same time a coexistence and convergence of media. Patterns of book production and consumption will also be highlighted.

In that context, this chapter will specifically discuss the strategies, policies and methods of the first printers/publishers during the long period of the maturing of the book, enlightening the ways by which they exploited the opportunities of the printing technologies, developed their promotion strategies and publishing policies, introduced new elements and features, collaborated with other stakeholders of the publishing chain (such as editors, authors, translators, artists, miniaturists, booksellers), and considered the needs and expectations of their reading audiences.

Specifically, we will focus on the defining and maturing of the printed page as strong information and visual device; inevitably, we will consider the impact of technologies, the role of the publisher and of the reading audience, the ongoing competition among publishers, financial reasons, the emergence of the role of the author not only in the publishing activity but also in the cultural environment, the augmenting demand for books, the book market, the printing and illustration techniques as well as the social, economic, scientific, educational, religious conditions of each period. Issues and elements of the printed page will be discussed such as the headlines and running titles, the rubrication, the foliation–pagination, the manicules, the head chapters, the tailpieces, the initials, headpieces and illustrations. As Bonnie Mak (2012: 5) states: "The architecture of the page is thus a complex and responsive entanglement of platform, text, image, graphic markings, and blank space. The page hosts a changing interplay of form and content, of message and medium, of the conceptual and physical, and this shifting tension is vital to the ability of the page to remain persuasive through time."

In order to investigate the structure and visual order of the printed page, we will enlighten and further interpret the nature, development, combination, evolution, and establishment of its parts and elements. We will try to shed light on the way that these parts and elements were developed and matured, on the factors that led to specific decisions and strategies, on their function and role in regard not only to the development of the page and to the book but also to the creation of print culture, of reading and consumer behavior, to the reception of text as well as to publishing policies. Additionally, by studying the development and nature of the page, we can discover and explain the role, history and contribution of each part so as to exhibit the influences from precedent forms of communication and expression, from reading and consumer habits, from aesthetic preferences and information seeking behavior; we can thus evaluate the role of tradition and innovation, discuss the relation of image and text, and highlight the impact of social, educational and cultural conditions. By deconstructing the page, we can understand its parts and elements in a wider framework that will enable us to interpret current trends and issues as well as to develop strategies nowadays. As it will be argued, the printed page—as established in early printed books and known for centuries—formed an important visual and information device, the components of which took a leading role in reading, communicating, accessing, consuming, promoting and creating. Nowadays, as the book is redefined and its typology is redeveloped, the knowledge of the history and development of the page and of the book -as visual and information mechanism- may enlighten the past, interpret the present and enable the suggestion of strategies and policies for the future.

Thereafter, the chapter highlights the development and evolution of the parts of the book looking at the development of paratext: frontmatter, backmatter, as well as of the cover and dust jacket. Transition periods in the history of publishing are of value for understanding our period of constant changes and turning points.

The chapter will claim that the printers—publishers of the first printed books developed their strategies, aims, techniques, aspects and policies in a complex environment and in complicated relationships as formed in the newborn publishing chain. Printers/publishers, editors, artists and authors explored and exploited the various opportunities of the new massive medium for the production, design, promotion, distribution and selling of books, taking into consideration the readers' taste and expectations as well as the reception of the text. Early promotion and marketing strategies developed by the publishers will be also discussed. It has to be considered that the publishing value chain was under development during this early period of printing, and the roles of each stakeholder were gradually defining and maturing. In that context, we will also argue that intermediation, communication, collaboration, convergence, information sharing, participation of various stakeholders, reader engagement had been key points.

The visual identity and typology of the book is a not only a matter of visual information, aesthetic value and visual perception, but as well of intermediation in complex environments in which we have to trace the promotion strategies and the publishing policy of the publishers, the taste and expectations of the reading audience, the different uses of the book, the evolution of the publishing chain, the book market, the consumer cultures, the technologies of the book and the influence from other media. The book as complex product can be a mirror of its Age as well as an innovative medium that may in turn revolutionize cultures, habits, and ideologies. By studying the past of the publishing industry and the transformations of the early printed book, we aspire to explain and interpret current issues and trends in an era in which hybrid forms, experiments, new assets, convergence of media, interactivity, new publishing models and new tools seem to be the rule.

The period for the maturing of the book cannot obviously be reduced to the incunable period and to the first decades of the 16th century, and it has been extended according to McKitterick (2005), Werner (2019), Smyth (2018), and others. From this point of view, the "experimental" period is broadened and we will focus initially on the printed book of the 15th, 16th, and 17th centuries, although this does not mean that changes were completed by then. The study will be expanded into the

30   2. Through the page: The evolution of the visual identity

next centuries so as to look at the evolution of the book as visual object. Undoubtedly, the incunable period and the 16th century form an exciting and worth studying period for a number of reasons including the interaction with the manuscript book. It is an exciting period for the reasons referred to the introduction of this book. As nowadays the boundaries of the book are expanded, and the transition from the manuscript to the printed book explains our hybrid era in which different forms of the book coexist and influence each other. This explanation and interpretation as well as the continuity of changes may lead to new promotion strategies, publishing policies, and suggestions on the visual identity of books.

It has, though, to be pointed out that in this chapter the analysis of the parts of the book and of the page does not aspire to be exhaustive but to focus on specific elements and to synopsize their evolution and construction in order to enlighten and exhibit their function and contribution to the development of the visual identity of the book. The printing types, the paper, the printing procedure will not be discussed; the chapter looks at the book and the printed page as visual and information device, as material object of aesthetic value and as an everyday commodity, familiar to the readers and users since the Renaissance, agreeing with Duncan & Smyth (2019: 4) that we aim to "conceive of the book not as a single stable object, but as a coming together or an alignment of separate component pieces." Thus, specific emphasis is given to certain parts of the book or elements of the page. Some of them may even seem to the reader to be of minor value or are expected to be there as indispensable part of the page without paying special attention (such as pagination, margins, running titles etc.). The chapter will also discuss the end matter of the book arguing that backmatter is as important as front matter.

In that context, the visual expectations of the reading audience will be discussed as well as the democratization of taste, term introduced (Banou, 2017) in accordance to the democratization of knowledge, which in this book will be further investigated. The development and establishment of an everyday visual culture of the book will then be enlightened, from Aldus Manutius and the Elzevirs to Penguin Books.

2.1.3 Setting the scene of books

The first printers/publishers inevitably aimed to provide to the existing reading audience a familiar and recognizable book which would easily be promoted and sold (Martin, 1995: 230; Baldacchini, 2009:46). Questions like "When the expectations and desires of the reading audience changed?," "When the demand had been differentiated?," "When the typographers/publishers started to experiment, to try something different, to suggest and introduce something new?" can be answered by exploring the significant changes that took place gradually during the 15th century and the 16th century.

As mentioned, publishing is an activity, a business, an industry based on both tradition and innovation; new techniques and technologies, challenges and strategies create needs, desires and expectations. The printed book as a dynamic new medium expressed and at the same time influenced every time its era; being a mirror of the Age, the printed book revolutionized, epitomized, and further encouraged reading, information dissemination and sharing, communication (Febvre-Martin, 1990; Barbier, 2001; Eisenstein, 1983; Johns, 1998; Braida, 1999). Familiarity with the manuscript book obviously had been inevitable at the early incunable period (Martin, 1995: 230–232; Zappella, 2004; Baldacchini, 2009; Miglio, 1983) but even from the first decades of printing, it was obvious that the printed book was a medium with new opportunities, expectations, challenges and needs. The visual identity of the printed book was gradually developed gaining its autonomy from the manuscript precedent due to practical, technological, aesthetic, marketing-commercial reasons. "After the advent of printing, visual aids multiplied, signs and symbols were codified, different kinds of iconographic and nonphonetic communication were rapidly developed" (Eisenstein, 1983, 58). The printed book was a mass information and knowledge medium for the wide reading audience and, as such, it had to satisfy needs, desires and expectations that previously did not exist.

Changes regarding the visual identity of the printed book were many and significant. The printed book exists as text (intellectual capital, intangible aspect) and as a material object (tangible). Nowadays, the visual identity of the book is of importance, although not material, not tangible; changes during the early period of printing decided and defined the page and the book as known for centuries and as exists nowadays even in other, "new" forms and devices. The typology of the printed book and its emancipation from the manuscript one consisted of both textual and visual issues, the latter being particularly powerful. The visual issues and the development of the printed page were of certain significance in creating the identity of the book as established and known since nowadays (Smith, 2000a; Morison, 1949). It was soon understood by all stakeholders of the publishing chain that the printed book was a much differentiated medium from its precedent with many opportunities, challenges and advantages that had to be explored and exploited. Inevitably new needs and expectations raised.

The printed book, since its beginning, was expected and is still expected to be friendly, portable, readable, marketable, accessible, desired, adorable, convenient, admirable, affordable. It was a commodity, a product, a work of art, a desirable object, a memory device, an information tool, a mass medium which at the same time existed as a unique object for its owner. Uniqueness in early printed books was achieved by hand illustration/decoration and unique binding. Beyond these luxury copies or the deluxe and limited editions, every book has its own history being a memory device and an object of personal history for the reader, as we will discuss in the third chapter.

In that framework, the visual identity of the book takes into consideration and engages the visual typology and organization of the page, visual information and communication, visual paratext, visual expectations, visual satisfaction, visual elements, visual hierarchy, visual history and visual excellence. In that framework, features and elements of the page and of the book will be studied as to point out the visual order of the page as well as the visual structure and mechanisms of the book. From this point of view, in this book we will focus initially on the incunables and the early printed books due to their experimental nature and evolving aesthetic−visual identity balancing between the manuscript and the printed book. As Marshall McLuhan in 1967 (1994: 173) stated: "Typography was no more an addition to the scribal art than the motorcar was an addition to the horse. Printing has its horseless carriage phase of being misconceived and misapplied during its first decades when it was not uncommon for the purchaser of a printed book to take it to a scribe to have it copied and illustrated."

In this horseless carriage period, we have though to wonder if this visual development of the printed book had been a struggle for innovation or a continuity and transition that took place gradually. The question "continuity or fracture" set by Lorenzo Baldacchini (1995−1996) is always of research interest. McKitterick (2005: 8) recognizes the 15th to early 16th centuries as "a period of innovation, experiment and compromise." Obviously, it was due to practical reasons that significant changes initially took place. The printed book ought to be readable, friendly, and convenient to the reader; it had to serve the readers' needs and showcase the text by verbal and visual parts that were gradually added or further used. Both frontmatter and backmatter, as well as the elements of the page (such as pagination, marginal notes, running titles, initials), guided the reader to the text giving him the tools so as to navigate in the content, to use the information properly, to interpret and to enjoy reading. Publishers aspired to fulfill and satisfy readers' needs and expectations.

It is noteworthy that the printing technologies and techniques remained unchangeable till the end of the 18th century and the beginning of 19th century. The printing machine used in Gutenberg times remained the same, with small additions, till the machine press appeared. Gaskell (1972) recognizes two periods: the hand-machine period that lasted till the Industrial Revolution and the Machine-press period. As Werner (2019:2)

2.1 The "horseless carriage" period: The early printed books

synopsizes: "But how type was cast and books were printed remained essentially consistent until machines entered the picture... What you learn about how a book was printed in Leipzig in 1502 will be relevant for a pamphlet printed in Boston in 1784."

Regarding the 15th century, an explosion in the production of books took place. Febvre-Martin (1990), Richardson (1999), and Fuessel (2005: 113, 77−104) recognize that about 30,000 editions were produced in Europe during the incunable period. This abundance of information and of books resembles to our information Age. Of the production named above, religious books, books on Law, and classical texts (Latin and ancient Greek) as well as comments on them, dictionaries and grammars form the majority of printed editions. The kind of text highlights the reading audience. Jones (2004: 10) refers that the books related to religion or theology are the majority of incunables, whereas the Canon and Civil Law "claimed a sizeable share of incunable printing." The author provides evidence for the publishing of Latin and Greek authors in his work recognizing 1475 separate editions of Latin authors (Jones, 2004: 21−22) and 26 editions of classical Greek texts (Jones, 2004: 22−23, 193−4) to which we have though to add grammars, dictionaries and comments on them.

This production of classical texts in Greek and Latin constitutes a category of specific interest since it is related to the wide humanistic reading audience, constituted by scholars, students, noblemen everywhere in Europe. It was a globalized, multicultural, and multilanguage audience and market for which the Latin was the *lingua franca*. Aldus Manutius initiated his publishing activity by printing ancient Greek texts. In that context, we can investigate the taste, aspects, experiences, and expectations of this audience that extended beyond geographic boundaries. Furthermore, these editions were initially printed on a better quality paper and in larger sizes in comparison to books for the popular reading audience. We have to consider that, according to Werner (2019: 3): "Some printed works were printed for survival −those heavy bound bibles. Others were barely intended to last through the week ...We work with what we have but we can try to remember there's a lot we don't have." Texts in the vernacular will be augmenting and it was not unusual to follow the edition in Latin. For example, the famous *Nuremberg Chronicle* was published by Anton Koberger in 1493 in about 1400 copies in the Latin version and about 800 copies in German (Fuessel, 2005: 118).

At the beginning of the 16th century the printed book, on the one hand, was rapidly been transformed in an object of everyday culture and life (friendly, affordable, convenient, accessible, portable such as the *libri portatiles* by Aldus Manutius, desirable, beautiful) and, on the other, maintained its role as a symbol of taste, power, wisdom, success, prestige, wealth, social class, cultivation—especially in the case of hand illustrated/decorated, specifically bound or printed on vellum copies. The transition from manuscript to the printed book and to the printed culture had gradually taken place. In that framework, we have though to remember that the printed book has to promote itself, to be the advertisement of itself. McKitterick (2005: 60) stated that "this period, in which new skills were established and old ones were reconsidered, lasted a century and more." Thus, the demand for an aesthetically desirable, friendly, readable, qualitative, affordable, convenient book should be considered alongside the need for a book that could promote itself and establish a recognizable identity for the publishing house.

We have to bear in mind that it was in the incunable era that two famous books, considered as masterpieces of typography, were produced with lavish illustration, the *Nuremberg Chronicle* (Anton Koberger, Nuremberg 1493) and *Hypnerotomachia Poliphili* (Aldus Manutius, Venice 1499) for which book historians and art historians still search, discuss, argue and comment. Both have to be studied in the framework of the art and printing techniques, of the social, economic and cultural conditions of the era. Both reveal also trends and issues of book consumption and of ongoing attitudes and ideologies. On the other hand, the virtues of the printed books for the wide audience—such as almanacs, calendars, fables—served the reader and at the same time developed a convenient, friendly, affordable and aesthetically admirable product.

2.2 The visual order of the page

The typology of the page had been gradually and systematically organized in such a manner so as both the text and the information on the text to be provided to the reader. Furthermore, guidance on the content and on the book as a whole was achieved; thus, the text has been framed in a page that offered visual and verbal clues in order to navigate the reader and to indicate, point out, clarify, enlighten specific issues and also to attempt explaining and interpreting the text. According to the kind of text, readers were used to a specific typology of the book. Tales, fables, almanacs, for example, had illustrations and large printing types. Taking for granted that levels of illiteracy were extremely high during the Renaissance, we can assume that not only illustration but more generally the visual order of the page provided the tools for understanding the content.

The visual order of the page was gradually developed and established by elements and parts such as headlines and running titles, pagination and foliation, manicules, marginal notes, tailpieces, initials, headings and other ornaments, illustrations, footnotes/endnotes, head chapters, tailpieces, catchwords and signatures at some incunables. Parts of the book that enforced the maturing of the printed book and the development of its typology and identity include the paratext such as title-page, index, contents, dedication, glossary, frontispiece, illustrations, maps. McLuhan uses the term "visual order" (1994: 174) so as to exhibit the features and virtues of the printed book as a mass media means: "The printed book based on typographic uniformity and repeatability in the visual order was the first teaching machine, just as typography was the first mechanization of a handicraft."

The printed page, as a certainty of our civilization, was developed in the 15th and 16th centuries. By bearing in mind that the printed book has to be friendly, convenient, readable, comfortable, it is easy to explain the changes made to the printed page so as to satisfy the reader's needs and to express the publisher's/printer's aims and expectations. Each page must serve the informational, practical and aesthetic—visual needs. Navigational elements were adopted such as headlines and running titles, pagination instead of foliation, rubrication, marginal tiles, ornaments. Mechanisms of promotion and marketing have also to be studied.

Genette (1997) has used the term "paratext" for describing these "thresholds of interpretation"; it is true that front matter is an introduction, a threshold to the text. End matter is as significant and has to be studied as well. The term "visual paratext" (Banou, 2017) has also been used in an attempt to describe the role and function of the visual paratext such as title-pages and frontispieces. In Smith and Wilson (2011) issues of Renaissance paratext are discussed shedding light to particular aspects of the printed book such as the running titles, fleurons and terminal paratext.

Furthermore, the visual identity of the page and of the book established a culture of reading and at the same time created a recognizable profile for the printed book. Additionally, by gaining its autonomy from the manuscript precedent, the printed book was rapidly defining and establishing its typology and visual culture being desirable and respectable to readers. Different audiences and different texts have different expectations. Classical texts, dictionaries, grammars, scientific editions for the humanistic reading audience have been different from almanacs, fables, manuals, tales, broadsheets for the wide reading audience. Even though, the visual expectations of the first readers had their origins in the manuscript book; the first readers of the printed book were waiting to find the known and recognizable parts, letters, decorations, illustrations. But the printed book was a different medium, massively produced with different mechanisms of communication, perception, understanding and sharing. The expectations created to the readers due to the new medium led to additions and changes. The readers,

36
2. Through the page: The evolution of the visual identity

especially the humanists of the era, soon understood that they needed new tools, mechanisms, strategies, devices for navigating in the text and for exploring the opportunities of the new medium.

Thereafter, we will study the development of the printed page that prevails till now. Each page is an expectation, each book is a new world, which the reader has to explore, navigate, discover. In that framework, suggestions, strategies, techniques, policies were developed and used, and we will try to enlighten how the page was matured, defined, and developed. The gradual development of the page had a cognitive and visual order, which led to maturing of the printed book.

2.2.1 Headlines and running titles

The opening, the beginning, the head of the page was and is the introduction to the reader into the text and into the contents of the page. Headlines thus formed a navigation tool for the exploration, use, and understanding of the content. The organization and the transformation of the head of the page is a good example for the new quests and the new issues related to the printed book.

Headlines and running titles, although used at the manuscripts, have been systemized by typography and thus constructed an essential part of the printed page and the printed book mainly as navigators to the text; they indicated to the reader the chapter or the part of the book and gave at the same time clues for understanding the text as well as for using it; furthermore, the structure and the typology of the page is further fulfilled by the headlines and running titles (pictures 14, 15, 16, 18). The headlines at the top of each page (apart from the first page of the chapter) provide information about the author and the chapter or about the contents of the page. Readers nowadays usually take for granted the headlines or/and the running titles; sometimes they do not even notice that there are headlines or they seem not to pay specific attention to them; it is one element of the page, like pagination, that we know it is there and attention is usually paid when something wrong or extraordinary happens or when we search for specific information and cannot find it. Gaskell (1972) provides the terminology while headlines are investigated in numerous works such as in Jennett (1951: 272–274) and Werner (2019). Further discussion regarding headlines is provided by Bourne (2019) and Day (2011: 34–47).

At the top of every page headlines are the opening, the introduction to the text; they inform the reader for the title of the book or of the chapter or of the part and for the name of the author. They are usually printed with smaller type fonts in comparison with the text and they are expected to form an informational circle: on the one page appears the name of the author and on the other the title of the book/chapter/part (picture). Gaskell (1972) synopsizes them as follows: "At the top of each page there is usually a headline, sometimes with a running (i.e. recurring) title reading across from the left-hand page of the opening (the verso) to the right hand page (the recto), sometimes with a separate heading of title on each page; and at the outer ends of the headlines are the page numbers" whereas Werner (2019: 175) writes: "the line of text at the top (or 'head' of the page, usually consisting of a book or book's section's short title and sometimes including pagination or foliation").

Although not an invention of the printed book (Bourne, 2019: 194), the headlines provided the printed page with a navigation tool proposed by the publisher and the editor that leads to the comprehension and interpretation of the text and transforms the printed book into a friendly and convenient medium. Furthermore, headlines and running titles promoted the book and might contribute to the understanding and reception of the text. Day (2011) enlightens the function and features of the running titles exhibiting their complex role and uses; for example, the author points out that the readers were aware of the role and significance of running titles which sometimes were the province of the author and not of the publisher.

Initially, the incunables did not have headlines and running titles; during the incunabulum period though, they were developed and appeared to a number of books so that in the 16th century they had been a feature and an element of the printed page. According to Bourne (2019: 195): "Printers appropriated textual arrangements."

Day (2011: 35) recognizes that "the failure of scholars to investigate the early modern running titles has perhaps derived in part from confusion about terminology." Sarah Werner distinguishes running titles from headlines (2019:20−21), running title being the title (of the book/ chapter/part) of the page, whereas the headline is the above part of the page that includes the running title and the number of the page; at the elements of the headline we can add the little fleuron or other small ornament used to embellish the headline. In Carter and Barker (2004: 121), based on McKerrow, it is also clarified that headline is a: "Line of type at the top of a page, above the text...; or if it consists of the title of the book (or of the section of the book) on every page or every opening (i.e. two Pages facing one another), sometimes a *running-title* or *running-head*. Properly the headline refers to the whole line, including the folio and the running title to the text part only."

In regard to the running titles, Jennett (1951: 272−274) distinguishes them in three categories: "running headline," "section headline," "page headlines." He is skeptical about the value and use of running headlines: "it is a habit; many people, publishers and printers included, never see headlines, and the running head is there because no one thought of omitting it" (273). Section headlines include titles of chapters, books, parts, so as to guide the reader (Jennett, 1951: 273). Jennett introduces the term "page headline" (1951: 273–274), defines and describes the "page headline" that offers information about the content of the page: "in wording summarizes the contents of the page over which it appears; or indicates the main topic of the page; or, and this is bad, pretends to be a witty or profound remark concerning it." It is true that this kind of running titles is laborious and time-consuming as it is different for each page and requires systematic work since it provides an "abstract" of the page in a few works. Rarely we find it; furthermore, the page line cannot be written until the book is in page proof. Jennett (1951: 274) calls it troublesome: "indeed, no headline is as troublesome as this one."

It is though noteworthy that the term "page headline" is survived, revived, and reused in the web pages nowadays. In manuals and guidelines about the design, use, and marketing of web pages, we come across the term. "The webpage headline is usually just a few words that appear in the largest size font at the very top of the page and contains the first words the visitor will likely read when they reach the page. A product web page headline anchors the reader with what the product is and what value it provides" (Farkas and Geier, 2024). Thus, the term "page headline" is used nowadays with the same meaning for a different medium; its function and value are the same and the disadvantages described by Jennett (time and trouble) decades ago have been overcome due to technology; page headlines are used as to promote and serve the needs of the web pages' users. In that case, the transition from the printed to the virtual page added value to the page headline which was adopted and used in a new environment. As we read on a 2012 guide: "a strong headline gives your visitors a reason to stay and digest more of the page content, the headline should ideally relate to solving a common need or be in a question format. Different variations should be tested to find the one with the highest positive impact on your conversion rate" (Ash et al., 2012: 243). Additionally, "page headline must have a clear purpose, and that purpose must be spelled out in a headline that spans the top of the page" (Ash et al., 2012: 70). As Jennett (1951: 274) stated, the page headline could provide "an amusing diversion for a bored reader."

"Early modern commentators seem not to have troubled to differentiate between the possible alternatives, commonly using the term *running title* as a catch-all phrase, or merely alluding to the top of the page" (Day, 2011:36). Terminology describes, explains, and categorizes the extensive use and establishment of the headline and of the running titles. Of special interest is the ornamental embellishment with fleurons. Apart from fleurons, other small ornaments were used at the headlines.

It is also of importance that during the first decades of printing, headlines at the top of the page, according to Richardson (1999: 129–130), appeared "often in red or blue," exhibiting thus that, although one of the new "navigational devices" and a part of the printed page, the headlines had the strong influence of the manuscript combining printing and rubrication/hand decoration in a hybrid book. In that context, rubrication—widely used at the incunable period—was adopted also at the headlines and at foliation or pagination during the early decades of printing. As we will discuss thereafter, rubrication is an excellent example of the coexistence of mechanical printing methods and hand-decoration/illustration providing recognizable visual identity to incunables.

The position of the headline was decided from the printers/publishers as to satisfy the reader and to inform, embellish and serve the harmony of the page (pictures 14, 15, 16, 18). Although usually centered across the measure, the headline may be sided so as to create a new visual-aesthetic proposal. We have also to consider that the headlines as navigation and information tools serve also the promotion of the book demonstrating the "new" features of the page as well as the artistic, visual identity of the book. The parameters of the tradition related to specific kind of text and the reading behavior have to be searched and discussed. As we will observe, it is due to the tradition and habits, based on formed strategies, that publishers/printers designed the book and adopted specific decoration and illustration.

The success of the headlines and running titles defers according to the kind of text and the period. Day concludes for the 17th century (2011: 38) that "both producers and readers of books in early modern England paid close attention to what came to be termed *running tittles*." It is noteworthy that headlines and running titles were widely used at religious texts (Day, 2011: 42–43) obviously in order to guide the users/readers not only at the study and reading but also at the missals and rituals when navigation to the text had to be immediate and simple. Later, headings will be established to other kinds of text. During the 19th century, they were used to novels and to works for the wide reading audience of the era (pictures 13–15, 17). The flexibility of the publishers/editors/designers in choosing the information provided to the headlines as well as its visual appearance led to a variety of combinations decided each time by the stakeholders. It has though to be pointed out that the rules were set by the printers/publishers, although there are no instructions or references at the first typographic manuals. According to Day (2011: 35) we can recognize four main ways "in which those involved in textual production used running titles: for advertising purposes; for religious reasons; to guide readers' reception of the text

40   2. Through the page: The evolution of the visual identity

and to engage in polemic, whether political, satirical, xenophobic or religious."

Furthermore, Werner (2019: 21) points out to headpieces as part of the skeleton since they were left on the imposing stone after printing at the printing shops of the era: "These elements that are reused from one forme to the next are known as the skeleton of a forme; they are the structural foundation that remains behind after the other parts are stripped away." From this point of view, it is noteworthy that by the use of the paratext we can understand the printing and working methods of the era and explain to an extent the strategies and the success of such "new" features of the book. Specifically, we can enlighten the work of the compositors and printers, as well as the printing process. "Using the direction lines, the compositor identifies where a page goes through signature marks and catchwords" (Werner, 2019: 15). After that, the compositor set the headlines. As referred in Gaskell (1972: 78), "the headlines for all but the first pages of the first few sheets of a book were added after the pages had been laid out on the stone, not before." We have to remember that printing was by then a new technology and a new art; thus, the stakeholders discovered the provided opportunities and set the rules for the new medium and the gradually developed techniques. The printed page, the mise-en-page, was structured according to the existing and to the exploited opportunities that were gradually discovered in accordance with the needs of the text and the reading audience.

Obviously, readers are familiar with the headlines and running titles; some even comment that are of no use. Jennett (1951: 272) stated that "there are times when a headline is of no practical use, but does act as a decoration, subserving the design, and there is then an argument for its presence that may, I think, be retained. On the other hand, the headline may be an invaluable part of a system of references, a signpost on an involved network of roads and bypaths, directing the reader quickly and efficiently toward the place he is looking for." Another practical use, that has to be considered, is that "running titles helped enable the readerly practice of gathering single-text books to get into bespoke collections" by indicating to the readers the books (Bourne, 2019: 200).

Headlines refer to chapters or parts of the book or to the whole book. They remind to the reader the part of the book, the topic/s, and the stakeholders. This is especially of value when the title of the chapter or of the part of the book appears (picture 14, 15, 16, 18). The two pages, recto and verso, facing each other complete a cognitive circle and provide knowledge on the whole book (author/book/chapter/part). Headlines sometimes are decorated and enriched with fleurons ("piccoli ferri tipografici" in Italian) or other small ornaments; thus, they constitute an introduction both verbal and visual to the page, reframing the text in a typographic and aesthetic order. Alongside with margins, head chapters and pagination, headlines and running titles place the text and cocreate the identity and the typology of the page as known for centuries. Obviously, the headline is a visual and informative introduction to the page as well as a navigator mechanism to the reader that indicates and at the same time may provide clues for understanding and interpreting the content. "Running heads" are a good example since they go beyond information and synopsize the contents of the two pages (Carter & Barker, 2004: 121). "If some running titles were unrelated to the text itself, others sought to use a running head throughout a text to offer a generic interpretation of the whole piece," according to Day (2011: 41) whereas "a far more common practice was the use of the running title to clarify or reinforce an aspect of the text."

The mechanisms of the page, whether verbal or visual, aimed to inform and navigate the reader to the text developing thus the identity of the printed page/book and providing at the same time clues, elements and mechanisms to the reader so as to understand and interpret the text. At the same time, these information and visual mechanisms added to the promotion of books and at the same time established an everyday visual book culture. The head of the page or the opening of the page has been an introduction to the text decided by the publisher/printer but also by the editor and the author whereas the readers were aware of their existence and use. The demand for books and the expectations and needs of the readers during the Renaissance further enabled and encouraged the publishers to establish the running titles at the head of the page combined often with pagination, and sometimes embellished with small ornaments or fleurons. Moreover, running titles contributed to the promotion and marketing strategies of the publishers and were used as both navigation and interpretation tools that not only facilitated the understanding and interpreting of the text but also contributed to the tracing of complex relationships in publishing and in the society of each era.

2.2.2 Chapter heads and subheads

The beginning of the chapter or part of the book has to introduce the reader to it and at the same time to give some keys for understanding and even interpreting the text. In the books of the first decades and centuries of printing the chapter head was often combined with the headpiece; it was a strategy that would gradually fade from the 18th century whereas during the machine-press period headpieces at the first page of the chapter would diminish. Chapter heads, printed with capital letters or with bigger type fonts, were sometimes embellished and combined with fleurons. Dames (2019) enlightens the function and evolution of chapter heads through the centuries synopsizing the "new" effects: "Signalling the opportunity of a break from sequential reading; teasingly referring to plot revelations or *cliffhangers*; echoing earlier moments to indicate a plot's architectonics" (Dames, 2019: 161).

The headpiece was printed at the top of the page, and the title and number of the chapter were printed below (pictures 9, 11); thus a visual and information combination was created constituting a balanced introductory part of the page. At the time of Bodoni, toward the end of the 18th century, the headpiece at the beginning of the chapter was no longer the rule. Chapter heads were printed at the beginning of the chapter in a simpler way, with the types used in the text. We have though to notice that the chapter head was and is not printed at the top of the page: "They are, in printer's parlance, dropped, and the distance from the top of the page to the first part of the chapter head is called chapter-drop. It is not unimportant, this space at the head of the chapter, for it has some psychological value not easy to explain" (Jennett, 1951: 288−289). We may assume that by this way the first page of the chapter is used so as to introduce the reader to its context, to relate it with the previous chapters, to divide the content successfully and create expectations. Since the text is inevitably shorter in this first page, the reader also takes this pause as to think and revise, to synopsize and begin the reading of the new chapter; in that context, expectations for the text are developed and the first page of the chapter recalls, connects and inspires reading. When an initial letter appears, apart from embellishing, it may offer a visual clue and tool for the context of the text. Sometimes fleurons or other small ornaments may be used.

The visual evolution of the chapter heads exhibits the ongoing changes in book publishing, in the design of the book related to the kind of text. The design of chapter heads became simpler although its decoration may be of interest even nowadays. The subtitle may be printed in smaller printing types whereas the number of the chapter can appear in various ways such as at the side of the page as a number without the word "chapter" or embellished with ornaments or placed in a different part of the page than the expected.

Subheads divide the chapters into sections; this is of value specifically for Scientific, Medical and Technical publishing as well as for educational editions where subchapters and subdivisions are extendedly used. Jennett (1951: 264−267) discusses the role and categories of subheads and describes five "varieties of subheads" as follows: cross heads, side heads, shoulder heads, cut-in heads, marginal heads. As the quest for information and navigation inside the book was becoming stronger, the titles were transformed and put in a way that served the needs and expectations of the readers, exhibited the text and sometimes even innovated and redefined the page.

Furthermore, they were part of the visual strategies and of the development of a recognizable identity of the publisher. Nowadays, in new forms of the book (digital publications) and due to the use of other media (such as multimedia), various types of subtitles serve the page and the information mechanisms of the book as not only to exhibit the meaning of the text and serve the needs of the readers but also to innovate and offer another point of view to the page.

2.2.3 Margins, marginal notes, marginal heads

Margins should be designed in the printed book in such a way so as to let the readers read in a comfortable manner and to note. The margins create the conditions for convenient reading, for understanding the text and for participating in the book. According to Gaskell (1972: 7): "The margins round the type on each paper are called the head, tail, outer (at the fore-edge), and inner margins." We are nowadays used to blank margins but during the first decades of printing and in the 16th century, comments, reference notes, titles and glosses were printed at the margins (Werner, 2019: 91). From this point of view, the margin was an important place for information, for reader engagement and for navigating into the book. Sometimes, notes were used so as to connect across the book. In some incunables the text was surrounded from the comments. Marginal notes thus helped the reader to understand and interpret the text.

In that context, marginal headings were used even from the incunable era in order to help the reader navigate into the text and to provide the necessary information for the understanding of content. As with marginal notes, their origin can be traced in the manuscript book. "[The marginal head] is placed on the fore-edge margin at the level required. There is no interruption of the text or of the colour of the page; but marginal heads do give a distinctive air, or atmosphere, if you like" (Jennett, 1951: 267). The type of marginal heads was different from that of marginal comments. Furthermore, shoulder notes, printed at the top outer margin of the page at the beginning of the text, synopsize the content providing to the reader information and key points for understanding the text; additionally, side notes give a synopsis or add comments.

Marginal printed notes or side notes were of special value since they commented on the text, indicated specific phrases or annotated the content. As in the manuscript book, the readers were familiar with them, so they were not surprised by coming across them in the printed book; being a feature from the past continued the tradition and guaranteed the quality of the edition. Furthermore, marginalia were associated with the work of the editor. For example, regarding the first edition of Chaucer's *The Canterbury Tales* published by Caxton in 1476/77,

Espie and Gillispie (2024: 50) recognize that: "Chaucer's reflections on the business of authorship now share space with the editor's. Every Canterbury tale, and almost all his other works, come framed with an editorial argument which identifies Chaucer's sources, summarizes the content and vaunts his talent."

Thus, the role of the editor and of the scholar is not only described and highlighted in introductions, prologues, and other paratext but demonstrated at the margins of the text, offering a vision, an explanation, a summary of the content. Alongside with the authorship that gradually emerged due to the printed book (Richardson, 1999: 77–104), the role of the editor was also advanced and emerged, being an important stakeholder in the publishing chain (Richardson, 1994). Especially in classical ancient Greek or Latin texts, the editor's work was valuable and necessary for the quality of the text. Aldus Manutius in Renaissance Venice based his reputation and his well-organized publishing policy and fame—among other features—to his collaboration with well-known scholars of the era who edited the ancient Greek and Latin texts. Some of them, like the Greek scholar Marcus Mousouros, highlighted their work in the introductions of the editions by Aldus Manutius; they described their laborious work, recognized the difficulties, analyzed their choices, exhibited their beliefs.

Noting, commenting, and indicating in the margins of the page was an issue and a habit of the manuscript book that passed to the incunables. In that framework, it can be assumed that editorship was exhibited whereas complex relationships between the stakeholders were developed; undeniably different points of view and interpretations of the text were offered while the reader could disagree or agree with the printed comments. As Sherman (2010: 7) argues: "By the end of the 16th century it had become increasingly common for readers to take their notes in loose-leaf or bound notebooks or erasable writing tables." Sherman also recognizes that by the middle of the 17th century "there were signs of a general drift" (from the use of marginalia to the blank notebooks). This is attributed to the cost of paper during the 15th and 16th centuries. In that context, we can trace patterns of use and consumption of the affordable, familiar and recognizable notebooks from the 17th century that then developed reading and research cultures. Noting on books is obviously a habit even nowadays but it is true that during the 15th and 16th centuries we find exhaustive and systematic comments by readers. Students were taught and encouraged to make notes on the texts they read. These notes comment on the edition while in some cases we can even find personalized indexes and tables of contents (Sherman, 2010: 9). Sometimes a dialog between readers can be observed at the margins of a book as different readers offer different points of view and different interpretations.

2.2.4 The manicule

The manicule is the little illustrated pointing hand at the margin of the book with the finger indicating the part of the text to which the reader should pay or have paid special attention. An adherent of the manuscript tradition, it is used as a guide and a clue so as to indicate text and encourage the reader to read, understand, interpret. By providing special emphasis on a particular part of the text, it should therefore be recognized as a tool that highlights content. Titles on the margin and other annotations served the reader as well. The manicule derives from the manuscript book and was adopted at the printed books of mainly the 15th and 16th centuries. It was a familiar and popular tool helping the reader to understand, to pay attention, to interpret, to comment. "Between at least the 12th and 18th centuries, it may have been the most common symbol produced both for and by readers in the margins of manuscripts and printed books" (Sherman, 2005: 2).

Sherman in his study of the manicule (2005) and in "Used Books" (2010), especially in the second chapter, investigated the historical background, the function, the role and the terminology of manicule, which has also been named pointer, (pointing) hand, fist, mutton fist; Sherman admits that he had found 15 names (2005: 9): "hand, pointing hand, hand director, pointer, digit, fist, mutton fist, bishop's fist, index, indicationum, indicator, indicule, maniple, and pilcrow," from which the last three are outright mistakes, according to the author.

Manicules had been designed and drawn in the margin of the printed page and sometimes between columns of the text. It is not clear if the author, the editor, the publisher or/and the compositor (in regard to technical aspects), or a combination of them, decided on the place of the manicule in the text, on its usage and on the its aesthetic aspect so as to force the reader to pay specific attention to those parts of the text. The printing revolution changed the concept of communication, and the visual order of the page was decided and arranged in a new basis related to the access to knowledge and information, to the aesthetic result and to the promotion of the book. In that framework, the manicule has been one of the popular navigating tools provided to the reader for indicating and interpreting the text. The printing techniques and opportunities were used so as to embed the printed manicule, as both an information device and a small symbol that decorated the margins. The little hand indicated to the reader what to comment, where to stop, what to study, where to give emphasis. According to Sherman (2010: 27): "The old practice of using symbols to—that is both, to classify and and to point out—particular subject matter took on new life in the early Age of print. It was quickly deployed by authors and editors as a means of giving order to their printed texts and it continued to be used by new

46 2. Through the page: The evolution of the visual identity

readers ... to give their own order to the growing amounts of information that made its way into their hands."

In this chapter, we focus on printed manicules that appear in printed books. The manicule goes beyond the ornament or the type being a central symbol to marginal annotation and contributing to the understanding, studying and sharing of the text. "Manicules could also be used to highlight passages that were added to a new edition of an old text" (Werner, 2019: 91). Thus, the manicules constituted an element of early printed books that not only continued but also systemized the tradition of the manuscript era in the new medium and established an *abitudine*, a habit of the reader. Additionally, the printer/publisher and in some cases the author took a leading role in marginal annotation which was supposed to be decided by readers themselves. Furthermore, manicules can be found not only in the text (content and titles) but also in paratext, in other parts of the book, such as in the index. Thus, the publishers intervened in the understanding, reception and interpreting of the text. In that context, the printed manicule becomes one of the publisher's tools suggesting and recommending to the reader, while the margin is a vital part of the page not only for noting but also for discovering the content and participating in a dialog between stakeholders. For example, at the first edition of the work of Chaucer *The Canterbury Tales*, published In 1476−77 by Caxton, "most pages contain manicules in the margins, illustrated hands that point out Chaucerian verses of special wisdom" (Espie & Gillispie, 2024: 51).

By suggesting, indicating, and pointing out, the manicule became the medium of communication between the reader and the publisher/editor. There was a dialog developed between stakeholders of the publishing chain. The reader could accept or reject the use of manicules and could draw others by hand. Thus, we can between the lines be aware of a dialog and collaboration that was developed alongside with cultures of participation, information sharing and recommendation which sometimes remind of our era. Participation of the reader seems to be among the main aims. It is also interesting to note that manicules were sometimes printed in red and that in a few cases they appeared at the title-page or other frontmatter material so as to point and direct the eye. They took a central role and constituted an active and useful tool for the access to the content. Werner (2019: 110) writes that notes printed in the margins act as navigational aids, references, cross references, and commentary: "the presence of marginal notes can be a sign of how the book was intended to be used." Alongside with other features and elements of the page—such as pagination or foliation, running titles, catchwords—they developed the visual order of the page and served as an information mechanism and a navigation tool. Their use goes beyond the books and

The Visual Identity of the Book

expands even to the recommendation technologies, multimedia and digital culture of our era.

Synopsizing, manicules indicate the beginning of the paragraph, mark new sections at the beginning or at the end of the text, point passages of interest and paragraphs, highlight passages that were added to a new edition; thus, they were a mark of annotation on behalf of the publisher or the author or the editor. Furthermore, they work as aids to memory or as guidelines and indications for reading and studying the text. From this point of view, they were among the first tools of communication and recommendation techniques between the stakeholders. "Manicules came to play an important role in the Renaissance culture of common placing" (Sherman, 2010: 44). Readers and scholars could then agree or disagree with the publisher's or the editor's or the author's annotations, suggestions and guidelines. In that framework, it would be interesting to study the readers' and scholars' hand notes in regard to the printed manicules. In some copies, we may be aware of a conflict between readers and publishers.

We have also to bear in mind that students during the Renaissance era were advised to note and to compile so as to use passages in the future. Manicules and other symbols may have been thought to provide this service (Sherman, 2010: 44–45), although readers were not always satisfied or did not agree with the suggestions made. Afterward, the manicule was also used in title-pages so as to emphasize and exhibit; Sherman writes that (2010: 41): "As the printed book hit its stride and title-pages began to come into their own, there was no section more in need of highlighting than the title itself." Additionally, the manicule/ pointing hand was and still is used in advertisements and posters in the centuries to come, becoming thus a tool for announcing events and advertising products (including books).

The case of Laurence Stern, author of *Tristram Shandy*, is noteworthy. In the edition of *Clarissa* by Samuel Richardson (who was at the same time the author, the designer and the printer of his works) in 1748, manicules were used as manuscript devices in the margins of letters of the heroes (Williams, 2021: 27). In the 18th century though the author's role has to be pointed out. "Whereas Richardson employs the manicule as a traditionally paratextual device, restricting it to the margin of one letter …, Sterne embeds the device as a feature of his creative practice. In employing it in the line of type, a domain traditionally associated with authorial control, he blurs the boundaries between author and printer, text and paratext, claiming power over the tools of the typesetter" (Williams, 2021: 28). As the novel started to prevail and the reading audience to be expanded and widened by new dynamic readers—such as women, children and working class—the roles of the writer, publisher, illustrator, editor in the 19th century will be altered and redeveloped. Furthermore, the role of the Press and the book reviews will take a leading role in communication, promotion, information sharing, recommendation, as well as in the dialog for books.

In conclusion, the manicule has been a tool of the author, publisher, editor, reader. As roles in the publishing chain were changing, the manicule had been a tool of both annotation and participation, a vehicle of dialog and recommendation, an information and decorative device. Nowadays, manicules may be observed in the digital environment as well as in advertisements. Annotation added value to the text as it offered guidance and information to the reader; the publisher, on the other hand, offered a vital service to the reader by marking the passages and indicating the text or the changes made to the edition; in this way tools for understanding and interpreting the text were provided. It is noteworthy that at the title-page of the Chaucer's edition in 1602 by Thomas Speght it is advertised that "sentences and provers noted" with printed manicules (Sherman, 2010: 44−45).

Houston (2013: 181) writes: "The printed manicule grew steadily more common as authors and publishers moved to protect the integrity of their work. In some cases the desire to guide readers to the 'correct' interpretation of the work became an all-consuming passion: entire margins were sacrificed to notes that rammed home the official line, leaving little or no room to the reader's own critical judgements." Manicules in the margins faded gradually during the 18th century but in the 19th and 20th centuries they were revived in advertisements, in manuals, in signs and generally in visual communication. As Houston (2013: 183) states: "…the demand of advertising caused fists to grow larger and more elaborate. Where once a simple outline had sufficed, type foundries now supplied fill variants to match the increasingly heavy letterforms demanded of them, and the biggest manicules moved from hot metal to woodblock printing to avoid the uneven cooling and cracking that affected lead type at large sizes."

The printed manicule is also of aesthetic value and it certainly has to be studied as part of the page and as a visual tool of the book. According to Sherman (2010: 29): "Some are clothed in the simplest of sleeves and others emerge from billowing cuffs with pendant jewels; some suggest the merest outline of a hand while others capture the sinews, joints and even nails with a precision that rivals the most artful anatomical study."

Thus, the manicule revived in the 19th century and mainly in the 20th century as an advertising and informative signal that served as navigation tool to the readers/users. It is noteworthy that its presence and use has been transformed due to their use, the new information needs, the different medium and the different audience; furthermore, in regard to the material aspect, the transition of the metal press to woodcut printing in the 20th century enlightens the constant use and at the same time the transformations and methods that go back in time. Manicules are used in the digital environment marking and indicating; they have survived and reappeared in digital reading environments being part of visual information, indicating, pointing out, exhibiting even recommending. As Houston (2013: 185) writes: "once synonymous with an existence in the margins, the manicule is in surprisingly good health."

2.2.5 Foliation, pagination, catchwords, signatures

Initially, only the leaves were numbered as an indication to the binder. Foliation also served the needs of the readers, such as of students and scholars so as to cite, to make references, to study, to compare. All these tools and elements guided the reader in order to have control on the book, to use it, to share information, to communicate and collaborate, to study. According to Gaskell (1972: 7): "In the sixteenth century many printers numbered the leaves (foliation) rather than the pages (pagination)." Margaret Smith (2000b: 149–151) writes that 16% of the books by the end of the 15th century used foliation and she highlights pagination and foliation in incunables: "Over the whole incunable period printed leaf numbering was quite rare, found just in over ten per cent of the editions," commenting that foliation was very often added by hand by the owner or by the rubricator. Foliation was still used and can be viewed even until the mid-18th century (Gaskell, 1972: 52; Richardson, 1999: 131).

The evolution and establishment of pagination is a very good example of the development of the order of the page. During the 15th and 16th centuries, the number of the page did not appear. It was only at the end of the 16th century that pagination was extendedly used; "by the late 16nth century the pagination with Arabic numerals had been nearly universal" (Oxford Companion to the Book, 2010: 994). Pagination provided the readers and researchers with an excellent tool for studying, citing, collaborating, communicating, exchanging information, and indicating parts of the text. Furthermore, it served the needs and working methods of printers/publishers: "Because the printer has to work in page units when he is imposing the type in the printer's form for printing onto sheets" (Smith, 2000b: 150). The number of the page was set either at the top of the page as part of the headline, or at the bottom of the page. When there were no headlines at the edition, the number of the page was printed usually at the bottom whether in the middle or the outer side of the page.

At the bottom of the page of the printed book, information mechanisms were developed so as mainly to guide the reader as well as to embellish the page. Catchwords and signatures were used in early printed books and were abandoned later. The direction line at the bottom of the page includes pagination or foliation, catchwords and signature marks in incunables, and sometimes fleurons or other very small ornaments; in the late 17th and 18th centuries the direction line may include—usually on a left page—press figures (Werner, 2019: 93). They were small numbers or letters or other symbols applied by the printers so as to identify which pages had been set.

Catchwords and signatures were also used during the incunable period as navigation tools for the readers and the binders. Footnotes were to be introduced later; comments were printed together with the text in the page at the early printed books. A signature, according to Werner (2019: 177), "is the mark at the bottom of the recto side of a leaf that helps ensure that leaves are gathered in the correct order." The catchword is "the word printed in the direction line at the bottom of the page that indicates what the first word of the next page is. Sometimes catchwords are used only on the recto of the leaf, sometimes on both recto and verso" (Werner, 2019: 172). These navigation tools during the incunable period guided the printers, the binders, and the readers. They were used at the bottom of the page being thus part of the direction line alongside with the foliation and probably fleurons or small ornaments. As the printed book was maturing, both catchwords and signatures were abandoned.

2.2.6 Decoration

Book decoration or ornamentation in printed books consists of initials, headpieces, tailpieces and other ornaments, including the fleurons. We will focus on the development of book decoration in regard to the development of the page. Ornamentation/decoration in printed books is obviously expected to decorate, to embellish the text, thus to have artistic−aesthetic added value. Furthermore, ornaments divide the text into sections, chapters, units, paragraphs; they also guide the reader and are successful visual clues constituting thus a navigation tool for the reader. Although sometimes such ornaments are taken for granted, they are the visual introduction to the text and by their pattern, theme, or repetition remind the topics to the readers; furthermore, they might help the reader to interpret the text by highlighting specific parts of the book or specific aspects. As with illustrations, ornaments may enlighten the plot or the meaning of the text, being thus explanatory or representational to it. From this point of view, they constitute a visual information resource and device for the readers.

Ornaments establish a visual culture and add value to the book. They are part of the visual identity of the book developed mainly by the publishers and artists. Rarely they are signed by the artist/designer not only during the Renaissance period but even till the first decades of the 20th century. According to Wilkinson (2019: 112–114), "the craftspeople who produced block ornaments in the handpress period are largely anonymous. Block ornaments were not normally included in printed type specimen, suggesting that their producers were probably independent craftspeople, rather than employees of foundries. Very precise copies were made of some popular design, presumably by more than one hand, and these were used by multiple printers." Repetition of decoration is a common practice; most of the ornaments have a decorative motive (floral, arabesque or even fauna) and thus they can appear in more than one editions or kind of text. Some of them are used extendedly in different books whereas it was not uncommon to pass from one printer to another.

Obviously, decoration promotes and advertises the book and thus develops a reading, consumer and visual culture. Ornaments are the mirror of the art of the era, express the aims and strategies of the publishing industry, exhibit the competition with other editions, and define opinions and aspects establishing in this way a decorative visual tradition.

2.2.7 Headpieces

At the first page of the chapter or sometimes of the part of the book (such as in the bibliography, index, glossary etc.) headpieces were applied. The opening of the chapter or of the part of the book had been designed by the printer/publisher so as to introduce the new content, embellish the page and enforce further reading as well as to engage readers. The visual introduction to the chapter or part, usually at the top of the page, was a headpiece often printed in red during the 15th and 16th centuries. These headpieces, recalling the manuscript book, were used in order to divide the parts/chapters, to decorate, to embellish, to give emphasis and introduce the reader to the text. Floral motives were widely used. According to Carter and Barker (2004: 122): the headpiece is "a type-ornament or vignette at the head of the chapter or division of the book." Headpieces were a vital element of the manuscript book and after the invention of printing they were successfully used at the printed book. The first woodcut headpieces were designed according to the manuscript aesthetic standards developing and using the popular floral or arabesque motives and in some cases fauna. Later on, fleurons were also used in order to design the headpiece. It is noteworthy that a combination of headpieces was also used so as to compose the title-page.

The headpiece is usually rectangular but, in many books, especially those of big formats (like the folio) it is like the Greek Π or like a bridge; the title could be printed between the two vertical sides of the headpiece. The ornaments were in many cases printed in red as well as titles, headings, subtitles; it was a strategy and a decision of the printers/publishers so that the printed book could recall and assimilate with the manuscript precedent. Furthermore, rubrication was used in the incunable period so as to divide the text and give emphasis to specific passages. Printing with red, although presupposed time and labor, as discussed below, was also extendedly used. Headpieces may either have a bordered framework or not; in the last case, the decorative patterns (such as floral or arabesque) were not limited and could be applied freely on the paper reminding the hand-illuminated headpieces and initials. Sometimes headpieces were combined so as to form a framework; this can be observed in title-pages. The aesthetics of the manuscript period were survived since the headpiece is a common element, adaptable to the new medium, used widely in the printed book.

It must be pointed out that the headpieces were designed together with initials as they were intended to appear together at the page. We though may notice that, although a number of research works focus on the initials, headpieces seem to be rather in the shade. It is true that initials appear from the Renaissance till nowadays (in a simplified manner though) while the headpieces' use had been diminishing. This can be attributed to a number of reasons including the space required for the use of the headpiece, the simplification of the page that was gradually achieved after the Baroque era, the aesthetics of the era and the gradually established habit of printing the chapter head not at the top of the first page of the chapter, as discussed above, thus the headpiece was of no practical function. As neoclassicism took the leading role at the end of the 18th century, headpieces changed in regard to their pattern being simpler and gradually their use was diminished.

Printed in red or black, with arabesque or floral or geometric or other patterns/motifs, the headpieces decorated the page, served as an introduction to the chapter or to the part of the book, provided clues for the interpretation of the text, related the content with a decorative tradition. Printers and publishers sometimes used the ornaments, both headpieces and initials, from their stock without paying attention to their relation with the text; unlike illustrations they seem to match to the edition since the motif is decorative and not illustrative. Headpieces and initials were repeated from one edition to another and sometimes were used so exhaustively by the printers/ publishers that in a few cases the wood was destroyed at the corners so that the ornament could not be printed properly. Moreover, headpieces are not always visually combined with the initial; it is more than obvious in many editions that the two ornaments have different origins and they were used from the stock of the publisher during the laborious work of printing; in that case, although the information order of the page guides the reader, the visual order seems to be capsized.

It is noteworthy that a few printers/publishers of the Renaissance printed their name or initials (or those of the patron) at the headpieces as in the case of the Greek scholar and printer Zacharias Kalliergis; at the headpieces, printed in red, of his famous edition of *Etymologicum Magnum*, Venice 1499, appears at the two bottoms of the headpiece the name of Nicolaos Vlastos, the partner of Z. Kallierges. Furthermore, in the edition of the work of Galen *Therapeutica* by Z. Kalliergis, Venice 1500, the headpiece is decorated in the middle with a vignette depicting the portrait of the author. Although the headpiece is printed in red, the portrait appears in black. This is a very rare case of combination of the headpiece with the portrait of the author. Galen is represented as a Renaissance scholar.

Furthermore, the head of the page, as already referred, guides the reader to the text providing the framework for understanding and interpreting the text; furthermore, it introduces visually the reader to the chapter. The headings have a long development in book history managing expectations, serving needs, mirroring the era of the period. Coming from the medieval and Byzantine ornamental tradition survived and flourished in the printed book. The headpiece at the beginning and the tailpiece at the end of the chapter complete a visual and comprehensive circle by indicating details, emphasizing the content, guiding the reader and embellishing the edition. The former introduces and the latter concluded visually the chapter or part of the book. From this point of view, the page is a micro-mirror of the book framed by the headline and the direction line whereas the chapter is framed by the headpiece and/ or the chapter head and the tailpiece.

The first page of the chapter had another design at the end of the 18th century and mainly in the 19th century. Chapter heads were printed in the upper half of the page, just about in the middle and not at the top of the page. Even though, mostly in novels, vignettes/illustrations took the role of headpieces and, on the one hand embellished and decorated the page and, on the other, had a strong visual connection with the text as they illustrated scenes from the work. In that framework, these vignettes in the place of headpieces introduced the reader into the text, revealing aspects of the plot and of the characters. By this visual foreshadowing, these images/vignettes further encourage the reader to read and created anxiety in regard to the plot.

At the edition of the "Voyages de Gulliver" by L. Hachette, 1872, at the top of the page at the beginning of each chapter, an illustration or even better an illustrative headpiece or "chapter-head illustration," according to Jennett (1951: 288–289), appears and illustrates a scene of the chapter. Additionally, the publisher provides a label with the title of the image and in parenthesis the number of page or pages to which the picture refers (pictures 14, 15, 18). For example, in the first chapter, which begins on page 3, the vignette-illustrative headpiece refers to page 7, and this is indicated at the label. Jennett (1951: 397) states that "headpieces really belong to the chapter head, but come in here in the sense that they are illustrations and not merely decorations." Anxiety and curiosity are thus cultivated to the readers. At the same time, the publisher or the editor or the illustrator exhibits part of the content offering clues for understanding and interpreting the text. In this way, the book passes "from illustrative book decoration toward the narrative woodcut" (Fuessel, 2005: 161) in competitive and complex environments. The criteria by which specific pages have been chosen to be illustrated and thus introduce the reader into the chapter had been obviously chosen by the publisher or the editor or the illustrator, who in this way made a choice and a proposal; the headpiece or chapter-head illustration attempts to visually synopsize the meaning of the chapter or provide visual clues to the reader by enlightening and emphasizing specific content.

It is noteworthy that tailpieces in this edition by Hachette are also illustrative representing scenes and heroes of the work (picture 15). In that framework, the headpiece and the tailpiece move from decorative to illustrative, from abstract to pictorial. Technically, this aspect diminishes the repetition and the extended use of ornaments as both headpieces and tailpieces can be used to specific books; this does not though prevent publishers from using them as ornaments for embellishing different works.

Thus, the head of each page is an introduction that uses either the headline-running titles, and at the first page the headpiece and/or the chapter heads. In that context, the material designed and prepared for the head of the page by the printers/publishers/editors/artists considers the informational and visual needs and expectations aiming to provide a visual guide and a navigator to the text. At the same time, the mise-en-page (the physical arrangement of the text) further promotes the edition and serves informational purposes.

2.2.8 Initials

Initials decorate the beginning of the chapter or the subchapter or the paragraph or the part of the book. They are printed; even though at the incunables and the printed books of the first decades of the 16th century they were sometimes hand illuminated by a miniaturist, as it will be discussed at the third chapter. During the first decades of printing, they might be rubricated in red and blue whereas very rarely they were printed or added in gold. When their use had been systemized, they were often printed in red, especially in religious—liturgical works, as well as in classic editions; although time-consuming, printing in red offered a privileged point of view, added value to the edition and at the same time promoted it. Alongside with the headpieces, the initials constructed a harmonious opening of the chapter and an introduction to the text that recalled the manuscript tradition but soon developed its own identity in the printed book.

Beyond visual and aesthetic enjoyment, the initials relate the edition to a specific decorative or iconographic tradition; especially during the first decades of printing, both headpieces and initials were designed according to the manuscript patterns continuing a long decorative tradition. The patterns used in the manuscript book were adopted and further systemized in the printed tradition so as to serve the needs of the readers and at the same time to further explore the opportunities of the new medium. In the manuscript book, the decoration at the first page of the text had a certain heraldic value by using the emblem of the family in the ornaments, especially at the bottom of the first page. This was maintained in the case of the hand-illuminated ornaments during the incunable period. But the printed book is a mass medium; the private becomes public and uniqueness is gained by the use and personalization of the copy.

Undeniably, initials were used in a repetitive manner and became part of the page and of the printing process. At the incunables the space for the initial was left blank so that the miniaturist could hand-decorate it whether before or after its purchase. A guide letter (a small printed letter) was printed in the middle of the blank space so as to indicate the correct letter to be drawn, painted, inserted by the artist and also to be taken into consideration by the reader/user. (pictures 3, 5). These hand-decorated and hand-illustrated copies were offered as gifts from the printers—publishers to the patrons of the edition as well as to wealthy and powerful readers of the era. Sometimes they were ordered by book collectors to booksellers or directly to the artists-miniaturists, as we will discuss in the third chapter (Werner, 2019; Armstrong, 2020, 1991; Zappella, 2001; Zappella, 2013; Marcon, 1986, 1987). Guide letters did not longer exist in the 16th century as printed initials and other orna-ments (woodcuts and engravings) were established.

Ornaments were repeated extensively from one edition to the other; their floral or arabesque patterns made them ideal for being applied in different kind of texts. Printers/publishers had in their stock series of initials and sets of headpieces and initials as well as other ornaments which they used for many and different editions. They were used repeatedly, almost exhaustively, in different kinds of text. This could be attributed on the one hand to their floriated or arabesque patterns that were intended to decorate different kind of texts and on the other to the printing methods of printers/publishers of the era who tended to use again and again even illustrations with no relation to the text. In the case of illustrated/historiated initials, it is obvious in many books that they are used in completely different texts from the ones that were initially designed and intended; thus, they had no relation with the content. Rarely the initials were designed and cut specifically for an edition.

In most cases the ornaments were expected, familiar, part of a decorative-iconographic tradition, already used in previous editions of similar texts (picture 9). These ornaments were recognizable and expected to be found. We can though assume that new, innovative, even experimental ornaments, which introduced not only new decorative patterns but also a new typographic and publishing aspect, had success. As tradition and innovation go hand in hand in the publishing activity, the reading audience, although expects the familiar, is adaptable to new elements.

The printed initials constitute a feature of the printed page significant for the development of the identity of the printed book (pictures 9, 11). The background could be of floral and plant repeated patterns (pictures 9, 11). In other cases, the initials were decorated and surrounded by plants and flowers with no strict framework. They were often designed together and combined with the headpieces. Jennett (1951: 292) writes that "even the most beautiful ornament or arrangement of flowers needs to be used with discretion and judgement. No ornament can of itself make a book design successful, but any ornament can, if not well used, prove an enemy that will ruin all. Ornament must contribute to the design, not strive to dominate it or impose disharmony or incongruity."

Zappella (1988a, 1988b, 1989, 2013) in her works has investigated, categorized, and systemized the initials discussing their function and evolution. Donati had also studied the initials of the early printed books. We may categorize and distinguish the initials as follows:

1. According to the framework: those with shaped and bordered framework and those with no framework, in which the decorative patterns and motifs were not restricted and could be developed and spread in the page. The latter recalls the manuscript tradition.
2. According to the decorative pattern: In the early printed books, the patterns and motifs derive from the manuscript tradition. Thus, initials can be floriated (with plants, flowers, vineyards), fauna (with animals), historiated (depicting people, figures, scenes, etc.),

2.2 The visual order of the page

arabesque (with repetitive patterns); all these may have an abstract, decorative, repetitive character. Rarely we may come across initials with crown, printed usually in early printed books (Donati, 1953). Additionally, initials might be iconographical/illustrative/ historiated, thus depicting scenes from the plot and illustrating the content; they are designed and cut so as to illustrate and accompany the text, to remind or synopsize the themes of the chapter, to introduce the reader into the text and to offer visual clues for the interpretation of the text. Nowadays, we rarely find initials decorated or illustrated. Even in historiated or illustrative initials, the memory of the iconographic theme and the combination with the text had often been lost. We have to point out that "occasionally, artists incorporated their initials into ornamental blocks, potentially allowing them to be identified" (Wilkinson, 2019: 114). Furthermore, simple initials, with no decoration, in the design and style of the type fonts are used.

3. According to the color of ink, initials may be either printed in blank or in red for emphasis, embellishment and for dividing the text. The use of red ink in the ornamentation had been expanded even from the incunable period.

4. According to the material and the technique used, initials can be distinguished into printed (woodcut or engraved initials), hand illuminated/decorated during the 15th century and the first decades of the 16th century (it will be discussed at the third chapter), hand-colored (woodcut initials that were colored) and hybrid. The last ones are stamped (with woodcut borders) so that the reader or the colorist could add the color and thus intervene. In Italian, the term "xilominiatura" is used. This kind of initial has its origins in the manuscript era; at the same time, it reminds us of the coloring books of our era. Moreover, we have to consider the factotum (printed borders that surround a blank space into which a normal printing type/initial letter could be printed). According to Gaskell (1972: 155) a factotum is "a square ornamental block with a hole through the middle into a piece of type could be wedged." This ornamental block could serve easily to the printers.

Sets of initials and headpieces were used. This ornamental suggestion and design gave to the printed page a harmony and an aesthetic order that could exhibit the new medium's value, especially to the readers that still recognized the manuscript book as superior to the printed or as a book of quality. In that way, the printed book reached the existed as well as the new audiences and confirmed its value. The printers/ publishers owned series of decorative initials (of various sizes so as to harmonized with the page), which they extendedly used. Two (or even more) initials may be observed at the same page, a large and a smaller one or two small ones. Especially in large format editions, usually printed in columns, at the beginning of the chapters two initials could be printed, often in red ink, so as to embellish the page and divide the text. Moreover, the patterns and design of the initials and of other ornaments related the book with a specific decorative and iconographic tradition. Thus, the typology and the visual order of the page matured; furthermore, there was a gaining balance between the verbal and the visual part that established the identity of the page. Initials alongside with headpieces at the beginning of the chapter, tailpieces at the end as well as other ornaments between the chapters and units strengthened the visual identity of the printed book by adding value and exhibiting that it was by no means inferior to the manuscript one or to the hybrid one (hand illuminated printed books).

Even though, it was not unusual to find at the same page initial and headpiece of different typology and patterns. Even at the editions of Aldus Manutius, we may find such combinations. This can be attributed to the working methods of the publishers (who used the ornaments they had in stock) as well as to the augmenting demand for books and the pressure of time for the new editions. On the other hand, as the ongoing printed page was under development, printers/publishers of the era introduced the "new" elements; most of them had their origin in the manuscript book but the new techniques and opportunities provided a new option and a new point of view. This experimental period of the book highlighted the advantages as well as the problems. For example, at the edition of the Bible by Zainer, printed in 1475–76 in Augsburg, 73 "pictorial" initials were used at the beginning of the biblical books. This was obviously of high importance for the decoration and embellishment of the text. But the initials were bigger that they should. As Fuessel (2005: 161) writes: "it so happened that these initials occupied a disproportionate two-third of the column width." Jennett stated that "decoration is better if it is discreet; the ornament should not overcome the type" (1951: 276). We might comment that it was also due to such troubles that the printed book matured.

During the first decades of the 16th century, when the *libri portatiles* of Aldus Manutius were having success and the size of the books in many editions was becoming smaller and more friendly, the initials alongside with other ornaments had to be designed, cut and combined in such a size as to fit the smaller pages and such a way as to serve the needs of the text. Books in Latin, as well as Latin and ancient Greek classical texts, constituted a vast proportion of the printed books of the 15th century aiming to satisfy the existed reading audience of noblemen, collectors, humanist scholars and students. Although their visual expectations were already shaped, the printed book brought about new elements that shortly after their introduction formed a tradition. Aldus Manutius used initials and headpieces with no bordered framework, simpler in regard to other editions of his era, and with floral or arabesque design. As we will discuss below, they were part of the friendly, convenient, portable book that established an everyday visual book culture. It is noteworthy that "Once given visual form, any text is implicitly coded by that form in ways that signal, however subtly, its nature and purpose and how its creators wish it to be approached and valued" (Gutjahr and Benton, 2010: 6). Each publisher created and developed his visual identity so as to express his aims, scope and policy, to promote his books and to establish a recognizable visual identity.

Obviously, initials may differ according to the kind of text. Classical texts, dictionaries, grammars, books in ancient Greek and Latin were often characterized during the incunable period by a more homogenous decoration, usually floral or arabesque. Even though, historiated initials were used too. From the 16th century, we may observe all kind of initials as described above. Although initials may be regarded to be in accordance with the headpieces, this would not always be the rule. Initials will be simplified toward the end of the 18th century; capital letters at the beginning of the chapters and parts would take the leading role. Nowadays, decorated or illustrated initials are rarely used; they might be applied to deluxe, limited editions or they might be redeveloped and used in specific kind of texts and mainly by specific publishers so as to reapproach visually the edition or propose another point of view for the visual identity of the book.

2.2.9 Fleurons—small ornaments

Fleurons or printer's flowers are small ornaments or "ornamental type" according to Wilkinson (2019: 111) that embellish the headlines or the end of the chapters or of the parts of the book; they are used in the printed book so as to decorate as well as to indicate and divide the text. Furthermore, they are the decorative and constructive basis of headings, initials, borders and other ornaments and framings. Having their origins in book binding, these small ornaments were extendedly used by the printers/publishers/compositors especially till the 19th century. According to Wilkinson (2019: 114–115): "from their beginning fleurons used a visual code that was already well established in a variety of media, from drawings to sculpture, architecture, lacework, and book binding." In Italian, they are called "piccoli ferri tipografici" declaring their origins in bookbinding. Jennett writes that (1951: 292): "Where ornament is used it may be of two kinds, either drawn or engraved or painted by some reproductive process, or built up from printer's flowers. The first

60   2. Through the page: The evolution of the visual identity

kind is usually made for a particular book; the second is made up of standard elements of type the arrangement of which is subject to infinite variation." This infinite variation provides the publishers with an effective tool that can be combined and used in all kind of ornaments (picture 11) and in most parts of the page, such as in running titles, initials, headpieces, tailpieces, between the subchapters, at the end of the chapters or of other parts of the book as well as in title-pages. Furthermore, because they had been widely used, fleurons were recognizable and popular to the reading audience.

Printers' flowers were placed when space was small or difficult to be covered by other ornaments, and we can observe them in different parts of the book. We could assume that they were a smart and convenient "solution" for when place was inadequate for other ornaments or for when no other ornament was suitable. Martin Fertel in 1723 clearly stated that fleurons could be placed "when there is insufficient place left to begin a new title, and also at the end of a whole part, when there is not enough room for a woodcut ornaments." Fleurons constituted thus an easy to use and combinable ornament that suited every kind of text and every format of the book. They were neither representational or iconographic; their scope was decorative but their function extends beyond the embellishment of the page as they were used for dividing the text, signaling the end of the chapter, decorating and exhibiting the running titles.

It was though in the "Mechanical Exercises on the Whole art of printing" by J. Moxon, 1683, that the term "flowers" was used. Moxon points out the use of fleurons writing that the printers ought to have flowers "to set over the Head of the page at the beginning of the Book." Fleming (2011) investigates the origins, function and development of the printers' flowers and provides an overview of their use and evolution in British publishing. In regard to the books of the 16th century in Italy, we may observe these small ornaments at the end of the chapters or between the parts of the text. Wilkinson (2019) also looks at fleurons and their use and function which are of value for the study of book history and book making since they reveal the printer's practices, collaborations and methods.

Additionally, by their repeatability and combination fleurons were used to compose patterns and form headpieces, initials and other ornaments and frames that appeared in the printed page. Sometimes, they appeared on the title-page either as ornaments or as decorative pattern of other ornaments and headpieces. This was a method developed initially in Venice in the first half of the 16th century and then spread in Europe. "Fleurons were cut in type metal by the type founder and sold to the printer along with founts of alphabetical type, to which they correspond in size. A foundry might produce specimen sheets suggesting possible arrangements of fleurons, but otherwise their design was left to the compositor" (Wilkinson, 2019: 114). Both Fleming and Wilkinson discuss the working methods of the compositors in regard to the ornaments developed by fleurons (Fleming, 2011: 60–64; Wilkinson, 2019: 118–120).

Printer's flowers constitute a convenient and recognizable method for embellishing the text and creating ornaments of practical-information use during the 16th and 17th centuries. Moxon wrote in the *Mechanick Exercises on the Whole Art of Printing* (1683: 17) that they were "much out of use." From the 19th century, fleurons "have continued to be a staple of small or private handpresses" (Wilkinson, 2019: 120). Although still appearing in publications, the use of fleurons has been altered and certainly has to be redefined. As the book is though constantly changing, fleurons might be an element not only of embellishment but also of participation, creativity and convergence with other ornaments, of suggestions and participation. Furthermore, they might be used for dividing the text and indicating content beyond decoration; they can be used in other forms of the book or for encouraging readers to create ornaments. Moreover, the role of the fleurons and their contribution to the visual identity of the book have to be further studied in regard to the publishing activity as they reveal the strategies, working methods of the publishers/printers as well as their collaborations.

2.2.10 Tailpieces

Tailpieces were used at the end of the chapter or of the part of the book, They were not designed and cut specifically for the edition; as with other ornaments, the printer/publisher usually used in the editions the already existed in his printing shop. As discussed, fleurons were often used for decorating the end of the chapter or of the part of the book. It is noteworthy that from the 18th century small vignettes/gravures appeared as tailpieces, which not only illustrated but mainly synopsized visually the content of the chapter shading light to a particular scene that provided a visual clue for the understanding and interpreting the text. In the case of Gulliver's travels published in Paris by Louis Hachette, in 1872, small vignettes appear at the end of the chapter that not only embellish and signal the end of the chapter but are thematically and iconographically related to the text (picture 15). From this point of view, they guide the reader to the understanding of the text.

2.2.11 Printing in red

Printing in red is one of the main features of early printed books. Although an inheritance of the manuscript book, titles, words, phrases and ornaments as well as illustrations in red ink served visually, commercially and practically the printed edition. Ornaments in red, such as headpieces and initials, added value to the edition offering an aesthetic satisfaction whereas titles, subtitles and head chapters were printed in red as to give emphasis and at the same time to divide and distinguish parts of the text; thus titles or words printed in red formed a navigation tool that served the reader and helped to the understanding and the division of the text. We have to consider that during the first decades of printing, hand rubrication was also used to a certain number (or hopefully to all the copies of the tirage) in order to exhibit the titles, subtitles, headings, marking capitals, enlarged initials.

"The development of colour printing techniques was not the result of a progression of visionary advancements by a small number of individuals but nearly coeval with the introduction of the printing press in many areas" (Stijnman and Savage, 2015: 1). Printing in red, although implied much more printing time and financial cost, was largely used even from the first decades of printing being thus a bridge with the rubrication in manuscript or even printed books. Specifically, in religious books it was used over and over through the decades and centuries, providing clues to the reader so as to navigate into the content; at the classical texts and dictionaries we may find extensive printing in red both at the ornaments and at the beginning of chapters and phrases either at initials or at words. Capital letters were often printed in red ink whereas "some manuscripts and some of the early printed books avoided paragraph divisions and ran all paragraphs on, indicating the commencement of each by means of a paragraph mark, which was sometimes printed in colour" (Jennett, 1951: 256). The visual order and typology of the page was thus maturing.

Printing in red goes back to Gutenberg's famous 42-line Bible as on leaves 1, 4, 5, 129, 130 the headings of the chapters were printed in red (Fuessel, 2005: 19). It is noteworthy though that this red printing was not continued to the reprinting sheets from the second typesetting. Fuessel (2005: 19) writes that "it is obvious that the two-fold inking and problems with impression were holding up the work-rate and giving unsatisfactory visual results, so he [Gutenberg] left further rubrication in the hands of the professional scribes as hitherto in the manuscript era." During the next decades printing in red will go hand in hand with the work of print colorists demonstrating thus the experimental period of printing and the hybrid books produced. These hybrid books, as we will discuss at the third chapter, exhibit the convergence of media and explain the gradual development of the typology of the printed book.

Unquestionably, printing in red was used extendedly at 15th, 16th, and 17th centuries, especially in religious books. This can be attributed to the printed tradition created in regard to specific kinds of text, to the visual expectations of the reading audience, to promotion strategies, to printing techniques, to practical reasons (as the red ink divides the text). "The first three centuries of exploration into the possibilities for printing in colour directly reflect the experimental climate that was furthering scientific discovery in general" (Stijnman and Savage, 2015: xvi).

Many experts have written and analyzed printing in red; it is a feature that nowadays is almost abandoned, applied, and advertised in deluxe or limited or excluded editions or in a few editions for the wide reading audience. Even though, it may be used more easily in regard to the past due to new technologies so as to indicate, divide, compare, enlighten, emphasize, combine, decorate. Moreover, it adds value to the edition by embellishing the text, emphasizing content and decorating the book. Alongside with ornaments, printing in red can be used for further encouraging reader participation and engagement.

2.2.12 Printing in gold

Printing in gold in incunables also exhibits the strong influences of the manuscript book, as well as the aim of the first typographers and publishers to imitate the precedent book in their effort to satisfy the needs and expectations of the existed reading audience. The addition of gold to the initials and other ornaments may be explained as an attempt to provide luxury, personalized copies to collectors. The term "illuminated" manuscript actually means that gold and silver were used. "The metals reflect light and therefore literally illuminate the page" (Boardley, 2019: 91).

As Carter et al. (1983) argue, printing with gold was very rare in the 15th century. Erhard Ratdolt is considered to be the first to use gold printing in some copies of the editio princeps of Euclid's *Elements*, Venice 1482. At least seven out of 300 surviving copies have their dedications printed in gold (Boardley, 2019: 93). It seems that Ratdolt changed the procedure and the method of the preparation of gold ink or shell gold in the printed books by initially "dusting the paper or parchment with a powdered adhesive and then applied gold leaf to the surface of heated type" (Boardley, 2019: 93). In 1505 E. Ratdolt published the work of Conrad Peutinger (Counselor to Emperor Maximilian and secretary to the city of Augsburg), *Romanae Vetustatis Fragmenta in Augusta Vindelicorum et Eius Diosci*. This was a luxurious edition, printed in vellum, in Roman font, aspiring to imitate the letters of the inscriptions found in Augsburg. Apart from black and red ink, Ratdolt used also gold ink. Fifteen years later, in 1520, the book was published without color additions in an edition on paper for the wide reading audience (Jecmen & Spira, 2012: 72).

64   2. Through the page: The evolution of the visual identity

Zacharias Kalliergis (or Callierges) was a Greek scholar, scribe, printer and publisher in Renaissance Venice. He started his activity as a printer/ publisher in 1499 in Venice with the publication of *Etymologicum Magnum*. Kalliergis has three periods of publishing activity each of them mirroring the age, highlighting the role of collaborations and of financial support, and exhibiting the publishers' strategies and policy as well (Layron, 1994). At his first publishing period in 1499 and 1500 Kalliergis printed four editions (*Etymologicum Magnum* and the works by Galen, Simplicius and Ammonius—all titles for the humanist reading audience of the era) which are characterized by the carefully and mature visual design that recalls the manuscript Byzantine tradition. At the *Etymologicum Magnum* bordered headpieces and initials (large and smaller), printed in red, decorate the beginning of each letter using floral patterns. A few of the copies of both the *Etymologicum Magnum* and of the work of Simplicius were decorated with gold. Kalliergis is recognized as one of the few to print in gold (Carter et al., 1983; Boardley, 2019: 93).

In the centuries to come, printing in gold was used rarely. Joseph Moxon in his manual (1683: 331-333) refers not to printing in gold but in applying gold by hand with varnish and gold leaf. Even though, gold will be maintained at the edges of the books in the next centuries, even at affordable editions for the wide reading audience as in the case of the famous series *Bibliotheque Rouge* by L. Hachette in the second half of the 19th century; the books are recognizable by the red hardcover on which the author, title, publisher and other information are printed in gold as well as for the gold edges that embellish and add value to the edition. The visual effect of gold seems to be significant providing the sense of luxury and of uniqueness; nowadays limited or deluxe editions, as we will discuss at the third chapter, use gold at the edges of the book; this is an element that further promotes the edition and has added value recalling past tradition.

2.2.13 Printing in color and colored prints

Undeniably, we can trace similarities between hybrid books of the past and of nowadays. During Renaissance, the printed book not only coexisted but interacted with the manuscript precedent. Apart from incunables that had unique hand-illumination from miniaturists, even from famous artists of the era (luxury copies for gifts or ordered), there was a method by printers/publishers so that a large number of copies or all the tirage was hand-colored after the ornaments and/or the illustrations had been printed in black ink. The print colorists applied the color as guided by the printed frames. This was a technique of use during the first decades of printing when difficulties and disadvantages in

2.2 The visual order of the page

regard to printing in color had not yet been overcome. Later on, although printing in red was time-consuming and laborious, it was widely used, as already discussed. Furthermore, printing and illustration techniques altered color printing.

Thus, between the unique hand-illuminated copy and the mass medium printed book decorated with woodcuts or engravings, we can recognize massive hand coloring according to the guidelines provided by the printer/publisher so that all the colored copies to be similar. This was decided not by the reader as in unique luxury copies but by the publisher as an effective and satisfactory technique for mass embellishment. "The introduction of stencil coloring, a technique that allowed for colors to be applied to a large number of prints consistently and efficiently, facilitate the application of transparent colors over large areas of printed designs" (Dackermann, 2002: 66−67). In "The Book of Trades" by Hans Sachs and Jost Amman, published in 1568 in Frankfurt, we can find the description of the job of the print colorist (briefmaler). As translated by Dackermann (2002: 17): "A briefmaler am I./I make my living with my brush/And add color to pictures/On paper or vellum of various hues/Or heighten them with gold./I look with disdain on stenciling;/It makes for poor workmanship/Resulting in a lesser reward." Thus, in the publishing chain of the incunable period, in regard to the visual identity of the book, apart from the artist, the designer, the block cutter, the engraver, we have to consider the print colorist (briefmaler).

Print coloring was known even from Gutenberg and Peter Schoeffer. The latter published in 1484 and 1485 a Latin *Herbarius* and the *Gart der Gesundheit* (Garden of Health); both had great success. Fuessel (2005: 56) writes about the edition of the *Herbarius*: "A total of 150 plants were depicted, mostly in outline, by woodcuts in its 148 pages. Hatched shadings are used sparingly, and most of the surviving copies have been fully coloured. Because the plants are represented so stiffly, it has been suggested that most of them may have been drawn from pressed flowers." The *Gart der Gesundheit*, a 720 folio book, was illustrated by 378 woodcuts; till 1501 fourteen editions of the work had been published. The woodcuts are in many copies hand-colored presupposing thus an organization in the publishing activity as the print colorists could color the woodcuts of a large number of copies. This method was probably decided as less time-consuming and more accurate in regard to printing.

The color added value to the edition whereas specific meaning may be traced in some cases. Some readers also colored their own copies as we observe in old books that reveal the uses and the habits of the readers. The printed book was an object not superb nor sacred but used and beloved from the reader who could experiment, intervene, note, color, underline, bind it. Thus we can observe reader participation and reader

66   2. Through the page: The evolution of the visual identity

engagement in the origins of printing. Moreover, the reader may also order to an artist or colorist the rubrication of his/her copy.

In the copy of the *Psalterium* printed in Milan in 1481 by Bonus Accursius (picture 2) we can observe initials rubricated in blue at the beginning of each psalm and part both in the Latin and in the Greek text. The initials of the copy of the Central Public Library of Corfu are all rubricated with blue whereas the small guide letter is visible. Both the letter O in the Greek text and the letter D in the Latin text are rubricated in the same style and the same color while beneath the rubricated letter the small guide letters O and D on the upper left side of the letter can be observed.

Levarie (1995: 87) among the factors of the use of hand-illumination and rubrication in printed books in Germany recognizes "the pressure from the rubricators' and illuminators' guild" attributing thus the "highest quality" of early printing to the competition against the scriptoria and "the excellent examples of format provided by manuscripts." Obviously, as their method was laborious and time-consuming, it was abandoned. We have as well to bear in mind that manuscripts were produced even after the invention of printing (Classen, 2014). According to Parshall (2015: xiii): "The first three centuries of printing in color were largely experimental and redundant, with few instances that can be claimed retrospectively as important technical, aesthetic, and commercial success." In regard to the edition of the *Psalterium* by Fust and Schoeffer 1457, Levarie writes (1995: 82): "It was the first book to carry out the printing of not only rubrics, but also elaborate initials in one and two colors—red and blue or grey."

Undeniably, there was a convergence of media in the 15th century that produced a hybrid book, typical of the period which consisted both on printed and on hand painted or hand colored material. That combination was intended to satisfy the needs and expectations of part of the cultivated audience of collectors. But the emerging expectations of a gradually widening reading audience as well as the exploitation of the opportunities of typography led to the development and establishment of the visual identity of the printed book and then to printing in color. It was not uncommon to find color prints with stencils (Boardley, 2019: 83). During the first centuries of typography, printing in red ink was used (and very rarely in gold), as discussed above, whereas attempts in color printing were made. Apart from coloring copies by hand, woodcut remained the main means of the empirical value of illustrations. Parshall (2015: xiv) recognizes the chiaroscuro woodcut as the "earliest, and in many respects most successful foray into multi-block colour printing prior to the eighteenth century." McKitterick (2005: 80) writes that, "while color was an embellishment for many books, for others,

The Visual Identity of the Book

and especially those in the sciences, it was a vital part of the author's and artist's meaning, and its absence in such books often remains an enigma. The printed book, ostensibly offering shared knowledge on the basis of standardized text and image, in fact provided only partial standardisation."

It was at the beginning of the 18th century that trichromatic printing, the forerunner of lithography and chromolithography, was invented by Jacob Christoff Le Blon (Stijnnam and Savage, 2015: x; Boardley, 2019: 89). In Stijnnam and Savage (2015) the evolution of printing color between 1400 and 1700 is investigated highlighting the techniques, methods, collaborations and receptions. Boardley provides an overlook in "printed polychromy" (2019: 79–89). Color impressions in the printed books of the first centuries are of great research value and exhibit the publishers' methods, strategies, policies, collaborations and innovations. As Parshall (2015: xiii) writes: "As commercial endeavours motivated by profit, but also intersections for the dissemination and exchange of learning, printing shops were in many respects the ideal laboratories for invention. …There were always reasons to improve the efficiency by improving mechanisms and modifying procedures, and in the course of doing business printers had regular contact with every sort of competence needed to advance their techniques."

Coloring books nowadays recall the colored copies of Renaissance. Readers are called to color the printed patterns and images by choosing the colors and offering their option; thus participation is encouraged; publishers, artists and graphic designers may provide instructions and the framework to the reader so as to create and be further engaged. It is noteworthy that the materiality of the book is still continuing and thriving in our virtual Age in which intangible assets often seem to take the leading role. Even though the success of coloring books, which we will discuss in the third chapter, has to be studied in a complex environment taking into consideration creativity, materiality of the book, interactivity, reader participation, technologies and techniques as well as marketing methods. Publishers diachronically exploit, take advantage, collaborate and innovate in order not only to advance their techniques but to gain a recognizable identity in a highly competitive environment. From this point of view, the publishing value chain is developed and enlarged with new stakeholders, either in the Renaissance with artists, woodblock cutters, miniaturists, type designers, engravers, scholars, "physicians, pharmasists," or even carpenters metal workers with mechanical expertize" (Parshall, 2015: xiii), or nowadays with game designers, multimedia artists, engravers, experts in virtual reality, etc. In this way, publishers innovate and redefine the publishing chain by their decisions, policies and collaborations.

68 2. Through the page: The evolution of the visual identity

2.2.14 Technopaignia (*carmina figurate*)

Technopaignia (*carmina figurata*) are poems, the text of which takes the shape of the object of the title. It is noteworthy that this tradition of Greek figure poems of the Alexandrian period is survived at the printed book. For instance, in the editions of the *Idylls* of Theocritus, printed by Aldus Manutius in Venice in 1494/1496 (editio princeps), by Zacharias Kalliergis in Rome in 1517 and by the Giunti in Florence in 1540, some of the poems such as the *Syrinx* (*Σύριγξ*), *Wings—Πτερύγιον*, *Axe—Πέλεκυς* are printed in the woodcut border of the title's object. The printed in black bordered framework shaped the object of the title, exactly as appeared in the manuscript tradition. The words of the poem are printed inside the woodcut framework which in this case borders text and the page as well since no comments or other text appeared on that page. As Reid (2019: 132) writes for Poly-olbion's page borders, they "help to structure the reader's interpretation and visual-material experience of the entire work." Similarly, in the edition of *Idylls* and in other editions of these Alexandrine poems [*Altar-βωμός* (by Dosiadas), *Egg—(Ωιόν)* by Simias of Rhodes had been printed in the same way], the structure of the page is redeveloped ad reshaped as to emphasize on the text and introduce "new" reading experiences in the printed book; furthermore, visual clues for the interpretation of the text are provided. Verbal and visual elements are thus combined and suggest another option for the order of the page considering that "much of the modern criticism (rightly) emphasizes the figure poems intermediality; the fact that they can be viewed as phenomena crossing rigidly defined boundaries of poetry and visual culture" (Kwapisz, 2019: 113–114).

Deriving from a tradition that goes back in time, *technopaignia (carmina figurata)* during the Renaissance continued in the printed book the visual tradition of the text and satisfied the scholar reading audience; readers of that kind of text were familiar with the manuscript tradition and their visual expectations were developed in that basis. In that context, typography proved its value by reproducing in a massive way the aesthetics of a long visual and textual tradition. Furthermore, *carmina figurata* embellished the page and the edition by combining word and image, text and picture, further establishing a reading and print culture.

Visual strategies were of use for embellishment, promotion and for the perception of text. Technically it was easy to design, cut and print such woodcut borders. Due to new techniques and technologies we can nowadays design and insert figure texts in new forms of the book in a variety of shapes obviously. This method can be applied in various kinds of text and for different purposes such as educational, and might encourage reader participation and engagement. Combination and interactivity between word and image, letter and picture in the printed

The Visual Identity of the Book

book has been used and may be used to highlight and emphasize, attract the attention of the reader and fulfill its scope: the understanding and perception of the text. The evolution from the manuscript to the printed and then from the printed to other forms of the book extends to reader participation and reader engagement and demonstrates the significant role of the publisher in deciding and introducing patterns, policies and strategies.

2.2.15 Volvelles and movable parts: Interactivity, reader engagement, and convergence of media

Movable parts in printed book are of specific interest as they reveal the evolving techniques and strategies of the publishers in order to enable the reader to use and understand the book and at the same time to participate more actively and to be engaged. A volvelle is a part of the book attached to the page. According to the Oxford Companion to the Book (2010: 1246), a volvelle is "one or more movable paper circles rotating on string pivots and surrounded by graduated or figured circles, used to establish astronomical positions, tides, etc. and attached to the papers of the book." Volvelles are made of paper or vellum and were attached to the page in such a way so as to enable the reader to turn and use them (Werner, 2019: 100−101). Moving parts of the book had been popular culminating in the 19th century when their use was mechanical. The word comes from the Latin "volvere" that means "to turn."

Volvelles were used initially at mathematical, astronomic, navigation, geologic, anatomy, and natural science editions and enabled the reader to make calculations, to understand the text, to study in detail. The book thus provided to the reader also the opportunity to search as well as to share and use the information provided. Furthermore, reader engagement was encouraged. As Leitch (2024: 21) writes for the early printed books: "Directing highly personal empirical experiences can be considered one of the primary goals of volvelles, or moving paper dials." The use of volvelles as well of movable parts would be of success not only in scientific texts but also in other kind of books (Werner, 2019: 100−101). Leitch (2024) in her work looks at the use and role of volvelles in early printed books as an effective readers' participation medium and "do-it-yourself" activities, recognizing that "volvelles had an enormously influential afterlife."

Alongside with the illustrations and the tables at the scientific editions, the volvelle was one more navigation tool of the printed book the origins of which go back to the manuscript period. We can assume that volvelles and other movable parts of paper or vellum are the precedents of the pop-ups. More specifically, the volvelle has been the first printed moving device attached to the book, dimensional and rotating. As it is described: "A paper or vellum usually circular disk, attached to a leaf in a book in such a way as to allow the volvelle to turn. The disk was attached to the leaf (usually in the center) by a small piece of cord or vellum. Usually, the printers left the points of attachment on both sides of the leaf blank so that the cords would not interfere with the printed text on the rear of the sheet. Some volvelles had more than one moving part: a circular disk on top of which was another moving pointer" (Berger, 2016: 227). The term "volvelle" has disappeared in dictionaries of nowadays printing and publishing as it is of no use; volvelles have been transformed into other printed or virtual parts of the book.

The first printed volvelle can be found in the work of Regiomontanus (Johannes Mueller), *Kalendar*, published in Nuremberg in 1474, where two diagrams appear, one movable and one with brass pointer. Regiomontanus was also a printer and publisher of his books and of scientific works trying to explore the opportunities of the printed book, to overcome difficulties and to provide the readers with the necessary information. He had established his printing shop in Nuremberg with the aim to publish his works. In that context, he used the volvelles and movable parts into his books. His 1474 edition, as well as the edition of the *Kalendarium* by Erhard Ratdolf in Venice in 1476, introduced new issues into scientific publishing. Regiomontanus published the calendar of his own astronomical observations both in Latin and in German editions. There are two diagrams of instruments (on leaves 19 and 32), each made up of two leaves pasted together. It is noteworthy that the last two leaves are printed on four pages of thick paper pasted together in order to form astronomical instruments. Furthermore, in the famous edition of Regiomontanus' *Kalendarium*[1] published in Venice by the Erhard Ratdolt, apart from the volvelles, there are a number of elements that had introduced and further established new trends such as the title-page (Fuessel, 2005: 63–64, 80).

Furthermore, the first printers–publishers (as well as authors and editors) had not only to overcome difficulties but also to explore and discover the opportunities of printing techniques in order to solve problems, to introduce new elements, to combine techniques and to suggest. The manuscript tradition could not provide the responses to new needs and questions set by the nature of the printed book. Thus, the incunable era is an era of experiment. Kemp (1996: 41–42) talks about "processes that lie behind the making of an illustrated scientific

---

1 Goff, F.R. Incunabula in American libraries, R-93. Copinger, W.A. Supplement to Hain's Repertorium bibliographicum, 13776. Catalog of books printed in the XVth century now in the British Museum, V, p. 243 (IB.20481).

text. These processes potentially involve, in a complex and not necessarily sequential manner, variant combinations of observation, visualization, graphic modeling, publication, communication, and reception. Furthermore, the framework within which a particular combination of processes is realized will differ substantially over time and even within the same period."

In that content, the visual identity of scientific and of other kinds of texts, as we will discuss, was developed. Movable parts of the book were used for various purposes. Flaps would also be popular. "These flaps were used to show before and after scenes, to view human anatomy and to complete diagrams" and served as early "computers" (Madej, 2016: 21). Flaps were adopted in other kind of texts so as to inform, delight, surprise, explore and encourage the reader to participate. Through the movable parts of the book, we can trace the development and encouragement of reader participation and reader engagement. The reader—apart from reading, noting, sharing, communicating, coloring—was also able to compete with the book, to use it in a material visual manner, to interact and to discover, to recall and comment.

"Turn-up" or "lift-the-flap" mechanisms were also of use in manuscripts and then were adopted by the printers–publishers. Separate leaves could be hinged together at the top and attached to a page. These folded plates and illustrations were of use in incunables and old books. The reader had to unfold the paper so as to discover the picture or map or table or the anatomy of the human body. In the famous work of Andrea Vesalius' *De humani corporis fabbrica librorum epitome*, published in Basel in 1543, we can find folded papers which we can unfold and observe the human anatomy in detail. Kemp (1996: 42–43) recognizes in the work of Vesalius "factors of communication to his audience through the particularly magnificent new medium of the large-scale printed volume. These factors embrace the aesthetics of what I will be calling the "rhetoric of the real" as well as more technical questions of what is actually possible in his chosen medium of illustration." In that framework, Kemp (1996: 43) refers to: "the use of recognizable visual signals of uncompromising naturalism to convince the viewer that the forms are portrayed from life."

Thus, in the printed books the following might be used: illustrations, diagrams, small inset illustrations, indices of figures/pictures, comments, labeling, folded illustrations/movable part. These techniques encouraged the reader to participate and to discover. As Pauline Reid (2019: 17) argues: "scientific and philosophical controversies were threaded throughout book visuals, even to the point of intending readers to choose a particular avenue or experiential attitude toward their text." Apart from scientific books, volvelles or movable parts were introduced in other kind of texts. In *Diversarum Nationum Habitus* (printed in

Venice in 1591), the artist Pietro Bertelli used "lift-the-plaps" for the costumes of the courtesan. "These works were at the leading edge of the tangible interactivity that would become very popular in print narrative in the next centuries" (Madej, 2016: 22).

At the end of the 18th century, these movable tools/devices were popular and were called metamorphosis, mechanicals, harlequinades, transformations, and turned up books. These mechanisms and methods further enabled and encouraged the reader to interact and participate. "The harlequinade was printed on one sheet that was cut and folded into flaps rather than pages" (Madej, 2016: 22). These revealing scenes exhibit a new role and a different aspect of the printed book while printers and artists of the era were extending and at the same time exploring the boundaries of the book.

Movable mechanisms and devices can be considered the ancestor of the pop-ups children's books. Layers of ready-cut pictures were folded and glued so that a three-dimensional picture could be seen. The question on the nature and function of these editions ("are these books or toys?") is a question of our era on the convergence of media and on reader engagement. Convergence of media in the printed book that goes back to incunables, which were sometimes hand-illuminated, is of interest in different eras enlightening not only publishing opportunities, initiatives, techniques and strategies but also strategies and policies of the publishing companies as well as the needs and expectations of the reading audience. The book as material object was changing by incorporating the technological novelties, expressing the art of the era, serving the needs of the market, setting promotion strategies, and disseminating knowledge.

2.2.16 Children's book publishing: novelty or toy books

Technological developments in printing, illustrating, papermaking influenced the development and production of novelty or toy books alongside with changes in the publishing industry and the widening of the reading audience with new dynamic categories (women, children, workers) in the 19th century. Books of flaps, "turn-up" books, movable books, paper dolls, panoramas, etc. constructed a category of popular books for children since the end of the 18th century. From then on, publishers of that kind of books exploited the new techniques, such as chromolithography, and experimented with the movable parts. Thus, they extended the boundaries of the book for children introducing new techniques and ways for taking advantage of the opportunities provided in regard to the paper, the illustration and the participation of the reader. This emerging and augmenting reading audience (of children, parents, teachers) set the framework for a heavily competitive environment.

Immel (2010: 133) writes that: "Related to the activity book are publications in which the illustrations include cut-out figures that engage the child in dramatic play. The earliest examples are the S. and J. Fuller paper doll book issued in the 1810s." The role of illustration is obviously significant and multifunctioned: "Illustration in children's books may also be designed to direct artistic play" (Immel, 2010: 133).

Series of movable books and lift-the-flap pictures had great success to the reading audience of children's books. Movable book artists were also known as paper engineers. Flaps, revolving parts, movable pieces, pop-ups, dissolving view books, panoramas and other mechanisms were used (Field, 2019). In that framework, the book as material and visual object broadened its visual, material, and functional borders; it reached new audiences and expanded the existing ones whereas at the same time a new kind of books/printed material was developing and establishing. Books were used simultaneously as text, toy, device, collaborative or do-it-yourself activity; they were regarded as constructions, movable books, educational books, and activities. All the above obviously encouraged and cultivated reader engagement and participation; the reader had an emerged, active role while convergence of media became a key point to the publishing activity.

Literature review is provided by Hannah Field (2019): "Children's panorama foldouts unraveled often continuous scenes across a number of panels. Pop-ups incorporated three-dimensional paper tableaux, with particularly sumptuous examples mounted from midcentury onward, each one like a miniature theater. Dissolving view books transformed one image into another using a system of interlocking slats, which were activated by at a tab at the bottom of each page." Mechanical books embedded movable figures in the pages as well as additional mechanisms. Thus, convergence of media and reader participation and engagement are among the main features of the 19th century—just as nowadays.

In a competitive environment, publishers introduced, developed, and finally established mechanisms and editions which exploited the provided opportunities, such as the chromolithography. Graphic and visual, word and image, text and picture, illustration and movable part, paper mechanisms and illustration techniques, toy books and activity books formed dynamic collaborations, a new successful kind of books and an interesting research theme. For example, Thomas Dean founded his publishing company at the end of the 18th century; he exploited the new printing and illustration techniques (such as lithography) and focused on "toy" or novelty books. His son George became a partner in 1847. The publishers became famous for their recognizable toy—movable books that were very successful and popular in the mid-1850s (Madej, 2016: 23, 142). These books were called "movable" or "toy books." Dean introduced, around 1856, a series of fairy tales and adventure stories titled *New Scenic Books*.

The reader had to be engaged; when the flap was lifted, a three-dimensional scene would pop-up. During the 1860s Dean established a mechanism that was moved by pulling a tab which was usually located at the bottom of the page and named by the term "living pictures."

In the case of volvelles and moving pictures, the reader has to explore physically the book, to act and discover so as to have access and understand the content. The materiality of the book is thus further pointed out while interaction is presupposed. Reid-Walsh (2017) refers to books with movable components and other more sophisticated devices stating that "each type of movable book possesses a unique style based on its particular arrangement." In a competitive publishing environment, publishers tried and managed to offer desirable, useful, and unique books by taking advantage of the new opportunities. Movable books are books to be discovered and constructed. They are moving and can be transformed or personalized like nowadays.

Additionally, paper dolls were very popular since the end of the 18th century and were produced by various publishers, some of whom introduced changes. The dolls were designed and illustrated with their underclothes on and pasted on cardboard. For instance, the publishing company S. & J. Fuller published a series of small books in verse between 1810 and 1816 each of which was accompanied by a paper doll and various outfits, hand-colored and cut-out (Madej, 2016: 25, 141−142). The neck served as a tab that slided into slots in the backs of the outfits. The small books were intended to children in an Age when stories and tales, combined with the participation of the reader and the gained pleasure, attempted to provide a moral framework to the reading audience. This was successful in engaging and convincing parents and teachers/educators to buy the books. We have to bear in mind that children's books have diachronically to persuade the child, the parent, the teacher, the educator satisfying the needs of all stakeholders at the same time. The paper doll was the main character in these stories and was dressed according to the plot in the (appropriate) manner requested and suggested.

Initially, these books had been quite expensive but afterward they were affordable to the wide reading audience. During the 19th century, they gradually became friendly, accessible, easy to be acquired and used, affordable, popular, convenient. The German publisher Ernest Nister published in the last quarter of the 19th century several series of movable, "pop-ups" books. Although not the first to use movable books and hidden pictures, he is recognized to be the first to invent automatic pop-up books which were afterward established. Before Nister, pop-ups/movable pictures had to be manually used into an upright position. Furthermore, color reproduction techniques of the era gave him the opportunity to develop visually these books. Children's books by

2.2 The visual order of the page

Ernest Nister used extendedly the movable parts (the term "pop-ups" was not of use by then). Ernest Nister "began a printing business in 1877 and created a large number of movable books that used all of the major processes of the time: dissolving and revolving transformational slats, rotating intersecting wheels, and stand-up plates."[2] Nister published series of movable books, usually of a few pages with colored illustration. The text was illustrated by scenes that changed when the reader turned the tabs. He held both English and German patents for the revolving books and dissolving pictures.

It is though noteworthy in regard to the relationship between publisher and illustrator that: "The illustrations in Nister's books—typically featuring affluent, well-dressed, cheerful children at play—were produced by many different artists. The artist's name, however, was often either dropped or missing, while the signature of Nister, as lithographer, was usually found somewhere on the work—thus leading to confusion about attribution. Nister frequently reused illustrations, occasionally adding picture elements that were not in the original work."[3] Nister's series of stories, of Christmas Books and of activities that used movable parts became famous. Beatrix Potter was among the authors who collaborated with him. At the bottom of the cover of his books the reader could read "hidden pictures," whereas at the title of many books it was referred "A Revolving Picture Book." The anonymity though of the artists and lithographers indicates their position in the publishing chain and their collaboration with the publishers.

2.2.17 The case of almanacs, calendars, manuals, and other practical books

Interactivity as well as reader participation and reader engagement can be traced back in the early printed books in vernacular for the wide, popular reading audience. Almanacs, calendars/calenders, astrology, manuals, and other practical books were used by the readers also as notebooks, as personal storage and memory devices, as material objects of everyday life. They were domestic objects that advised, commented, gave instructions and provided solutions. Moreover, at their blank pages readers/users usually noted, commented, stored knowledge; thus the copies were personalized, customized, and had significant value as unique objects and devices of memory, of work, of family history and

2 "Movable books and Pop up books", in *The Oxford encyclopedia of Children's literature* (2006), ed. Jack Zipes, Oxford: Oxford University Press. (date of last access 19/3/2024)

3 "Ernest Nister", in *The Oxford Encyclopedia of Children's Literature* (2006), ed. Jack Zipes, Oxford: Oxford University Press (date of last access 19/3/2024).

relationships, of obligations. These hybrid books are of research value obviously being the precedents of nowadays hybrid books. They can even be used as a paradigm for combining printed material with personalized notes, comments, and drawings.

Leitch (2024: 5–6) argues that the visual program of certain early printed books mandated a systematic visual engagement with the world, commenting that: "calendars and almanacs were record keepers for wide usage and often covered a range of materials.... Calendar books printed with blank fields encouraged readers to pencil in activities as to-do lists." Reid (2019: 63) comments that "Memory was intensively material and visual in early modern culture on the printed page ... Memory is transformed from imagined mental spaces to material, physical spaces."

Manuals, calendars, almanacs, pamphlets were among the kind of books that claimed and presupposed reader participation and engagement due to their materiality, nature and function. The visual identity of these books encouraged the user/reader not only to read and learn but also to come back, to underline, note, recall, and insert personal information, transforming these into diaries. These hybrid books developed print culture and established an everyday culture of the book. In the 16th century, almanacs included "blank pages that invited the reader to participate in recording and prognosticating" (Reid, 2019: 98) as well as to comment, note, and thus be a memory and storage device. Smyth distinguished "almanacs with inserted vacant pages" as blank and the regular ones as "sorts" (2018: 204). The earliest known in England survived "blank" almanac was printed in 1579.

Publishers thus offered to the readers/users the object, the book—notebook—information/memory storage device so as to satisfy their needs. This multitask book was often considered "provincial" and "uneducated"; Smyth investigates the annotators of the almanacs and also looks at the opinions for that audience (2018). Reid (2019: 62–112) discusses in depth the early annotated almanacs by studying Edmund Spenser's *Shepheardes Calender*. In regard to the visual identity of these books, she writes (2019: 69): "gothic or *black letter* type, occasional printed commentary I separate sections and typefaces, woodcuts of astrological symbols and parts of the human body, and even a thematic focus on memory as a *topos*."

The case of almanacs and calendars exhibits interactivity and convergence of media. These hybrid books, as already referred, are the precedents of other forms of the book in the decades and centuries to come till nowadays. Furthermore, they are of research interest as they were books customized and used by a wide, often considered "uneducated," audience, different from the collectors who expected hand-illuminated copies or limited—deluxe editions. The almanacs and manuals exhibit the visual book culture of particular social classes. The boundaries of the book were thus reset and redefined by these hybrid objects: Just like hand-illuminated early printed books, affordable and accessible almanacs and calendars, children's books and movable books introduced a new culture and typology of books and a new aspect for the customer-reader behavior while they established reader participation and engagement. Nowadays, as other "new" forms of the book prevail and reader engagement is a value of our era, multifunctional books, that can be customized and augmented, are not only of research interest but can be further explored and enriched.

2.2.18 Illustration

When we discuss on the book as material object with artistic value, the reader usually bears in mind lavishly illustrated books or editions famous for their illustration or/and for the artists engaged. Even though, as we have discussed, the visual identity of the book goes far beyond that and relates to the typology of the page, to the combination of verbal and visual elements, to the balance between the different parts of the book as well as to the convergence of media. Thus, the visual identity of the book depends on its design and typology that mainly are decided by the publishing policy, aims and scope of the publishing company and by the collaborations. Undeniably, illustration has many, complex and important roles and functions. The embellishment and illustration of the text may seem the most obvious but, as in every work of art and in every part of the book, the role and aims are more complicated and ought to be studied considering various parameters such as the art of the era, the cultural and social conditions, the printing and illustrating techniques, the role of the artist-illustrator in the publishing chain, the publishing series, the publishing policy, the tradition of the publishing house, the impact of new technologies, the kind of text and its visual tradition as well as the needs and expectations of the reading audience. The function and value of book illustration is obviously complicated.

In the early printed books, woodcut illustrations and ornaments demonstrated to the reading audience the power, beauty, and opportunities of the new medium adding thus value to it. From this point of view, illustrations in the printed books offered to the readers the sense and the privilege of owning a work of art, a massive work of art that could be personalized by the reader's use (notes, comments, even drawings and coloring). This was of special interest and emphasis especially during the first century of printing when changes in regard to the manuscript book were significant and the comparison between the two forms of the book was ongoing. We take as starting point that the printed book, apart from mass information medium, was the first mass work of art and device of visual communication that altered reading and consumer behavior, the reception of texts as well as information sharing. We have also to consider the different uses of the book which is not intended and supposed only to be read but also to be enjoyed, exhibited, showed, collected, shared, noted, commented, colored, offered as gift. Sometimes it is used as the personal memory and device of the reader−user−collector. "Illustrated books alerted the eye to a new consciousness in the early sixteenth century. Self-confident agents of learning, these heuristic tools aimed to help navigate the viewer's visual horizons" (Leitch, 2024: 3).

Printed illustrations, alongside with other visual parts of the book such as the ornaments and the title-page, added value to the edition and demonstrated that the printed book was also a potential and affordable work of art for each reader. Apart from luxurious or expensive editions (in which we will focus at the third chapter), the illustration and decoration in printed books offered to the reader the opportunity to own a desirable, enjoyable, beautiful, carefully designed, of high quality and value printed book leading in this way to the democratization of taste. According to the kind of text, the illustration and decoration were decided mainly by the printers−publishers, sometimes in collaboration with the editor or author or artist. Books for collectors, noblemen, patrons were initially supposed to have decoration and illustration of higher quality than books in the vernacular for the wide popular reading audience, which had a lot of pictures but were printed in different quality of paper.

Progress in illustration techniques has obviously to be considered, from woodcut illustration during the incunable period to intaglio processes, such as copper engraving and later mezzotint, to lithography (Blocklehusrt and Watson, 2015: 39−67; Goldman, 2010) and then to photography. Thus, the medium developed new types of visual communication and information sharing; it might also emphasize and synopsize offering visual clues to the interpretation of the text. During the 17th and 18th centuries, the woodcut illustration coexisted with the intaglio, copper-plate ones, the former mainly used to embellish mostly popular books whereas the latter related to more luxury and expensive editions. The rise of other kinds of text brought about developments in illustration. As religious books lost their protagonist role, scientific works, literature (novella) and books of travel as well as atlases were raising (Levarie, 1995: 217−218).

The "Age of metal" followed the "age of woodcut" (Goldman, 2010: 108−110). "Following the advent of the woodcut, copper engravings and etching were the two most important techniques for producing images for illustration" (Goldman, 2010: 138). The "Age of stone" thereafter, with the advent of lithography changed the scene. It is noteworthy that woodcut was successfully used in the 19th century and even in the 20th century. For example, in the edition of "The Adventures of Odysseus" of Homer, by Marvin-Mayor-Stanwell, published in 1942 by J. M. Dent & Sons, both the title-page and the frontispiece recall the aesthetics of the woodcut Renaissance borders used centuries ago (picture 25). It is noted on the verso of the title-page that the "paper and binding of this book conform to the authorized book economy production standards".

From woodcut illustrations at incunables till woodcut engraving and gravures at mass produced editions during the nineteenth century (pictures 14, 15, 16, 18, 21) this technique often prevailed due to several advantages including the convenience since blocks could be set up and printed "with the letterpress at the same time" (Goldman, 2010: 143). Luna (2019: 316–318) highlights the evolution and impact of the technologies available from woodcuts and wood engravings to engraving techniques and lithography, discussing the changes in the printing procedure, production and promotion.

We have to bear in mind that the illustrations embellished the first printed books so as not only to embellish the text but also to guide the reader; "The image was often a proposal or a protocol for reading, suggesting to the reader a correct comprehension and a proper meaning for a text. It could fulfil this function even it was a reused plate and not cut for the text it accompanied...It could be used as a place in a mnemonic system, crystallizing in one representation a story, a propaganda message, or a lesson; or it could serve as a moral, symbolic, and analogical figure that gave the overall sense of the text, which the reader might fail to grasp in an intermittent and distracted reading" (Chartier, 2014: 5). The truth is that illustration was not the rule at least for the very first printed books. Richardson (1999: 193) writes that the "the proportions of Italian fifteenth-century books which were illustrated were low: about 7 per cent in Bologna ...; 12 per cent in Rome (but rising to nearly 30 per cent in the 1490s) and 17 per cent in Naples."

The use of illustration and decoration was spread and systemized during the last decades of the 15th century and mainly in the 16th century. This may be explained by the further combination of available printing and illustration techniques, by the gradual maturing of the printed page, the promotion and aesthetic strategies, and the readers' expectations. Blank spaces at the initials with a guide letter that waited for the illustrator to hand illuminate them were gradually diminishing toward the end of the 15th and almost abandoned at the beginning of the 16th century. Illustrations were popular in books for the wide reading audience in the vernacular, such as almanacs, calendars, fables. In religious books and classical texts images were a few and illustration appeared initially in accordance with the typology of the manuscript book. Other kind of books, such as manuals, chronicles and "travel" texts (such as the description of the voyages to "terram sanctam"), were lavishly illustrated. "Illustrations can refer to the world beyond the page and participate in a wider conversation about the book that involves the social status of the particular codex, its designers, and its owners" (Mak, 2012 17). In that context, the reader-user-customer expected the decoration and the illustration which was mostly related with specific kind of text. Furthermore, both illustration and decoration were considered to be a promotion method for the edition, a feature of value that even could be exhibited and praised at introductions and book catalogs, and in the next centuries at the advertisements, reviews and book announcements.

It must though be considered that illustrations were very often imitated or repeated from one edition to another or from one printer to another, losing sometimes their relationship with the text (Dondi et al., 2020). Publishers used to illustrate different editions with the woodcuts or engravings available at their stock whereas it was not unusual to buy ornaments and illustrations from other printers and reproduce them often in different texts and in pages with different size or typology.

Repetitions may be observed from one edition to another or even at the same edition. According to Richardson (1999: 133): "The expectation that certain kinds of book had to be illustrated meant that printers might resort to insert depictions of subjects which had little or no relation to the text." Even though, we have also to consider that "when a woodblock appears with an entirely different text, we can assume that the printer found it expedient to use his or her existing stock, but this does not mean that the use was careless, or that the image was meaningless," according to Alexandra Franklin (Franklin, 2019: 216). It is true that, for instance, a view of a city was sometimes used to illustrate others. Repetitive decoration and illustration is an aspect of printers' methods (Dondi et al., 2020: 842–843). Repetitions were extended at title-pages and at ornaments, such as initials and headpieces, as we will discuss thereafter. Thus, imitations or repetitions of popular, successful iconographic themes were reproduced because they were already known, tested and successful. The reading audience recognized also the editions from the printer's mark at the title-page. The expected illustration in the pages of the text and/or paratext was an asset and one of the factors that decided the success of the publication; readers, especially in regard to novels published in the 19th century, did not probably paid specific attention to the illustration but took it for granted; it was expected that pictures were to embellish the text, constituting thus one of the features of the book just like the headlines or the pagination.

It is noteworthy that we may trace the influence of the printed book to the manuscript one. "The development of illustration should be seen as a process parallel to the history of the printed word. Just as printed images could be copied or adapted to other media altogether, such as maiolica, metal work, stained glass or interior decoration, or to portrait head on metals, or to paintings, or to sculpture, so too they had their effect on manuscript illumination" (McKitterick, 2005: 58–59).

During the 19th century, the typology and visual identity of the printed book was further developed and systemized in order to serve the needs of the readers, to promote the book to the rapidly augmenting reading audience and to compete in highly risky business. Book series were very popular to the reading audience, and highly estimated and used by the publishers of the era, as we will discuss. The machine-press period, as stated by Gaskell (1972), brought about significant changes in book design, production, and promotion (Barbier, 2001). The publishing companies exploited the new opportunities and technologies for the production and the illustration of the book whereas the role of the artist–illustrator was upgraded so as to be even introduced to the title-page (Berg, 2007). We have to consider also the Reading Revolution that took place during the industrial 19th century; new dynamic parts of the reading audience—women, children, working class—took a leading role by their demand, needs, expectations, recommendations, participation, taste and information sharing (Lyons, 1999). Although the role of the Press, of bookstores and libraries was significant in the promotion of books, the "word of mouth" prevailed. It is in this period that we can recognize the first organized reading communities; thus consumer and reading behavior were changing and developing rapidly. New promotion strategies and information–communication mechanisms were used, in which the role of the Press was central. Novels were also published in newspapers and magazines of the era creating a massive audience, not only anxious for reading and consuming, but also for talking about books, recommending, reviewing, debating, sharing information, participating in ongoing dialogs. In that framework, illustration served the needs of the reader and of the text.

For example, in the translation in French of *Gulliver's Travels* by Jonathan Swift published in 1872 in Paris ("nouvelle edition" as stated at the title-page) by Louis Hachette[4] in his famous series *Bibliotheque Rouge Illustree* (in 16o format), at the beginning of each chapter a small illustration, an illustrative headpiece, a "chapter-head illustration"

---

4 Swift, J. (1872). Voyages de Gulliver à Lilliput, à Brobdingnag et au pays des houyhnhnms: traduits de l'anglais et abrégés à l'usage des enfant. Nouvelle éd. Paris: Hachette et cie. BNF – Catalog General, https://catalogue.bnf.fr/ark:/12148/cb31424129k (date of last access 14/4/2024).

according to Jennett (1951: 288–289), as discussed above, is printed in black and white (7.5 × 4.5 cm approx.) (picture 15). It is a visual introduction to the text that embellishes the page and the beginning of the chapter, and at the same time represents and explains the content to the reader shedding light to specific parts of the book and offering as well a tool for its understanding and interpretation. Furthermore, the illustration is accompanied by a label underneath, constituted by a phrase from the text with the number of the page in parenthesis so as to guide the reader. This illustration is a strong visual device at the beginning of the chapter that explains and introduces the text helping thus the reader to navigate into the book; furthermore, the reader is informed of the content of the chapter by this illustration which may synopsize the plot and theme of the next pages offering a visual tool for the interpretation. At the end of each chapter, in the place of the tailpiece, a small gravure (approx. 4.5 × 2.5 cm) is printed as an epilogue that indicates the end (picture 15). Apart from enjoyment and pleasure, these gravures offered important visual information to the readers; moreover, their systematic use at the beginning and at the end of the chapters created expectations to the readers and developed a printing and visual typology and habit.

At the title-page it is referred "with 57 gravures," the illustration being thus an asset that adds value to the book and advertises it. At the first two parts of the books, the ten chapters are illustrated each by one larger gravure (approx. 7.5 × 9.5 cm), not fully paged. At these illustrations a line-label was printed as in the chapter-head illustrations: an one-line extract from the text with the number of the page in parenthesis (picture 15). The illustration was placed in the middle of the page; two lines of the text were printed above and three beneath the gravure. The running titles consisted of the title of the part of the book and the pagination (picture 14). Even though, at the last chapter (*Voyage au Pays des Houyhnhnms*) there are five full-paged illustrations for which the whole leaf is used printed in recto page, while the verso is always left blank. At this part of the book, all gravures at the beginning and at the end of the chapters as well as the full-page pictures are illustrated with horses due to the theme. These five full-page illustrations at the last part, different from the ones at the previous two parts in regard to their size and place, offer to the reader a more privileged aspect.

This hardback edition follows the previous ones by L. Hachette and by other publishers, and has to be studied in the long tradition of the translation and publication of the book in French by Pierre-François-Guyot Desfontaines (whose name is referred at the "avertissement" of the edition, p. V-VIII) and of the illustrations by Jan–Jacques Grandville. This friendly, affordable, convenient, portable book in 16o was easily recognizable due to the series "Bibliotheque Rose Illustree" and due to its popularity. It was a hardback edition with gilded edges, recognizable red cover on which the title and information of the edition were printed in gold. It is noteworthy that at the labels beneath the illustrations the number of page was always printed so as to indicate the text guiding thus the reader and constituting an information mechanism. This typology of the book and the use of illustration in the text or at the beginning of the page was very familiar aiming to satisfy the developing needs and expectations of the augmented reading audience. Louis Hachette created a publishing and bookselling empire which lasts to nowadays being one of the publishing conglomerations.

The illustrations at the beginning of the chapters were not used in all the books of the series by L. Hachette. Additionally, the full-page illustrations were usually printed in a different leaf with the verso of the page left blank. This is the case, for example, in the edition of the book "Des Pauvres Petits" by Aime Giron, published in 1882 and illustrated by "B. De Monvel, A. Ferdinandus et Sandoz" (picture 16). The illustrations are mainly full-paged and printed in recto pages while the verso of the leaf is blank. Labels followed the pictures guiding and explaining the theme to the readers. There are no ornaments at the edition. It is noteworthy that the works of three artists are used[5]: the French artist Louis-Maurice Boutet de Monvel, the Polish artist Adolf Karol Sandoz who had worked as an illustrator for a number of publishing houses including Hachette, and Alexandre Ferdinandus.

Both the demand for novels and the competition were high during the 19th century. Editions, especially in the second half, were produced in large tirage and designed as to satisfy the wide reading audience. Another good example is the edition of Pierre Perrault's "L' apprentice du capitaine" published by Armand Colin in 1898 and illustrated by Marcel Lecoultre (picture 18). The name of the illustrator is printed at the title-page . It is in that era that the work of the illustrator was recognized and acknowledged at the title-page or at other parts of the book. The end of each chapter is embellished by a small illustration that differ in size as well as in the use of framework; sometimes the picture is printed in a framework as in page 85, sometimes partially in a framework as in page 21 or without framework as in page 47. The illustrations, whether full-sized or not, are always accompanied by a label with theme. There is no illustration or ornamentation at the head chapters. The title-page is embellished only with the printer's mark. The series is called "Bibliotheque du Petit Francais" and, like Hachette's books, the edges were gilded while the hard cover is red on which the information is printed in gold apart from the title of the series which is printed in black at gold background (picture 17).

---

5 https://www.bm-tours.fr/notices/ces-pauvres-petits Bibliotheque du Tours. (date of last access 14/4/2024)

84 2. Through the page: The evolution of the visual identity

At the frontispiece a catalog of other books produced by the publishing company is sometimes printed. Although promotion methods had been augmented due mainly to the Press, to the development of bookstores, to publishing and bookstore catalogs sent vial mail, the book had always to be the advertisement mainly of itself and additionally of other books by the publishing company.

Illustration may be used to guide the reader so as to understand the text (Banou, 2017); this was more than obvious in editions in the vernacular during the first centuries of printing when the reading audience was gradually augmenting and some readers could hardly read or learned to read by the intensive reading of specific books that owned or to which they had access. This aspect of the illustration is not as simple since it engages and combines various and sometimes complex functions, issues and aspects. The illustrations may be explanatory to the text indicating and helping the reader to interpret and explore meanings. Most of them were related to a specific iconographic tradition that sometimes went back to the manuscript book. In that context, specific themes were related to specific texts and the reader expected to find them in every edition. For example, a vignette representing David usually decorated the title-page of the *Psalterium*. In the same line, the portrait of the author was often printed at the frontispiece. The visual expectations were in this way developed. Even though, innovations were based in the element of surprise that introduced different ways of illustrating, decorating, and reading.

Apart from the obvious artistic—aesthetic value, the illustration promotes the publication, as in the case of the Italian edition (1887) of Atala, illustrated by Gustave Dore, published in 1887 and offered as a gift by Corriere della Sera to its subscribers (pictures 20, 21). The Illustration was used also in the announcements and descriptions of books to be published whereas information on the illustration can be found at the title-page, the cover, and the colophon. Illustration inevitably adds value to the edition. At the subscription model used since the mid-17th century, popular during the 18th and 19th centuries, illustration and decoration alongside with the typefaces were exhibited by the publishers in their announcements of the publication so as to inform about the future edition and thus to attract the subscribers. The future illustration was praised either for the artist, the quality, the use of "new" techniques, the number of illustrations, the themes and their relationship to the text, whereas the decoration was pointed out as a feature that embellished the page and visually guided the reader indicating the part of the book or of the chapter.

Concluding, as illustration offers visual information, it is a strong information device and resource. Moreover, it reminds the topics to the readers or may divide the text into sections or chapters; sometimes by its frequency it creates an abitudine, a habit in the book and the reader is expecting to find the illustration at specific part of the book. Small illustrations, mainly since the 19th century, were used so as to outline and decorate the beginning or the end of the chapters or of other parts of the book (such as prologues, letter to the reader, introduction, index, glossary). As the headpieces and the decorated initials were gradually vanishing in the 20th century, small illustrations took the place of the headpieces so as to introduce the theme to the reader and/or of tailpieces in order to conclude and synopsize. Even though, we have to recognize that changes and innovations in publishing take place in different ways, with different priorities and hierarchies, in different countries. Although publishing is a globalized industry and activity, even nowadays the introduction and reception of new, different methods, models, techniques, technologies, media, aspects, strategies and policies have to be studied in regard to the specific features of its publishing industry. Usually in small publishing markets and industries, the new elements may differ to the time and grade of introduction, use, development and establishment.

Inevitably, illustration in printed books develops and establishes a visual culture, which relates to the consumer culture offering at the same time enjoyment and entertainment. New issues, themes, styles and trends are sometimes introduced; thus innovation and experiment offer a privileged point a view, and the expected goes hand in hand with the unexpected. Illustration is closely related with the art of the era and obviously competes not only with other editions by different publishers but with other competitive media. It often plays a key role becoming thus part of the text as in children's books or in lavishly illustrated books; in silent or picture books it takes the leading role. Illustration may also comment on the text, interpret, exhibit, emphasize, enlighten. Thus, it adds, apart from the aesthetic capital, to the symbolic capital of the publishing house.

Nowadays, as we will discuss, illustration may be a key point for creating readers and expanding to new audiences, for further promoting the book, for encouraging reader participation and engagement, as well as information sharing and the development of reading communities. In a competitive world of convergence of media, of information abundance, of new publishing models and "new" forms of the book, the visual identity of the book may serve as a key element for the readers so as to explore and exploit, to approach and interpret content, to share and exchange opinions, to further search and interact. Nowadays, the protagonist role of the picture and illustration is unquestionable. Coloring books are based on the illustration, sometimes even of classic texts. Silent books and picture books, for children and adults, have great success introducing them to the text as well. In that framework, reader

86

2. Through the page: The evolution of the visual identity

participation, as we will discuss, can further be explored. In an era of visual communication, book illustration is an asset.

2.2.19 Folding pages

Even from the incunables we can find folded illustrations or tables or diagrams; the reader unfolds so as to discover, study, be informed and enjoy. Apart from the aesthetic impact, folded pages encourage anxiety and reader participation cultivating the element of surprise and of discoverability. In the famous edition of the work of Breidenbach *Peregrinatio in Terram sanctam*, published in 1486 in Nuremberg, the woodcut illustrations by Erhard Reuwich were in some cases double-paged whereas the view of Venice "folds out to a leaf fifty-seven inches long plus its facing page-room... A map of Palestine is almost as long" (Levarie, 1995: 103). Since then, maps and illustrations are sometimes folded. In children's books this is an element of exploration and engagement and we can view editions in which folded material for coloring extends to meters. In that case, the book expands into its environment whereas colored material can be used also for decoration. The borders of the book also have been extended. In virtual publications and electronic books, new technologies—by the use of multimedia—can extend and augment the book and its content into space and time.

2.2.20 The edges of the book

The edges of the book (fore-edge, bottom edge, top edge) are usually with no decoration and no markings. But even from the incunable period some of the copies were decorated in gold or were painted; this was obviously a heritage of the manuscript book that survived in the first printed books, mainly classical texts and dictionaries, in an attempt to provide a luxurious aspect to the printed book and continue the tradition. In the next centuries decorated or painted or marked or gilded fore-edges can be viewed in different kind of texts till nowadays. The gold coloring/embellishment used sometimes in the incunable period is survived to the editions of novels in the second half of the 19th century (such as in books by Louis Hachette) in a most massive and democratized framework. Manuscripts had their edges sometimes gilded with burnished gold; obviously, in printed books of the centuries to come, the procedure and material changed. Hachette's "Bibliotheque Rose Illustree" as well as books by Armand Colin had fore-edges painted in gold, a feature which in accordance with the hardback red cover (pictures 12, 17) constructed on the one hand a recognizable identity and on the other offered a luxurious detail and feature to a mass market book intended to the wide reading audience of the era.

Sometimes titles were inscribed on the fore-edges of the book. Werner (2019: 75) writes that: "The edges might be decorated by staining, gilding, gauffering (cutting designs into them), speckling or marbling. In the middle of the 17th century, fore-edges were sometimes decorated with pictures, either painted when the book was closed or when the pages were slightly fanned, so that the image was hidden when the book was closed." Inevitably, this was a visual tool that added value to the book, satisfied the reader, promoted the edition and contributed to the making of the visual identity of the book. It was in the competitive 19th century that fore-edges were painted or colored so as to attract readers and to add value to the book. Furthermore, a tradition and a habit was developed so that the reader expected to find colored or gilded fore-edges in specific series or books.

Nowadays, in limited, deluxe, collectable editions, the edges of the book are decorated or gilded; this is referred, demonstrated, and advertised as one of the specific features of the uniqueness and the visual identity of the edition, as we will discuss in the third chapter. On the other hand, nowadays we can find instructions on how to paint the edges of the book, thus how to customize the copy or the copies by adding an element that recalls the manuscript tradition and the first printed books. It is noteworthy that in our digital era, features of the printed book, that go back in time, prevail and are reused, rediscovered and redeveloped.

2.3 Information mechanisms of the book: Parts of the book

2.3.1 The opening of the book—frontmatter

After the invention of printing, the printed book was developed so as to serve the text on the one hand and on the other the needs and expectations of the readers. It had been obvious since the first decades of printing that the new medium had its own opportunities, advantages, challenges, features and needs. The parts of the book were thus developing and the book was maturing as typographers/printers explored and discovered opportunities and as the reading audience was gradually widening. Frontmatter (parts before the text), and backmatter (parts of the book after the text), were developing, constituting what Gennette (1979) has named "paratext."

The title-page was the introduction to the book and at the same time had the role of the cover, before the cover appeared. The manuscript had no title-page since it was unique and the first page of the text was also the first page of the book. But the printed book had different needs and features, being a mass medium that had to inform the readers and introduce them to the text. Additionally, it had to promote itself. In that context, most of the parts of the book before the text (front matter), as we know them, were gradually developed and established since the first decades of printing: title-page, dedication page, table of contents, foreword–introduction–preface, frontispiece, etc. were added as verbal and visual information mechanisms and tools. As we will discuss below, the transition of information from the colophon to the opening of the book was due to practical, decorative, information and promotional reasons. Thus, aspects of book protection, promotion, discoverability, copyright, information sharing, communication, advertisement have to be regarded.

The strong information and visual mechanisms of the (both introductory and ending) parts of the book, consisting of verbal and visual elements, were developed from the Renaissance to nowadays, as follows:

- From the colophon to the title-page/frontmatter.
- From the title-page to the cover and dust-jacket.
- From the cover/dust-jacket/blurb to hypertext

Considering the first transition, information and visual elements (such as the title, the author's name, the printer's mark, information about the edition, ornaments) were transferred from the colophon to the title-page. When the industrial cover was developed and established, the visual and promotional function of the title-page was mostly transferred to the cover. The title-page then became part of the inner parts of the book with strong information value.

2.3.2 Title-page

Much has been written about the title-page; probably it is the most celebrated and discussed part of the book. We take as starting point that the title-page was introduced and developed after the invention of printing and that it is a feature of the printed book. The manuscript book did not have title-page as there was no need for it; it was unique and expensive and thus the "Incipit" could inform the reader on the text. But the printed book was a mass medium aiming to reach a wide reading audience; furthermore, this new medium had to be introduced to the reading audience as well as to introduce the readers to its content. Thus, verbal and visual elements were combined. The term title-page and frontispiece (Baldacchini, 2009: 26–37) might be confusing terms (in Italian "frontespizio" still means the title-page). Having as starting point the term "frontispiece" as used in architecture (the principal front of the building/a decorated pediment over a portico or window), the title-page signaled the beginning, the entrance, the introduction, the threshold (Gennette, 1979) of the book. Bertram et al. (2021: 6–7) discuss the terminology of frontispieces and title-pages and the research made on a "national focus" (2021: 10–16) and according to the disciplines (2021: 17–27).

Stanley Morison (1949: 5) in his preface to "Four Centuries of Fine Printing" writes that: "In most instances the title-page best displays the book's typographical character and presents s representative exhibit of the style and skill of the individual printer." Being a mirror of the printer/publisher, the title-page was a strong information and visual device that informed, engaged, promoted, competed, advertised, exhibited, introduced to the book, encouraged, provided the tools for interpretation.

Bearing in mind that the book had to be marketable, alongside with being friendly and desirable, publishers exploited the opportunities of the title-page for informing the reading audience and promoting their book. The visual identity of the title-page and of the front matter was decided and designed according to the reading audience, the kind of text, the decorative–illustrative tradition, the competition, the publishing policy and aims of the publisher. It was already recognized that the printed book, as material object, could be a valuable object for different audiences and for different purposes. Apart from book collectors and bibliophiles, the literate as well as the wide, popular reading audience (which was augmenting) bought and collected books, was informed about books, and shared information about them. As for the series in the centuries to come, the cover or/and the title-page constituted an important issue of the visual recognizable identity of the book.

In that framework, the title-page has to be studied on the one hand as part of the book and more specifically as visual and information device, and on the other in accordance with the social, cultural, artistic, educational and financial conditions. Much has been written about the title-page. Research has been done by Smith (2000a), Baldacchini (2009), Barberi (1969), Bertram et al. (2021). As it has been pointed out, the title-page is the child of typography; it did not exist at the manuscript book as there was no need for it.

Obviously at the first printed books the colophon included the information on the production and the identity of the book (such as place and year of publication, printer/publisher, title of the work). The importance of the colophon is further exhibited by the fact that the printer's mark was printed at the same page, whereas there were efforts to embellish it. For example, the text of the colophon ended sometimes in an inverted triangle or could be embellished by small ornaments such as fleurons or asterisks.

Due to practical, commercial, informative, advertising-promotion and aesthetic reasons, the title-page emerged initially as a blank page protecting the first page of the text so as not to be lost or damaged (Smith, 2000a; Baldacchini, 2009: 38–56). As the title-page was gradually developing from the intentionally left blank page, the information from the colophon was transferred to the title-page. Obviously this blank page could not serve the complex needs of the publishers/ printers, binders, distributors and readers. It was confusing for readers (who could not be informed properly at the bookstore or elsewhere), for book binders, for distributors, booksellers and publishers. Whoever entered a bookshop of the era would have seen similar blank pages without been able to identify the titles, the author and other information before opening the book. So, the first step in the evolution of the title-page was this blank page which gradually was enriched both verbally and visually. It was in this blank page that initially the title and then the author of the book were printed. Afterward, information from the colophon was transferred to the title-page so as to inform the reader and promote the book (Baldacchini, 2019: 38–56). The title and the author were initially printed with small letter types in black. Rapidly enough, the letters became bigger and sometimes were printed in red.

Information at the title-page was augmenting. Among the information provided, we can find the title, the author, the publisher/printer, the place and year of publication, the translator, the privilege and then the license, sometimes the editor and rarely the artist-illustrator. The printer's mark appeared at the title-page, sometimes printed in red ink. Moreover, subtitles, epigrams, even small poems or texts appeared later in the 16th century with the aim not only to inform but also to attract, to persuade the reader on the value of the book and thus to promote it.

The title-page was thus embellished and decorated. The printer's mark/device was an element of both information and visual value (Zappella, 1998) which could be printed in red. The visual part of the title-page was rapidly developing; vignettes and/or decorative borders were often used. As we will discuss thereafter, the architectural title-page would be of success. Thus, as the title-page was enriched with new verbal and visual elements, the stakeholders were discovering and further exploring and exploiting the opportunities provided by the printing and illustration techniques; printers/publishers developed their promotion strategies in accordance with the title-page. In that framework, the rise of authorship can be traced (Richardson, 1999) and studied alongside with the rise of editorship (Richardson, 1994) and certainly with the rise of the publisher/printer. Both the title-page and the frontispiece have to be studied in accordance to the book itself and to the changes in the publishing chain and industry.

Furthermore, the title-page served and cultivated the needs, expectations and taste of the reading audience. Types, cultures and tradition of the title-page were recognized by the readers. Printers/publishers discovered a very successful book part for promoting their books, declaring their role, advertising their company and products, reassuring the copyright, competing in a rapidly augmenting book market, informing the reading audience and creating a recognizable visual identity. It was a time of innovation and experiment as well as of repetitiveness and tradition. The title-page was enriched both verbally and visually so as to meet the various stakeholders' expectations; inevitably, new mechanisms—mainly visual—were introduced and developed not only for informing but also for introducing themes, reminding topics and relationships, providing clues for the understanding and interpreting of the text, communicating ideas, even expressing and declaring on ongoing issues.

We have also to consider that the title-page was not intended only for those who had not yet read or wished to read the book but also for those who had already read the book and kept it in their library or discussed it with their friends or lent it or shared information on the edition. The title-page had thus to remind the topics of the book, to recall the experience of reading, as well as to help the readers revise the topics or the meaning of the book. As reading was intensive and not extended during the first decades of printing for the popular reading audience, the title-page could be a synopsis of the content creating at the same time a visual print culture. We have to consider that the title-page played the role of the cover since covers and dust jackets did not exist during the first decades and centuries of printing. Thus, the title-page was the important and crucial part of the book that not only informed, promoted and introduced the book to the reader, but also created an almost permanent relationship with the book per se, as material object. In that framework, the rise of authorship and editorship can be observed, the protagonist role of the publisher is demonstrated, the democratization of taste, alongside with that of knowledge, is further established. Additionally, the title-page contributed to the creation of consumer and reading habits, and to the encouragement of reading networks.

In that context, the title-page was established as a complex and much valuable device. Its design and use sheds light to publishing strategies, printing techniques, collaborations, competition, innovations, aesthetic values and visual expectations. The typology of the title-page, as developed and used for centuries, is the combination of the above. Illustration and decoration at this part of the book go beyond embellishment and interrelate with aspects of communication, information, interactivity. Information was presented in such a way so as to enlighten, communicate, persuade, compete and promote. The arrangement of both visual and verbal parts are of specific interest. Verbal parts, apart from informing, exhibit to the reader the quality of the book as content and as visual object; sometimes, later in the 17th century, information was provided on the benefits of the book, thus advertising and explaining to the reader why the book was useful. It has though to be pointed out the balance and the combination between text and image, between verbal and visual elements of the title-page. The influence from the art of the era, as well as of social and cultural conditions, is obvious. For example, during the Baroque era the title-pages were lavishly decorated and illustrated.

Furthermore, we will discuss the relation between tradition and innovation and how the visual expectations of the readers were developed. This is of interest since there was no precedent form at the manuscript book; the title-page was born and developed in the printed book and gained its typology rapidly in the 15th and the first decades of the 16th century. Famous artists had collaborated with the publishers and worked for the title-pages, such as Albrecht Duerer, Lucas Cranach, Peter-Paul Rubens, Hans Holbein the Younger, Jost Amman, Agostino Caracci, Guido Reni, N. Poussin, and later G. Dore and Honore' Daumier. Even though, the names of the artists are in the vast majority in the shadow of publications, even during the 20th century. Apart from illustrious case studies, the work of the artist, designer, cutter was not generally recognized neither acknowledged during the first centuries of printing. In regard to the techniques, as mentioned above, woodcuts and then engravings were used; relief and intaglio processes (Blocklehusrt and Watson, 2015: 17−65; Goldman, 2010) have been the protagonists for the first centuries of printing.

During the first centuries of printing, books were sold unbound, just sewn. The title-page had thus the function of both the cover and the dust jacket which were established afterward. Thus, it had to attract, persuade, inform, intrigue, delight, engage, promise; it had also to be recognizable and of artistic value. As tradition was developing, innovations and experiments were also introduced. On the one hand, the already known, tried and tested (for example, the vignette depicting David praying at the *Psalterion*) might be recognizable to the reading audience reassuring for the quality of the edition. On the other, new proposals and patterns were introduced and had success. Even nowadays, books are promoted and discovered due to the cover (Matthews and Moody, 2007).

Inevitably, the development and establishment of the cover altered the typology of the book; the title-page, although still important for the information provided, became one of the internal parts of the book, of the frontmatter. Its information value is high since it is this part of the book that the librarian, the reader, the bookseller, the researcher visits for obtaining the full and correct information in regard to the publication. However, by becoming one of the internal parts of the book, the title-page lost its illustrative and decorative features. Even though, at the title-pages in the 19th century, small ornaments and in some cases the printer's mark can be found.

The title-page and then the cover and dust jacket are expected to be a visual synopsis or synthesis or representation of the ideas, plot, themes of the book. But obviously it is more complex than that; among the factors that decide the typology of the title-page, we may count promotion methods, the visual order of the book, the publishing and aesthetic identity of the publishing house, the role of tradition, the work of the artist, the ongoing competition, the series. For example, imitation and reproduction of the already tested, known, and successful title-pages can be observed extensively. Printers/publishers reproduced or imitated the already known ornaments or illustrations or innovations and elements. On the other hand, new iconographic and illustrative types, new arrangements of the page, new proposals were introduced. As there was no precedent for the title-page, tradition was developing and gradually building every day. New roles and ideas were tried and inevitably innovation and experimentation played a key role; it is noteworthy that very quickly they were adopted and spread in such a way that formed a tradition of the title-page. In that content, the "expected" and "trusted" were developed in an Age of constant changes and ongoing developments. From this point of view, the period of the early printed book has much in common with our period of changes and challenges. So, what we may call "tradition" was constantly under development; it was establishing, and at the same time it was due to changes.

A categorization of the title-pages has been proposed and used in bibliography based on the arrangement of visual issues and the use of illustrative/decorative elements. According to Smith (2000a), we may categorize the title-pages as follows: the blank page, the label-title, the label-title-plus-woodcut and/or printer's mark, and the decorative border. In this chapter, we will not discuss exhaustively the categories of the title-pages since on the one hand bibliography on the theme is rich, and on the other, we will look at the evolution of the title-page as an information/visual device, as part of the mechanisms of the book and as an issue of the strategies, working methods and aspects of the publishers'. From this point of view, we will comment on the impact that the title-page and the cover had on the visual identity of the book as well as in book promotion, information sharing, communication, and reception of texts. The categorization below synopsizes the proposed main categories of the title-pages so as to exhibit its emerging visual functions and look at its impact on the development of the visual identity of the book. From this point of view, it does not obviously aspire to be exhaustive.

1. *Title-page with the printer' s mark/device*
   This simple kind of the title-page bears as the only visual-decorative element the printer's device which is multifunctional. On the one hand,

the printer's mark informs, guarantees and reassures and, on the other, exhibits the benefits and policies of the publisher reminding of previous editions. The printer's mark is one of the most popular and successful information and visual devices of the Renaissance book (Zappella, 1998). The added value was related with the fame and work of the publisher/printer, who enriched the title-page visually. Appearing usually at the bottom middle, it embellishes the title-page creating thus a type of decoration that interrelates with the information on the book and the brand name of the publishing company.

Aldus Manutius in his title-pages used extendedly, as the only ornament, his famous printer's mark with the anchor and the dolphin. In the case of the work of Ovidius, published in Venice in 1502, the title-page is typical of Aldus Manutius (picture 4). The printer's mark is printed in black at the bottom half of the page; the name ALDUS appears on the two sides (AL–DUS). At the upper half of the title-page there is rich information about the edition, such as for the index and the "orthographia dictionum graecum per ordinem literarum," as well as for the privilege of Aldus Manutius to publish the work. It is noteworthy that the title of the book is printed in the middle of the title-page, after the verbal introduction to the edition. Thus, the title-page at the upper half informs the reader about the edition and verbally promotes the book exhibiting its advantages. This simple title-page was popular, successful and coexisted with the impressive and lavishly illustrated ones. It will continue to appear in the book through the centuries and at the end of the 18th century, this type of title-page will prevail till nowadays (pictures 13, 22, 24). Artistic, social, economic, cultural issues influence the development and visual order of the title-page which also has to be studied in accordance with changes in the publishing activity and in the publishing value chain.

The printer's marks/devices might be enriched with borders, printed in red and certainly might be modified in specific details. Thus, printers' devices of various sizes existed at the stock of printers/publishers so as to fit the size of the page.

2. *Title-page with vignette/illustrations*
The title-page was often embellished with a vignette related to the content (Baldacchini, 2009: 57–66; Smith, 2000a). Tradition was created rapidly enough so as to establish specific iconographic types related to specific kind of text, especially in religious books. For instance, a depiction of David praying very often appeared at the title-pages of the editions of the *Psalterium*. Themes, like the Crucifixion or the Resurrection, were also popular. These vignettes were usually reproduced from one edition to the other, and from one printer/publisher to another. In that context, changes and

2.3 Information mechanisms of the book: Parts of the book   **95**

innovations can be observed due to the changes in printing and illustration techniques, in the book market, in the readers' needs. The Elzevirs used in Leyden during the 17th-century illustrations for embellishing and constructing the title-page even in small format books such as in the edition of "De Bosporo, Thracio Lib. III I " in which three illustrations are used (picture 8).

3. *Title-page with portrait. The rise of the authorship*
   The printer's mark added value to the title-page. Additionally, the title-page with the portrait of the author was based on the fame and symbolic capital of the author, such as in the edition of Shakespeare's works (1616). The rise of the authorship has been recognized as an issue of early printed books (Richardson, 1999). Obviously, the role of the author was upgraded in the publishing process and his/her work was disseminated to a broader reading audience. The portrait of the author was very often appeared at the frontispiece, as we will discuss. It embellished the page, related the book to other publications and to the literary tradition, added fame and recognition to the author, introduced the text and the author to the reader, made the book recognizable. The author as celebrity, even as brand name, is further exhibited in the portrait and adds value to the title-page and to the book; publishers exploited this opportunity. When the cover and the dust-jackets established, the portrait and then the photograph of the author appeared either at the ear of the book/dust jacket or at the backcover together with a shot bio and information on the author. This is of use and of value nowadays, in all forms of the book. In an Age of social media, communication, convergence of media, the role of the author in book promotion and marketing is significant (Murray, 2019), and authorship has to be studied in a complex network of relationships and shared information.
   Phillips (2015: 213) writes: "The publishing reality is that readers want to see authors, and authors need to be seen in order to sell their books whether in the media, at literary festivals, or on book jackets." Portraits of the authors nowadays recall that tradition and exploit all media so as to reach communities of readers and potential readers. The author has always been a celebrity, and in a world of celebrities, the roles and strategies are further developed.

4. *Title-page with printed decorative framework/borders*
   Even since the origins of the title-page, decorative frameworks determined the visual identity, order and space of the title-page. The famous *Kalendarium* of Regiomontanus is a very good example as well as the *Horae* published by Aldus Manutius in 1494. The decorative borders, with arabesque or floriated decorative patterns,

96   2. Through the page: The evolution of the visual identity

were used during the Renaissance and the Baroque Age, so as to construct a framework for the title-page. Decorative frameworks/ borders structure the title-page and define the visual and information mechanisms so as the reader can discover, understand, decide, proclaim; thus the reader can be both informed and attracted. It was not unusual to find different woodcut parts, which had served as headings, that composed the title-page as well.

This type of title-page has survived through the centuries although altered as to the design. In the 19th and even 20th centuries it was mostly constructed by decorative typographic lines, often printed in red, as in the case of the edition of "Black Arrow" by Robert Lewis Stevenson (published by MacMillan in 1925) (picture 24). These lines frame and structure the title-page as to exhibit the stakeholders, highlight the title and define its value.

5. *Architectural title-page*

The architectural title-page is typical of the Renaissance and the Baroque era demonstrating the aesthetic values of the period as well as the visual issues and attitudes related to the printed book. This kind of title-page offered a much recognizable and successful visual introduction to the text; the façade, the entrance of the building is decorated with flora, fauna, books, arms, putti, emblems etc. This is a threshold and a dramatic opening in an era in which these elements were much appreciated (picture 10). Inevitably, such kind of title-pages were used repeatedly by the printers/publishers, and the same title-page can be observed in many different editions of the publishing company; similar title-pages were printed exhaustively by different publishers in a much competitive environment. At the space in the middle, which was left blank, the printer could print the details and information of the edition such as the author, the title, the place and date of publication, the privilege or/and license, even a small epigram, or text, praising the edition. In some cases, an oval framework, the "occhietto" (Baldacchini, 2009: 57–66), was used for providing specific information, both visual and verbal, to the readers.

Obviously, the architectural title-page visually synopsizes the introduction of the reader to the book. The facade of the building is the entrance to the world of the book; we may even assume that it is a temple of knowledge, information, communication, sharing, learning, interpreting. Allegorical figures, emblems, books, scrolls, putti, arms, flowers, vineyards, mythological figures, anthropomorphic motives were largely used in order not only to embellish the introduction to the book but also to provide the visual clues for the understanding and interpretation of the text. Furthermore, the decoration of that kind of title-page promoted and advertised the edition. As the title-page

The Visual Identity of the Book

had the role of the cover during the first centuries of printing, the information was often embedded in the illustrative and decorative tools which took thus a leading role in the marketing of the era. This lavished visual introduction to the book was gradually to be abandoned toward the end of the 18th century.

6. *"Simple" title-page*
This title-page informs and promotes the book without using specific decorative or illustrative elements (pictures 13, 22). Initial letters or words are often printed in red so as to emphasize and promote. Long titles, often combined with epigrams and the contents of the book, served both as a kind of summary and as a promotion tool during the first centuries of printing. As already mentioned, the establishment of the cover and the dust jacket, altered the visual identity and function of the title-page the role of which was diminished to verbal information, being part of the front matter of the book.

In conclusion, as the function of the title-page extends to practical, artistic, visual—aesthetic, advertising, promotion and information patterns, we may assume that its evolution expresses the visions, aspects and issues of the era and of the publisher. Undeniably, the title-page has been an important promotion device. Da Costa recognizes the title-page as one of the marketing tools of the printed book (2020: 18—19). In that framework, the role and the recognition of the author and of the publisher, and sometimes of the editor and the artist/illustrator, have to be studied. Printers/publishers experimented and innovated. Innovation patterns surprise, promise, encourage and intrigue the reader who may further participate, discover and explore the book. In a competitive framework, the cover thus had to prevail and often to keep the balance—being at the same time recognizable, desirable, satisfying. Nowadays, the visual introduction and getaway to the book has been and can be further enriched; the cover and dust jacket still take a leading role (Phillips, 2007). Even though, both front matter and back matter are of great significance. In accordance with the new opportunities and challenges, the visual introduction to the book is not limited to the cover and to the title-page but expands to the front matter and back matter.
It is true that information, both visual and verbal, augmented. Apart from the information regarding the publishing of the book, the reader could find epigrams, poems and small texts in which the utility and the beauty of the book was praised. Furthermore, the parts and advantages of the book were highlighted (such as the edition, translation, illustration, decoration); the paratext (such as prologues, introductions, glossaries, dedicatory poems, bibliography, letters to the reader, epilogues and afterwords) added value to the edition and were also advertised and exhibited at the beginning of the book and at the cover.

98   2. Through the page: The evolution of the visual identity

The lavishly illustrated title-pages of the Baroque Era (decorated with flora, arms, books, trophies, putti, mythological figures, vineyards, emblems etc.) as well as the architectural title-page not only introduced the reader into the world of the book but also expressed their era using the common motives. Even though, as specific title-pages were repeated from one edition to another, it depended on the publisher to decide, to modify and provide specific guidance to the readers. It is worth noting that different title-pages were used by the Elzevirs so as to repromote and redistribute editions of their stock. In the case of omnibus (a book consisting of two or more parts that have already been published separately, maybe by the same author), the title-pages, as the editions were bound together, continued to have their central verbal and visual role.

2.3.3 The frontispiece

The origins of the frontispiece can be traced in the manuscript. In the printed book, it was and is usually printed on a verso page that faces the title-page. "Occasionally it is on a recto before the title-page," according to the Oxford Companion to the Book; the term derives from architecture as it refereed "to the façade of a building or to an ornamental pediment on a door or window" (Oxford Companion to the Book, 2010: 737). "The frontispiece provides a face to the book," (Cale, 2019: 27). As with the architectural title-page, the beginning of the book resembles to the entrance, the introduction, the threshold not only to the text but to the books as visual object.

Initially, the portrait of the author or a full-paged woodcut was printed at the frontispiece (Cale, 2019: 29–31). As discussed above, the title-page, especially since the end of the 18th century, became simpler and without illustration, thus the frontispiece—when existed—was the only visual part of the front matter. From woodcut to engraving and then to lithography, the techniques changed according to the era, expressing the art, culture and society each time. The visual information provided by the frontispiece guided the reader to the understanding and interpreting of the content by pointing out to specific issues and patterns. The frontispiece was a visual comment. As an introductory and navigation tool for the reader, it recalled the manuscript tradition and at the same time used the printing and illustration techniques of the era.

Frontispieces were very popular during the 18th century due to a number of reasons related to the typology of the book as well as to the needs and expectations of the reading audience. As mass-industrial bindings were establishing, the cover prevailed and the title-page lost its protagonist role and visual function; it was part of the front matter

2.3 Information mechanisms of the book: Parts of the book 99

with enlarged role in the bibliographical information but the visual element had been transferred to other parts. Thus, the only purely visual part of the front matter was the frontispiece that faced the title-page. It is interesting to note that in Italian the word for frontispiece is "antiporta" whereas in other languages the terms may be confusing.

During the 20th century, the frontispiece rarely appeared. Combined with the title-page, it might constitute a visual introduction to the book. It is true that the front matter is mostly verbal since the illustrative and visual elements of the title-page have been transferred to the cover and dust jacket. In that framework, the frontispiece can play a significant role as a visual introduction to the text that goes beyond embellishment and extends to providing clues for interpreting the text and exhibiting the key points of the book. Additionally, it can visually interact with the title-page; "the two are sometimes designed and treated as a double-page spread (Oxford Companion to the Book, 2010: 738)." This is the case of the title-page and frontispiece of the edition of the Adventures of Odysses by Marvin, Mayor and Stanwell, published in 1942 by J.M. Dent & Sons (picture 25). Both the title-page and the frontispiece have the same typology and constitute a visual entity. At the frontispiece the portrait of Homer appears recalling thus the tradition.

Whether in printed or in other forms of the book nowadays the frontispiece can have a central and augmented visual role by embellishing the book, extending the borders of the book, being combined with the title-page, offering a visual option of the information of the title-page, enlightening the themes of the book. For example, at the paperback edition of the "Printing Revolution in Early Modern Europe" by E. Eisenstein (1983), at the frontispiece appears the engraving of Prosper Marchand (1740) "The Press descending from the heavens." In that context, the frontispiece can be used as a visual introduction to all forms of the book.

2.3.4 The portrait of the author and the rise of authorship

The portrait of the author mainly appeared at the frontispiece and in some cases at the title-page further developing authorship in different environments. Authorship from Renaissance (Richardson, 1999: 77−104) since nowadays (Murray, 2019) is highlighted by a key word: democratization (Phillips, 2014: 1−23). The invention of printing led to the rise and democratization of authorship; by the printed book, the author could reach large audiences and gain fame; furthermore, communication with the reading audience and other authors further enforced information sharing, interactivity, dialogs and empowered the author' position in society. Additionally, "print publications undoubtedly

100 2. Through the page: The evolution of the visual identity

enhanced the general recognition of the identity of the author as the creator and owner of the text" (Richardson, 1999: 101). The printed book undeniably provided to the authors not only the medium for the transmission of their works but also for the building of their fame and the creation of the author as "celebrity."

In that context, the portrait of the author added value to the edition since the fame of the person illustrated as well as the success and impact of previous editions not only promoted but also guaranteed the quality of the edition. Furthermore, the author's fame was further established. The printed book also signals the move from patron to publisher and the publishing activity, thus to a more collaborative and democratic activity. Nowadays, new information and communication technologies, new publishing models (such as self-publishing, collaborative projects, crowdfunding), new business models, social media as well as the convergence of media create the framework for changes in the whole publishing chain and for further "democratization" of authorship (Phillips, 2014: 4–18).

2.3.5 The end of the book, back matter

Back matter or end matter or endlims or postlims or subsidiaries follow the text and is as important as front matter; back matter may conclude, epitomize, synopsize, provide further material, highlight aspects of the text and of the biography of the author, anticipate future research and further reading, navigate the reader into the book and in new paths. Although not studied or exhibited as the front matter, the end parts lead to the conclusion and to the end of the book cultivating further expectations and providing the "aftertaste" of the book (or of the series). Apart from the navigation/information tools (such as bibliography, index, errata, timeline, glossary), the epilogue or coda or afterword or other texts may provide a vision, synopsis and explanation offering further clues on the perception of the book and broader vision on themes to be looked at in future research. Texts on the period or on the author and short biographies sometimes enlighten, after reading, the content of the book in a decisive manner.

At the end of the text the reader may find afterword, epilogue, bibliography, index, timeline, errata, glossary, endnotes, register (in incunables), subscription list, colophon, advertisements and information for other editions, illustrations or maps or diagrams, tailpieces and other ornaments, printer's mark. In regard to the visual identity, illustrations, maps, and tables are sometimes placed at the back matter (whether folded or not). These parts were found at the end of printed books, after the text, especially when the illustrations or maps were printed on a better quality paper. Moreover, the tailpieces and other ornaments are of interest. The end of the book, due to the usual availability of blank pages, is used by the publisher so as to inform and promote new upcoming titles or other titles by the author or the series of the company.

Sherman (2011: 65) introducing the term "terminal paratexts," refers to Genette's classic work in regard to the end of the text: "He does not devote a single word to the conventional forms developed to bring books to close. Gennette never intended his account to be exhaustive...." The back matter till now forms a strong part of the book, especially in STM or educational books since we find bibliography, references, index, glossary, epilogues and afterward etc. Whereas, many publishers printed and sometimes still print the contents at the back matter.

2.3.6 Colophon

The colophon had been an important part of the book, both manuscript and printed, although the latter gave emphasis to the title-page. As discussed above, during the first decades of printing, information regarding the edition could be found at the colophon (picture 6). The birth and gradual development of the title-page led to the transfer of significant information to the title-page. Even though, the colophon coexisted with the title-page, and it was in this part of the book that till recently (and even nowadays) we search when we want to find more precise information not mentioned on the title-page (such as the place or date of publication, the book binder, the number of copies, the printer, the editor, the quality of paper, the artist). It is noteworthy that the colophon, although seemed to decline after the "invention" of the title-page, it did continue on the one hand to provide information and on the other to close the book signaling the end of the internal parts of the edition; these detailed colophons can still be found in some publishing companies and are of value for book historians, bibliographers, researchers, and librarians since they provide detailed information on issues of book design and production.

Apart from verbal information, the colophon provided visual information and furthermore embellished the end of the book. Sherman (2011: 71) writes that "[the printers] often incorporated or concluded with a visual device or illustration of some sort." Indeed, the printer's mark was printed at the end of the book after the colophon, as in the editions of Aldus Manutius (picture 6). Sometimes red ink was used. This was a strong visual notification of the publisher/ printer that empowered and demonstrated his role. We can thus trace and understand the changes in the role and position of the printer not only in the

102 2. Through the page: The evolution of the visual identity

value publishing chain and in the publishing process but also in the society and culture of the era. At the colophons of early printed books, the printer/publishers often were not even mentioned; for example, we all refer to Gutenberg' s editions in which though his name was never printed. As the stakeholders and the printers came to understand not only their role and responsibilities but also the features and challenges of the new medium and of the publishing activity, they realized that the books had to be signed by them. The augmented competition further forced them to "sign" their products so as to be recognizable and thus trusted by the gradually augmenting reading audience. In that framework, the colophon verified the edition and visually demonstrated the identity of the book. The printer's marks were very often the main visual and decorative element of the title-page, sometimes embellished with borders, lines, asterisks or small ornaments (picture 6).

We have to recognize that the colophon was designed in such a way as to embellish the end of the book. Sometimes, colophons were designed in inverted triangle or other schemes. More specifically, the words were printed in such a way that they formed an inverted triangle which could be decorated by a set of asterisks (more commonly) or other symbols. During the 15th century, we can trace valuable information about the printing methods and promotion strategies since the colophon combined verbal and visual elements.

Apart from the title, the author, the place and year of publication, the publisher/printer, other details had been included in the colophon, which were gradually transferred to the title-page. For example, Anton Koberger at the colophon of his *Bible* of 1483[6] refers to the illustration: "and with splendid pictures" (as stated in Fuessel, 2005: 162). During the 16th century, although the title-page and frontispiece took the leading role both verbally and visually, "textual endings continue to be signalled by visual as well as verbal clues" (Sherman, 2011: 71). Furthermore, small ornaments such as tailpieces or printer's flowers (fleurons) accompanied the colophon and thus embellished the end of the book. Recalling the manuscript tradition, the colophon remained an important information device and visual part of the book. Sometimes publishers tried to innovate the end of the book by adding visual elements. The use of colophon tended to be reduced toward the last decades of the 20th century. Even though, it is still of use and value in some editions. Furthermore, the appearance or not of the colophon is a choice and decision of the publisher in all forms of the book, printed or not; it can be embellished and provide further information on the book which does not exist at the title-page and at the verso of the title-page (such as the tirage, the corrector, the editor, the quality of paper).

6 Goff B-632.

The Visual Identity of the Book

2.3.7 Cover and dust jacket (or book jacket or cover jacket)

During the first centuries of printing, books were sold unbound, just sewn. "Books were almost always sold unbound" (Dondi, 2010: 56). As already discussed, the title-page had the function of the cover. Prior to the 1820s, most books were issued as unbound sheets or with disposable board covers. "It was until the mechanization of bookbinding in the nineteenth century that publishers begun to issue works in standard bindings, whether cloth or paper, that could be applied to an entire series" (Luna, 2019: 314). Hardback books, whether paper or cloth bound, appeared and changed the visual identity and order of the book. Apart from protecting the text and the book, the cover informed, promoted, advertised, and delighted. Furthermore, the book was more convenient, friendly, affordable, manageable for the reader, and obviously desirable. Thus, the industrial cover further democratized the book; binding was not any more the privilege of those who could order and pay for it. It was a privilege of every reader who could buy, read, collect books and have a personal library. In that context, the spines of the books had a strong information and visual impact; apart from informing, they were part of the identity of the book, exhibited at the bookshelves and useful for recalling the plot or features of the book.

Publishers recognized in the cover another asset for the promotion and marketing of their books that further developed their publishing policy and created a recognizable visual identity. The color and the aesthetics of the cover signalized the visual recognizable order of the series, as for example in the case of *Bibliotheque Rouge* by L. Hachette or in books by A. Colin (pictures 12, 17). The title, author, and information on the book appeared often in gold. Machine binding (Jennett, 1951: 166−178) changed thus the book as material object for the wide reading audience. At the large-sized edition of Atala in Italian, 1882, which was given as a gift to the subscribers of the Corriere della Sera the cover is red with decoration and title printed in gold. (picture 20).

Dust jackets to hardback or paperback books derive from the need to protect the cover and the binding of the book, just like the blank page—that created the title-page—derived from the need to protect the first page of the text from being damaged, lost or inked. In this way, dust jacket and title-page have parallel origins that are due to practical needs for the protection of the book which then expanded to aesthetic, visual, promotion, marketing issues.

More specifically, the origins of the paper dust jacket (also called book jacket, dust cover, dust wrapper) can be traced back to the first decades of the 19th century (Partington, 2019). In 2009, at the Bodleian Library was (re)discovered a dust jacket of 1830, which is considered to be the oldest surviving one (Cock-Starkey, 2017: 87). It is a dust-jacket, paper wrapper for a gift book, bound in silk, entitled "Friendship's Offering." Obviously dust jackets have not survived in their majority as they were lost or destroyed. Initially, dust jackets were made by wrap paper as to protect the binding and cover of the book; these plain paper wraps were taken away after the book had reached its destination at the bookstore or other retail points or libraries. With no aesthetic or informational function at the beginning, they were intended only for protection, just like the blank page at the beginning of incunables. It is though noteworthy that sometimes windows were left at the paper so as the title could be read and the book to be recognized—exactly like the titles of the book that were printed at the blank page of the early printed books so as to indicate the edition and guide the reader, the bookseller, the binder.

These windows were obviously born from the need for protection and the demand for being the titles recognizable; at the same time they gave ideas to the publishers for further exploration and use of the dust jacket in their books both for protection and for promotion. Publishers understood the advantages of this new tool, which soon became a part of the book; thus they explored and exploited the dust jacket's opportunities for book embellishment and promotion, for providing information and introducing the readers to the book. "What has previously been a largely plain protective layer began to fill with text and illustration" (Partington, 2019: 15). Apart from the information provided in the cover and title-page (author, title, date and place of publication, publishing company, translation, illustration), the dust jacket's information exceeded to the price of the book, extracts, reviews on the book, advertisements for other books, later the ISBN and other details. Thus, the dust jacket has since then been a powerful multifunctional tool, important in the visual order and identity of the book.

During the industrial 19th century, when significant changes took place in the production, distribution, promotion and sharing of books, the book per se had to be rediscovered. As the reading audience was enlarged with "new" dynamic categories, (women, children, working class) and the demand for books was augmenting (Lyons, 1999), the book had to satisfy their needs and be affordable, friendly, portable, desirable, admirable, accessible. Competition was hard. In that framework, the book had to attract readers and the dust jacket was the appropriate tool since it could be lavishly illustrated in order not only to promote but also to exhibit and synopsize visually the content of the book. A short description of the book, known as blurb, so as to attract the readers and outline the contents and main themes of the book, appeared at the back of the dust jacket. Sometimes an extract from the book or reviews were printed. The folded flaps of the dust jacket were used for printing the short biography of the author or for providing information about other books of the series or of the publishing company. Some readers may also use the flaps as book marks.

With the progress in illustration techniques, dust jackets could be more precise, desirable, competing. Often designed by well-known artists or graphic designers they form the outer threshold of the book which visually exhibits the identity and scope of the publisher as well as the content of the book. This is more than prevailing in book series, which visually declare the criteria and ideology of the series.

Toward the end of the 19th century, dust jackets with a significant visual information function, especially after the 1870s, were established and broadly used. More specifically, after the first decades of the use of dust-jackets, the title and the author were printed at the spine of the book; this helped the readers, booksellers, librarians to be informed on the book and also to arrange the shelves of the bookstore/library. Lewis Carroll in a letter to his publisher in 1876 asked for the title of his work "The Hunting of the Snark" to be printed on the "paper wrapper" so that the book would remain in "cleaner and more saleable condition." (Partington, 2019: 15). Nowadays, dust jackets are extremely important in hardback books.

2.3.8 Slipcases

Slipcases for one or more books were and are used for practical and aesthetic reasons; on the one hand, they protect the book or the books they contain, especially when they are of large or small sizes; these books might be of high quality, of deluxe or limited or collectable editions. The slipcase specifically protects the cloth or leather binding, as well as the cover. It is noteworthy that nowadays slipcases are referred and advertised as one of the features of the deluxe editions. The spines of the books in the slipcase are visible in the bookshelves so as to exhibit on the one hand the visual identity of the edition and on the other to help readers, booksellers and librarians navigate into the shelves and libraries and identify the books (picture 23).

Even though, not all slipcases accompanied and accompany deluxe editions; slipcases were and are used for affordable editions intended for the wide reading audience (picture 23). Experiments and innovation in slipcase can be observed in the 20th century. Furthermore, slipcases are used for trilogies or tetralogies as well as for books of the same series; in this case, the books included in the slipcase, apart from being recognizable and desirable, have a tangible, visual advantage that further promotes them. In that framework, experiments have taken place. For example, the slipcase might no longer be a box or sleeve but may look like an envelope. "Some slipcases were decorated in a matching or uniform style to the cloth covers or dust wrapper of the book they contained" (Oxford Companion to the Book, 2010: 1161). Undeniably, the visual identity of the slipcases has a close relationship with the cover and dust jacket, with the content of the book, with the iconographical and illustrative tradition, of the identity of the publishing company or of the series. Slipcases are also used for children's books or for celebrations when the box contains all the titles of collectible value. Additionally, publishers select books of the same author or of series, which are sold in the slipcase; in that case, the publisher recommends specific works that are related with each other even thematically or by the author.

2.4 The democratization of taste and visual expectations

2.4.1 The democratization of taste

Printed illustration and decoration became part of the printed book since the first decades of printing, cocreating thus a material culture that led to the interpretation and understanding of the text as well as to the promotion of the book. In some cases, printed illustrations were combined in the book and converged with other media. This material culture inevitably changed patterns of book design, production and consumption. Even since the first decades of printing, woodcuts (illustrations and ornaments such as headpieces and initials) were used by the printers/publishers for a number of reasons beyond embellishing the text. Thus, the printed book was further established not only as an information medium but also as a desirable object with artistic value that could be at the same time an affordable work of art and an everyday object. In that context, the printed book has been the first mass work of art that changed patterns of taste, visual culture and information, visual communication, information sharing, and thus introduced new consumer and reader behaviors. The printed book led to the democratization of taste, as already discussed, since it gradually revolutionized all forms of learning and developed taste in augmented audiences (Banou, 2017).

The impact of new techniques and of innovation patterns ought also to be enlightened. The resemblance of the printed book with the manuscript one was an issue of success during the incunable period. The printed book was thus recognizable and trusted by the existed reading audience which initially was the same with that of the manuscript book. But soon it had been obvious that the printed book was a new medium with innovative, extended and discoverable opportunities, methods, strategies and techniques which publishers and other stakeholders explored. It was in the 15th century and the first decades of the 16th century that the elements of the page and most parts of the book were developed as visual and information devices. But it was for centuries that the printed book matured.

Undeniably, the printed book and more specifically its visual identity since its origins led to the democratization of taste. Visual communication and visual information had been vital. The printed book as a material object developed consumer, aesthetic and reading aspects, concepts and behaviors related to the social, economic, cultural, educational, scientific, religious and political conditions of each era. The cultivation of taste and the emergence of visual expectations to the expanding reading audience went hand in hand with the innovation and introduction of new or redeveloped features of the book. According to Chartier (2014: 5−6): "Linked to the essential acts of life and to important decisions and engagements, the image was invested with an affective charge and an existential value that made these objects, printed in vast numbers, unique to their possessors."

The visual−aesthetic expectations of the readers were further cultivated, defined and developed (and redeveloped) according to the era and the policies/strategies of the publishing houses. The chapter takes as key element that the visual identity of the book has been of central role in regard to issues of information, reception of the text, consumer/ user behavior, promotion and marketing, communication, interactivity. Woodcuts and then engravings were adopted for the illustration and ornamentation of the printed books; the printers/publishers explored and exploited the opportunities and traced the parameters of the visual identity of the book so as to develop the quality of the book, to systemize and organize the work in the printing shop, to reach the reading audience, to augment sales and gain success. In that context, the printing/publishing houses developed and established a recognizable identity that added to their fame. We have to bear in mind that the printed book had been a democratic, friendly, easy to use, affordable, convenient and successful medium; simultaneously, this printed book had been understood to be a material object that not only took a leading role in communication and information sharing but also inspired and cultivated quests and desires in regard to the visual needs. So, one of the main patterns is what we will call the "visual expectations" of the readers and how they evolved.

2.4.2 The visual expectations of the readers

Typography altered the ownership, collection and use of books since it offered to the wide reading audience the opportunity to own books

108   2. Through the page: The evolution of the visual identity

and to create personal collections. The book was thus a potential work of art, an art object that was not any more a privilege of wealthy aristocrats but a privilege of every reader that could afford to buy the copy. The feeling of the ownership of books is strong even nowadays. Thus, the printed book contributed to the personal story of the reader being a memory device and often a notebook or diary. In that context, the copy that the reader/owner has read, bought, offered or being offered as a gift, underlined, noted, put in the library, colored, showed, becomes a unique copy.

Prologues and introductions to the early printed books highlighted new cultures, new methods and new pleasures of printing and reading. Issues and patterns of taste emerged for the publishers as well. In introductions and prologues the publishers and editors outline the visual features, aims and aspects, praise the book and sometimes refer to the difficulties faced. The so-called taste was maturing rapidly in an age of great expectations that derived from new printing and illustration techniques alongside with scientific discoveries and social changes. Inevitably, the book, as the medium for information and the transmission of ideas, created visual expectations according to the kind of text, the reading audience, the series, the illustration techniques and innovations in a broader social, economic, cultural framework.

We may refer to two different parameters: tradition and innovation. The unexpected and the expected is the twofold of the desires and consumer cultures of the readers whereas the twofold "tradition—innovation" is the bedrock of the publishing industry. Publishing has always been a business and an activity of innovation that takes risks beyond the known and tested. Although tradition is one of the main values of the publishing activity and the symbolic capital plays inevitably an important role, publishers have diachronically introduced and proposed new texts, new trends, new authors, new aesthetics, new techniques, new strategies, new design. They have proved to be adaptable and successful since they have explored and exploited the opportunities of each period. Keen on discovering, the publishers offered a new and usually privileged point of view to their readers and to their era. They redefined taste, communication, recommendation, consumption, interactivity and often set new rules; nowadays, in a world of information abundance and of updated publishing opportunities, they go beyond the initial shift adopting new terms of convergence and discoverability, new promotion methods and valuable services to their readers/users which we will discuss in the fourth chapter.

Although tradition in the visual identity of the book was always strong, it had always been easy to be overcome. In that framework, the expected and unexpected were in a constant dialog. Readers' visual expectations are often formed, based on the tradition as established by older publications and by the reader's previous experiences. For example, the readers-users of the *Psalterium* during the 16th century were used to see a vignette illustrating David praying at the title-page. In the incunable period, wealthy collectors expected editions that looked like the manuscript book in terms of illustration, ornamentation, binding, organization of the page. Their aesthetic order demanded a book as valuable as the manuscript one; this need led to hybrid, hand-illuminated printed books that will be discussed in the third chapter; then the printed book developed its specific identity not by struggling to prove its value but as a continuity in which new opportunities and techniques were adopted, explored and demonstrated. It is not always enough to offer what the reader expects and already knows. This would be a rather boring publishing world. The element of surprise in publishing is significant (Calasso, 2015: 31).

Convergence of media has been undeniably a significant feature since the incunable period. Interactions between the manuscript and the printed, between the mechanical produced and the unique handmade book were inevitable. The hand illumination, apart from being expensive and time-consuming, was a method for a unique, not massive medium. The desire for the printed book in a globalized sphere will be based in the introduced techniques and policies that go beyond the unique and thus establish print culture and then reconstruct the unique through not only the personalized-customized services but mainly through the personal stories and uses developed for each copy.

2.4.3 Information, discoverability and visual dialogs

Augmentation in book production led to the development of promotion methods and strategies. Discoverability was realized from first printers/publisher to be a key issue for their printing shops/publishing houses. As the uniqueness of the manuscript belonged to the past, they were aware that they had to reach augmented, even differentiated and potential audiences. In that framework, the printed book had to be the advertisement of itself by its materiality. The book as a visual object and an information device provided information on it and at the same time attracted and visually satisfied the reader. In that context, the book was designed and produced so as to be readable, friendly and desirable as visual object, not only for the illustration and decoration but for the visual order of the page and of the book. The reader was informed for the new editions and the publishing activity by media and ways that were gradually augmented (word of mouth, bookstores and other distribution and retail channels, printed catalogs, advertisements, the Press, bookmarks, posters, book presentations etc.)

Readers diachronically wanted and want not only to read but also to be informed, to participate, to be engaged, to be members of a community, to share and communicate. Information regarding new titles, news from the publishing industry, discounts, upcoming events (such as presentations) had been of interest. Although in a different manner and with different strategies and methods, the reader participated in the publishing activity and in the development of reading communities since the invention of printing. Information is a prominent value and an asset not only of our era. Back in time, readers expected and desired access to information and to knowledge via the printed book for which they had expectations, demands, preferences, desires. Scholar communication in Renaissance Europe exploited and experienced the opportunities of the printed book so as to communicate, share, exchange, create, solve, cooperate, exchange, introduce, evaluate, promote and reach potential readers (Richardson, 1999; Eisenstein, 1983).

Thus, the printed book as the first mass information and communication medium provided not only access to information and knowledge but also participation in growing communities of readers. We may recognize the ownership of the printed book and the creation of personal book collections, whether small or not, as important factors for the democratization of knowledge and of taste, explaining at the same time the complex role of the reader and of the augmented reading communities. The reader did not only read, understand, enjoy, discover, explore, interpret, share, learn; before that the reader discovered, selected, decided, argued, shared, was informed (sometimes in a personalized manner), and acquired or lent the book which then could recommend or review or describe or offer as a gift. Owning the copy as a visual object democratized patterns of taste and reading. This parameter has been of great significance as the reading audience was enlarged with new readers who could never have afforded the cost of the manuscript book neither could have used the existing channels and services for ordering (bookstores of the era, miniaturists, binders etc.) and acquiring manuscripts. The ownership of the book led to the development of the book as an everyday object of personal value that defined customer-reading habits and print culture.

Obviously, the democratization of knowledge and of taste led to changes not only in reading (silent reading was spread and established) but also in using, owning and collecting books as well as in communication, information sharing, development of scholar communities. Silent reading altered the reading habits and behavior. Furthermore, communication was introduced and appreciated between the stakeholders in the publishing value chain during the Renaissance. Editors as well as authors and humanist scholars wrote the introduction or the prologue/foreword/epilogues with the aim to highlight the value of their work, the difficulties faced and usually overcome, the benefits of the text, the methodology, collaborations and even future editions or series. In these texts, at the front matter usually or at the back matter, the stakeholders referred to the design of the book and more specifically to book illustration and ornamentation, to the type faces and the paper and more generally to the quality of the edition and to the book as material object providing further information and praising the visual identity of the book. This visual identity was not something additional but indispensable feature of the book that had also a practical impact.

We can also find descriptions of the typographic, visual identity of the books in preorders when the subscription model was introduced in the publishing activity. Thus, after the decades of 1640–1660 (Barnard, 2001) and during the 18th and 19th centuries, information on the visual identity of the book can be found at the announcements made by the publishing companies at the Press or at the last pages of their editions or at printed single leaves by which they informed the potential readers–subscribers about future editions in order to encourage or persuade them to subscribe. Information could focus on the illustrator/artist, the editor, the decoration and illustration, schemes, maps, printing types, quality of paper, binding, cover, printing and illustration techniques. Sometimes, the gifts and the rewards to the reader for his/her subscription could be a printed illustration, a gravure, a map or a discount or an offer of more copies (Banou, 2017: 92–93). The role of visual information and communication at the subscription model and at the preorders of each period is significant and of research interest.

Thus, in the pages of the book a visual dialog and communication between the reader on the one hand and the publisher on the other was developed. This dialog was further cultivated and enforced later via the newspapers, magazines, advertisements, publishing catalogs, announcements for editions, subscriptions, reading societies, reading communities, book clubs. Furthermore, different usages of the book can be observed, as we will discuss below. Publishers by understanding the needs, taste and expectations of the readers, introduced new visual mechanisms and strategies not only in order to cultivate and create new expectations. Interaction, communication, information sharing and exchanging would be key points for the publishing chain.

One of the diachronic issues of the publishing industry is the development of a recognizable identity by the publisher. This identity relates and is created on the one hand by the titles published, by the backlist and frontlist, and on the other by the visual identity of the book. Every publisher aspires to gain a recognizable visual identity. In that framework, the book had to be desirable by either being recognizable or innovative. A recognizable book is a trusted and successful book. In the case of book series, the reader recognizes the book by its visual identity as defined by the format, binding, cover, decoration, dust jacket, the order of the page, etc. (Banou, 2017: 104–105). Series are based on the twofold: content and visual identity, the latter constituting an important factor for the success. The readers recognize, thus trust the books of the series whereas sometimes collectability is an important parameter. The reader-user-customer may acquire the books not only for reading but also for collecting. Publishers invest on series as they might be popular, trusted, beloved, collectable, friendly, familiar, bibliophilic, and recognizable.

Readers during the first decades of printing not only trusted but actually expected the known and tested, the familiar and successful which usually recalled the manuscript tradition. In print culture, the visual tradition is developed and established fast enough according to a number of factors named above. Readers usually expect the next book by recalling the visual order of previous editions of the author or of the publishing house. Visual tradition is also related with the kind of text. For example, religious works were illustrated and decorated according to the manuscript and iconographic tradition. Furthermore, visual expectations are related with specific parts of the book. For instance, a portrait of the author usually appeared at the frontispiece whereas the title-page was decorated by the printer's device apart from other illustrations. The colophon was accompanied by the printer's device and by the end of each chapter, a tailpiece was expected to be printed. On the other hand, as the publishing industry is an industry of discoveries and innovations, the reader explores, discovers, and may be surprised. The unexpected, the innovative, the element of surprise takes a leading role, as discussed in the conclusions of the book. Actually, the reader waits for the unexpected.

2.5 Establishing everyday book culture from Aldus Manutius to Allen Lane

From Aldus Manutius in Renaissance Venice and the Elzeviers in Holland to Allen Lane (founder and publisher of Penguin Books) till nowadays, we can observe changes and "revolutions" that established an everyday culture of books; they created books readable and at the same time friendly, accessible, affordable, desirable, portable, nice, of aesthetic value.

Numerous books and papers have been published and research is still conducted for Aldus Manutius. Being a scholar and a teacher of ancient Greek, Aldus Manutius dominated the printing activity in Venice at the turn of the 15th century, at a crucial and much challenging period (Lowry, 1979). Between the incunable and the printed book of the 16th century, between the ancient Greek texts to books for a wider reading audience, between *Hypnerotomachia Poliphili* and portable books, Aldus Manutius is commemorated for his innovations and developments. He explored and exploited the opportunities of the new medium expanding thus the boundaries of the book, developing the visual identity of the book and establishing the book as a convenient, affordable object. Alongside with other printers/publishers of his era, he transformed the printing activity into a publishing activity.

Aldus Manutious was a publisher, who developed his publishing policy and strategies by deciding on the titles to be published and on the visual identity of his books. The printing of ancient Greek authors was among his priorities. Barker in order to study the Greek types developed by Aldus Manutius, looks back "to the roots of Aldus's enthusiasm for the Greek language and literature" (1985: 11). Aldus Manutius had been famous for both Greek and Latin/Italian types. As for the former, in 1495 "Aldus applied to the Signoria for a privilege for twenty years for the books to be printed with the *lettere greche in summa belleza di ogni sorte*, achieved by the two new methods of printing Greek, *much better than it is written with a pen*" (Barker, 1985: 55). The high quality of the printing types is highlighted by comparing the printed with the manuscript script text, the former declared to be better. As a scholar and then as a publisher Aldus collaborated with well-known contemporary scholars, Greek and Italian, for the editing of his books. Every book had been highly curated and well prepared both as text and as material object. The editing and publishing of the ancient Greek works was not as easy work during the first decades of printing; well-known Greek scholars, exiles to Venice and in general to Italy after the fall of Constantinople, collaborated successfully with Aldus Manutius: apart from other parameters, they had to face difficulties in finding the manuscripts for the preparation of the editions.

Additionally, Aldus Manutius is famous for the design and establishment of the much appreciated, well-known and broadly used italics (picture 5), that passed successfully from the printed to the digital text. Italics appeared for the first time in 1501 in the edition of the work of Virgil; Francesco Griffo was the designer and punchcutter of the types and he is praised by Aldus Manutius in the introduction of the edition.

One of the great innovations of Aldus Manutius are the "libri portatiles," portable books, that revolutionized the book and developed an everyday book culture at the beginning of the 16th century (pictures 4–7). He used smaller sized books for the editions of the much recognizable and appreciated ancient Greek and Latin works offering thus to the reading audience affordable, friendly, convenient books of classic works carefully edited and curated. Books of high quality and highly praised editions were in this way affordable, easier to be found and to be read/used in comparison to the large-sized books which were

114 2. Through the page: The evolution of the visual identity

previously used for the printing of classic works. Aldus Manutius was obviously not the first to adopt the small size which was already applied in almanacs, tales, calendars, texts for the popular reading audience. He is acknowledged to be the first to use and establish the small sized books for classic works of high quality, carefully curated by editors—scholars; at the same time these books were of aesthetic value as they introduced a visual culture to the reading audience. Thus, Aldus Manutius innovated and revolutionized the book for augmented audiences of scholars and students in the same way that Allen Lane would do centuries later in England, in 1935, with Penguin Books. The "libri portatiles" by Aldus Manutius—by being affordable, friendly, convenient, accessible—further encouraged studying, researching, reading, collaborating, exchanging ideas, expressing opinions, writing, sharing and creating. They developed scholar communication and inspired new modes of reading, noting, studying.

The visual order of the page in Aldus Manutius' editions was developing according to the evolution and "new" elements of the era. Headpieces and initials embellished the text in such a manner so as to accompany the text and decorate the beginning of the chapter. Illustration was not used extendedly; in the Greek editio princeps of the work of Musaeus "Hero and Leander" [Τα Καθ' Ηρώ και Λέανδρου] published in Greek in 1495 (Barker, 1985: 52) and in Latin in 1497—1498, two woodcuts embellish the text depicting the two heroes. The same woodcut is used both in the Greek and the Latin text; on the right page it accompanies the text in Latin (p. 13 v) and on the opposite left page in ancient Greek (p. 14r). The repetition is like a mirror of the image/illustration with the text in different language.

We do owe to Aldus Manutius the publishing of one of the most lavishly, beautiful and enigmatic books not only of Renaissance but of the centuries of printing. *Hypnerotomachia Poliphili*, published in 1499, is considered to be a masterpiece while a lot of researches, monographs, conferences, studies, discussions focus on this exceptional edition and its stakeholders; questions regarding the author and the illustrator have raised (Casagrande & Scarsella, 1998; Lowry, 1979). *Hypnerotomachia Poliphili*, which will not be further discussed in this book, provided another point of view and aspect for the printed books as a work of art, as an exceptional volume with added value, as an illustrated masterpiece.

Undeniably, Aldus Manutius' editions were famous for their high quality of text and of comments. Introductions by the editors-scholars accompanied the editions highlighting the process of editing and printing, the difficulties faced, the decisions made, giving information for the book as content and object. The success of these books was admirable and the demand augmented so that many pirate editions were printed.

The Visual Identity of the Book

The books by Aldus Manutius were recognizable and highly respected for their visual identity. The visual order of the page was decided in such a way so as to be friendly and comfortable for reading and for noting as well. Initials and headpieces were used as to decorate the beginning of the chapters whereas in the pages of his books we can find all the innovations and new elements such as foliation. We have to point out that in his editions blank spaces at the initials with guide letter might appear even at the beginning of the 16th century as in the portable edition of Ovidius in 1502 (picture 5). Ornaments in Aldus Manutius' editions are rather simple, without shaped borders, usually not historiated, with floral patterns that could suit more than one kind of text. By their repetition in different editions they created an *abitudine* of the printed book; thus, the decoration serves the text and the order of the page. Through his classic (ancient Greek and Latin) editions that formed a kind of series, Aldus Manutius aspired to create a loyal reading audience that would appreciate, interact and promote his editions.

Aldus Manutius invested in collaborations with experts, scholars and other stakeholders in the publishing chain, in the high quality of the text, in the designing of the types, in the innovations mentioned above and in the visual development of the book so as to be friendly, affordable, convenient, nice, readable, portable and of high quality. Illustration was not used apart from a few cases such as in the edition of the work of Musaeus. By the production of *Hypnerotomachia Poliphili* Aldus Manutius pointed out to another, exceptional kind of book aimed to the bibliophilic, scholastic audience creating thus a different, valuable, memorable, and remarkable book as object. The case of the lavishly illustrated *Hypnerotomachia Poliphili* is exceptional for Aldus Manutius and for the Renaissance printed book. He produced a typographic enigma, a masterpiece for which both book historians and art historians tried and try to find the keys. The book created a strong visual experience further exhibiting the potential visual identity and power of the printed book. The edition, both as text and picture, as image and content, through the questions gained provided a corner stone for a privileged dialog between art history, book history, literature studies, and publishing.

Obviously, the editions of Aldus Manutius developed and established what we might call an everyday culture of the book by introducing the book as a respectable, qualitative, affordable, convenient and friendly object, part of everyday study and life, which the reader could carry and enjoy, share it and note on it; harmonized with the developments of the era in regard to the visual identity of the book, he used headlines, foliation, pagination, decoration and other elements that matured in the page. His decisions and choices proclaimed the balance between the text and the visual identity of the book, between context and material object.

He also took a leading role in the publishing value chain highlighting the work and value of the publisher, not only as a printer, but as a cultivated scholar who could decide, develop the publishing policy, introduce, select, innovate, collaborate with other stakeholders and add value to the book. He developed a publishing policy that influenced his time. Additionally, as a publisher he took a central role in the social and cultural framework of the era; he developed and promoted by his decisions and strategies the scholar dialog and introduced a cultural mass medium. Furthermore, his printing shop in Venice was a place open for all scholars, a meeting point for intellectuals. In conclusion, Aldus Manutius offered an everyday visual book culture: books friendly, economic, accessible, nice, portable, affordable, accessible. There was a visual culture of the page and of the book in its materiality.

As for every day visual book culture, we have to point out to the activity and the books published by the Elzevirs in the Netherlands in the 17th century. More specifically, thirty-five volumes were published in the series *Respublicae* or *Republics* or *Petites Républiques or Repubbliken*, between 1626 and 1649, in pocket—very small—size (duodecimo), by Bonaventure and Abraham Elzevir (picture 10). Each of the thirty-five volumes in the series focused on one country or city or region, and gave information on the history, geography, inhabitants, culture, science, economy, monuments. The books were illustrated and decorated; the architectural title-page was lavishly illustrated providing information to the reader. Leitch (2014: 18) writes for that kind of books that: "Printers cultivated empirical engagement with the world and argued that the purchase of their books could make readers visually astute by providing ersatz empirical experience that rivaled the firsthand experience that came with travel... Such ersatz acts of "eyewitnessing" were cultivated by a range of books that recommended readers' engagement with the world. Sometimes their images took the shape of things to observe, methods of measuring, or profiles to assess."

Furthermore, the Elzevirs published a series of classic Latin texts, in pocket size (duodecimo). Lyons writes that "these pocket editions of the classics were quality products: scholarly, reliable and reasonably priced" (80). These very small in size books by the Elzevirs, printed in Latin and carefully illustrated, continued the tradition of Aldus Manutius and further established and enforced the book as a viable everyday object.

Centuries after Aldus Manutius, Allen Lane (Lewis, 2005) revolutionized the publishing industry and the book when he found Penguin Books in 1935. Obviously, we will not study in detail Penguin books but we will take a quick look at the visual identity of the books that further created and promoted everyday book visual culture as Aldus Manutius did approximately 450 years ago. Allen Lane further established the paperback pocket, affordable, convenient, friendly book for classic or quality works; additionally he introduced series such as for fiction, biographies, science that approached the wide reading audience. Like his precedent in Renaissance Venice, Lane designed and created a friendly, affordable, and beautiful book, which was recognizable, respectable and different from the others. Penguin series gained a huge symbolic capital, being recognizable to the reading audience by their design (Baines, 2005). The design of the books and the logo by Edward Young offered another point of view and approach. "The design of the books—also by Young—was simple but striking. And a reaction to the decoration or illustrative whimsy found on many other books" (Baines, 2005: 13). Furthermore, the first books had dust jackets highlighting how elements from the hardback tradition were maintained as the aesthetics of the pocket, paperback books were rapidly establishing. "Lane's true originality lay in his confidence that good books could be sold in large numbers, and in his willingness, at least at first, to use unconventional channels of distribution in order to achieve this" (Feather, 2006:175).

Penguin series and books had been recognizable by their design; the color often signaled the series, the identity, and the content. Series such as *Pelican Books, Penguin Specials, Penguin Classics, Illustrated Classics* (short-lived before the World War II), *Penguin Crime, Penguin Books, King Penguins, Penguin Biography, Penguin Poets, New Penguin Shakespeare* created an everyday visual book culture, highly appreciated and marketable. The design of the covers, with either the horizontal or the vertical grid, simple or illustrated, with a patterned background bearing in mind the end-papers of old hardback books, with works of art or photographs or graphic design, or totally in black constitutes a visual suggestion that might characterize the series and the time of publishing, creating reading, aesthetic and consumer habits.

The evolution of the visual identity of Penguin Books in the 20th century and during the first decades of the 21st century is of worth studying since the design of books each time epitomizes the needs and visual expectations of the readers, synopsizes changes in the publishing activity, exhibits the publishing policy of the publisher and reflects the taste of the era. At the same time, this visual identity further highlights the culture of books and establishes the use of the books as viable material objects, even in our digital era of coexistence and convergence of media.

New generations of readers discover the classics and explore the fiction and nonfiction through these convenient, affordable, accessible, friendly, easy to be found, portable, paperback editions that visually either recall the established tradition or innovate. Additionally, existing readers rediscover beloved or classic works either in the familiar visual identity and manner or in innovative patterns and suggestions. A crucial theme for the publishing companies is the publishing of the classics and their introduction to new generations of readers who may discover them on various forms of the book. In that framework, the visual identity of the book is significant. Apart from illustration and decoration, the order and typology of the page, the cover and dust jacket, the verbal and visual paratext may be used as to inform, attract, and engage readees.

2.6 Conclusions of the chapter: Defining the page, maturing the book

During the "horseless carriage" phase, the opportunities, techniques, and challenges of the book were explored and exploited by printers/publishers, readers, authors, artists, book sellers, and other stakeholders of the newborn publishing value chain. "New" aspects of the page and new parts of the book were introduced developing the visual order so as the book to be friendly, readable, accessible, affordable, nice, portable, desirable.

It is noteworthy that globalization in publishing goes back in time. As already referred, the reading audience of the first printed books was, to a high percentage, globalized and multicultural whereas the book market was also globalized. Humanist scholars, noblemen, students, scientists, collectors, wealthy patrons constituted the homogenous, throughout Europe, reading audience. Meanwhile, the "lingua franca" for scholarly communication was the Latin as nowadays is the English language. So, the first printers/publishers, alongside the wide reading audience who read books in the vernacular, had to satisfy this already shaped, existing, globalized, multinational and multicultural audience. In that context, due to the success of certain editions or series, the fame of publishers, authors, editors, artists exceeded the borders of their region and their works were recognizable in different countries. The editions of Aldus Manutius, Christoph Plantin, and the Elzeviers are a good example. Meanwhile, bestsellers were intended through their translations for a globalized market in which "global consciousness" (Briggs and Burke, 2005: 33) could shape the taste for books.

We discussed the democratization of taste; one may also wonder what taste is in the publishing industry. Kurt Wolff (1991: 9) wrote: "By taste I mean not only judgment and a feeling for quality and literary values. Taste should also include a sure sense for the form—format, type area, type face, binding, dust jacket—in which a specific book should be represented," whereas Roberto Calasso (2015: 131) stated that: "When Kurt Wolff, a century ago, published young prose writers and poets such as Franz Kafka, Robert Walser, Georg Trakl, and Gottfried Benn in his 'Judgment Day' series, those writers immediately found their first few readers because there was already something attractive about the appearance of those books, which looked like slim black exercise books with labels and came with no program announcements or publicity launches. But they suggested something than could be already sensed in the name of the series: they suggested a judgment, which is the real acid test for a publisher." Taste, decision, judgment, and experience led to the development of publishing policies and have to be counted among the parameters that shaped the visual identity of the book.

As investigated, the visual order of the page was structured and developed gradually during the first centuries of printing so as to create a multifunctional device due to a number of reasons discussed above. The visual identity of the book does not imply only illustration and decoration but extends to all elements of the page, both visual and verbal, and studies their introduction, appearance, provenance, creation, development, printing, combination, function, influence. The page was defined and constructed, and the parts of the book were developed in complex environments and for complex reasons. Beyond the obvious parameters and reasons (technology, techniques, publishing strategies, policies, kind of text, reading audience, social–cultural–economic and other reasons), we traced and enlightened aspects of prestige, desires, fears, needs, expectations, taste, aims, ambitions, habits, relationships, discoverability, reader engagement and reader creativity, convergence, interaction. We highlighted as well the uses of the book discussing it as an everyday object, a memory device, an information medium, a storage device, a symbol of power and prestige, a personal object.

In that context, emblematic books and illustrations characterize and epitomize our civilization; illustrations from books such as Cervantes' *Don Quixote* and L. Carroll's *Alice in Wonderland* have (re)-defined and synopsized the text, thus giving the visual clues for their understanding and interpretation. Furthermore, they have created a visual tradition in regard to the work and the text which next generations of readers, publishers, and illustrators have to reapproach. Innovation and experimentation offer another point of view by redefining the known and established. Convergence between the printed and the manuscript book, between hand illumination and woodcut illustration, between the mass medium and the book as a unique work of art during the first decades of printing defined the visual identity of the book. Convergence is among the main issues and trends of the publishing industry that diachronically establishes patterns of continuity and interaction between media and between different forms of the book. In that framework, a creative visual dialog is developed.

In the next chapter, hand illumination and decoration in printed books will be discussed and these "hybrid" books of the Renaissance will be highlighted so as to exhibit printing strategies, convergence of media and reader engagement as well as issues of taste and power. Hand-illumination and ornamentation to early printed books is a crucial issue on which we will focus so as to demonstrate how this hybrid form of the book, the one hand, led to the maturing of printing and, on the other, is the precedent of luxury editions and copies as well as of personalized publishing services till nowadays.

CHAPTER

3

Converged aesthetics: Personalized publishing services

Publishing could be described as a hybrid multimedia literary genre. And hybrid it certainly is. As for it becoming mixed up with other media, this fact is now obvious. But publishing, as a game, is nevertheless fundamentally the same as the old one played by Aldus Manutius. *Roberto Calasso (2015: 11).*

3.1 Converged aesthetics: The evolution of "luxury" copies and deluxe editions

3.1.1 Defining luxury copies and editions

Hand decoration and illustration in early printed books was very popular especially in editions of classic texts for collectors, wealthy patrons, humanist noblemen. In that framework, the term "luxury copies" has been introduced. Furthermore, the coloring of prints had been a method of embellishment in early printed books. In that context, we may wonder on the unique copies which we often study in libraries; we even can wonder on the term "luxury" copies. Inevitably, a great number of unique copies may be called "luxury," which required time, money, specific work and obviously were not affordable to the majority of readers. Even though, in this chapter, we will try to investigate as well other methods and strategies that created or even systemized the production/creation of unique copies, thus of copies that were different from the printed book as produced by the printing presses. Personalized publishing services since the invention of printing will be presented in this chapter and discussed focusing on the publishing, aesthetic and ideological aspects of the era, taking also into consideration the kind of text and the reading audience. A categorization will be

The Visual Identity of the Book
DOI: https://doi.org/10.1016/B978-0-443-19167-1.00003-6
Copyright © 2025 Christina Banou. Published by Elsevier Ltd. All rights are reserved, including those for text and data mining, AI training, and similar technologies.

121

attempted with criteria based on the typology as well as on the uses of the book and on the services provided by stakeholders of the publishing chain, such as the publisher, the editor, the patron, the reader, the bookseller; the categorization attempts to outline reading and collection behavior, to enlighten publishing strategies and to explore influences from the manuscript and from the art of the era, as well as issues of competition, convergence, taste, fame and power.

During the incunable period and the first decades of the 16th century, hand-illuminated and specifically bound copies can be observed. Bibliography is rich, studying specific case studies, exhibiting fabulous hand-illuminated printed books and enlightening the specific social, cultural and other conditions related to the creation of these copies. Works such as by Armstrong (2020, 1991), Marcon (1986, 1987, 2003), Smith (2000b), Werner (2019), McKitterick (2005), Smyth (2018, 2024) shed light to this crucial moment of the printed book.

Unique hand-illumination by artists/miniaturists of the era was time-consuming and much expensive, considered as a work of art. The coloring of prints was another method which was systemized and obviously more affordable. Binding was also an element of uniqueness while cut-and-paste methods constituted another category of unique copies. Hand illumination, although not vanished, diminished in the middle of the 16th century. Even though, deluxe, limited, or exceptional editions were produced aiming to satisfy the needs and quests of specific reading audiences till nowadays. During the 19th century, new printing and illustration techniques, the establishment of covers and the advent of dust jackets, alongside with the widening of the reading audience and the reading "revolution" brought about significant changes, offering other options. Thus, we will not focus only on hand illumination; as discussed in the second chapter, the visual order of the page and the creation of the parts of the book as information and visual devices are not diminished to illustration but related to a number of elements and parts that were studied and exhibited. These elements may be visual or a combination of visual and verbal. Sometimes we can trace the origins or we may understand influences, policies and aspects in specific details. In that framework, we will investigate the evolution of these unique copies so as to shed light to the methods and techniques used, to the convergence of media, to the reasons for their existence and success focusing on consumer and reading behavior, print and collection cultures, the impact of technology and the art of the era. The uses of the book will be exhibited.

Initially, the reasons that enabled the production, circulation and success of these copies will be approached and a categorization will be attempted. Complex relationships and ideological uses of the book during the incunable period will be looked at. Luxury copies, colored prints, unique copies, "post-luxury" copies are terms that will be used in this chapter so as to clarify and illuminate the methods, strategies and features of these unique copies and editions.

Thereafter, the evolution of special, deluxe, limited, collector's (collectable), exclusive editions, from the 16th century to nowadays, will be highlighted so as to enlighten publishing strategies and policies, consumer−reader behavior, the complex uses of the books, the development of the publishing value chain, as well as issues of taste, collection, communication and prestige. In that context, we will investigate the customization/personalization regarding books and publishing services nowadays, taking as key point that such methods and aspects derive from strategies that go back to Gutenberg's Age and are redeveloped and restructured. It is also noteworthy to look at the exploitation of the opportunities provided by information technologies and social media. Nowadays this unique, personalized "luxury" copy or edition on the one hand is produced as a material, printed object and, on the other, it may be accessible and affordable to all users/readers just for a few euros/pounds/dollars; it can be commissioned through a webpage. We will highlight the evolution and visual identity of these printed editions considering the impact of technologies. Furthermore, new publishing services will be investigated considering the impact of technology, interactivity and communication. Thus, a new ideological context is created with emphasis on interaction, participation, aesthetics, convergence and new services to customers/readers. In that framework, the term "post-luxury" copy will be introduced.

Thus, from the unique printed hand-illuminated and specifically bound book of the Renaissance to the luxury, limited, collectable, exclusive editions, and then to the potential and affordable personalization of the book nowadays, we will discuss the visual experiences and parameters which are obviously significant in terms not only of production but also of promotion, marketing, consumption, information sharing, prestige and creativity. We can recognize three phases and ways of customized books, as follows:

Fifteenth century and first decades of the 16th century: Luxury, unique hand-illuminated printed books or a certain number of copies with specific, added by hand, features (such as rubrication in initials, headings, titles, etc.)

Middle of the 16th century to nowadays: limited, deluxe, collectable, exclusive editions with specific features that regard all the copies or numbered copies.

Nowadays: Co-existence of the above mentioned limited and deluxe editions with customized, affordable books by personalized publishing services; these copies are already designed and can be produced massively. The impact and challenges of new technologies will be discussed.

Luxury, hand-illuminated and decorated printed books, bound uniquely, often printed on different material (such as vellum or parchment or paper of better quality or colored paper) during the first decades of printing have been discussed in monographs and papers that often look at case studies (Armstrong, 1995, 2020; Marcon, 1986, 1987, 2003; Werner, 2018). That kind of hybrid, converged books produced mainly till the first decades of the 16th century in a world between manuscript and printed tradition constitutes a special category of great research interest that can also explain current trends and issues of our hybrid era. Such "luxury" copies with hand illustration-decoration and binding have been studied as material objects, as exceptional booksworks of art that have been produced so as to satisfy specific needs of part of the reading audience. In that context, issues of book production and consumption are investigated whereas the book as symbol of taste, wealth, power has been highlighted.

McKitterick (2005: 60) writes that "international demand for de luxe manuscript, both secular and religious, continued long into the 16th century," and "the taste for lavishly decorated copies of printed books in Venice in the 1470 s, the penwork on bibles and other books from the northern Netherlands, and the rapidly executive flourishes on myriad books either ordinary in themselves or destined for an ordinary market, all speak in their different spheres for a period of accommodation." Armstrong (2020: 777) writes that thousands of incunables were *"finished* with initials and borders painted, that is hand-illuminated." That kind of decoration was executed by professional miniaturists. Margins of the book were also decorated with painted borders, whereas initials were painted or rubricated and other ornaments were added by artists. Margaret Smith (2000b: 146) recognizes that "one way in which the early printed book continued to follow the manuscript was in its variety."

The transition from the manuscript to the printed book implies an area not only of coexistence but also of convergence. Unique copies enlighten issues of taste, fame, power, desire, prestige, collectability, interactivity, collaboration, participation, and engagement. Sherman writes that (2008, xv): "Books no less than tools, apparel, and habitants can show signs of wear, but their markings can be far more eloquent of manufacturing processes, specific of provenance, telling of human relations, and suggestive of human thought." Especially, unique copies enable the researchers to study the complex relationships in the publishing chain. At the same time, these unique books shed light to the publisher's decisions, policies and strategies, and enable us to study the development of the publishing value chain with emphasis on the role of the printer/publisher, the artist, the patron, the reader and the bookseller. We can also trace and understand the visual development, order, and construction of the printed page.

3.1 Converged aesthetics: The evolution of "luxury" copies and deluxe editions **125**

Obviously, the coexistence of the manuscript with the printed book provides the framework for explaining the convergence of media and the role of hybrid books. Margaret Smith (2000b: 146) writes that "one of the circumstances that allowed printing to get started at all was that the printer would call on these other craftsmen to 'finish' the copies he churned out. This is the better way to understand the handwork in incunables: not as the proof of the intention to make the incunable 'look just like the manuscript' but as the part of the previous system of book production that allowed the printer to replace the text scribe without having at the same time to replace the whole system."

We have to recognize that hybrid forms of the book and convergence of media cannot be simply attributed to the "imitation" of the manuscript book. The latter was obviously the only known module for the printed book; first printers/ publishers aspired to produce and design books that could satisfy the needs and meet the expectations of the existing (and rather diminished) reading audience by producing in a massive way the book as known for centuries. Neither the material—the paper—was changed, neither the typology of the book which resembled to that of the manuscript book. We have also to consider that the first printers/publishers were not usually humanist scholars but craftsmen, technicians, merchants, businessmen, goldsmiths. They explored and discovered the opportunities, features and advantages of the new printing technology alongside with readers, booksellers, authors, editors, artists, rubricators. Thus, the manuscript book had been the "guide book," the module, which they aimed to reproduce; due to initially practical reasons all stakeholders discovered that the printed book was a mass medium that had other needs and demands as well as plenty of opportunities.

It is noteworthy to consider the book professions and expertize during this interesting and crucial period of the early printed book that has much in common with our era. The existing book professions were not abandoned with the advent of printing although changes were significant. Illuminators, rubricators, artists, book binders, booksellers continued their work either on manuscript or on printed books collaborating with the "new" professionals such as editors, correctors, block cutters, engravers, type designers and certainly printers/publishers. The production of printed books was obviously augmenting and in that framework we can recognize the need for the printed page to be visually completed in regard to ornamentation and rubrication; this demand was augmenting for a few years till on the one hand the woodcut ornaments, illustrations, visual elements, and on the other the printing techniques, such as printing in red, were established. McKitterick defines that need (2008: 101): "The rapid escalation of the numbers of printed books from the 1460s to 1470s onward also raised issues of how these extra numbers were to be finished for readers." The augmentation of the number of editions and

The Visual Identity of the Book

126   3. Converged aesthetics: Personalized publishing services

thus of copies enforced printers/publishers to serve the need for massive book decoration and illustration for all the copies of the tirage; it was also clear, in a rapidly competitive environment, that the edition could be further promoted and advertised by being decorated and illustrated. Not only woodcuts and engravings but also the visual order and typology of the page added value to the edition and helped the publisher to obtain and establish a recognizable identity.

Publishers were thus obliged to face the needs and quests by exploiting the new opportunities. Although the first printers/publishers thought of the printed book in visual and even commercial terms of the manuscript precedent, it was quickly more than obvious that the new book had innovative opportunities and advantages so as to be developed, designed, promoted and distributed massively. The transition from the luxury unique copy to the desirable, decorated and illustrated copy for all exhibits the democratization of taste, that took part alongside with the democratization of knowledge. Furthermore, the parallel use of miniature/hand-illumination in printed books offered a privileged point of view on the combination and convergence of media highlighting at the same time aspects of taste, patronage, book collection, information sharing, prestige, communication; these aspects were taken into consideration by the printers/publishers. It was the time that the work of the publisher was prevailing and differentiating from that of the printer, as it was discussed in the second chapter in the case of Aldus Manutius.

In that framework, we have to enlighten the coexistence of different elements in the printed page, which recall the manuscript tradition and at the same time bring about new elements developed by the long interaction between different media. This is of value for our digital Age, in which new media are combined with traditional ones, new forms of the book coexist with the printed material, and convergence of media seems to be the rule. In this chapter we will focus on the transformations and the evolution of personalized publishing services and on "luxury," unique copies and editions, from the Renaissance to nowadays.

3.1.2 Categorization of luxury copies: questions and quests during the early period of printing

During the 15nth and the first decades of the 16th century, luxury copies were ordered by the booksellers for their bookshops or by the readers-collectors for enriching their libraries; sometimes these hand-illuminated and bound books were created by the printer-publisher so as to be offered as privileged gifts to powerful "patrons" and collectors (noblemen, cardinals etc.) who had financed or encouraged in various ways the publication

(Armstrong, 2020, 1991; Richardson, 1999; Marcon, 1986; Banou, 2017). This hybrid printed book—which on the one hand was produced by the printing technologies and on the other reproduced and recalled the manuscript visual aspects—had been of success to specific readers and collectors since it satisfied needs related to issues of fame, prestige, taste, cultivation and power. The combination of a mass medium, such as the printed book, with methods that derive from the manuscript tradition (such as hand-illumination, specific binding, printing on vellum/parchment/other quality of paper) express the complex relationships between stakeholders in the publishing chain enlightening thus the transition and the continuity between the printed and manuscript book.

Alongside, the printed book gradually gained its autonomy from the manuscript precedent and developed its own identity by using visual and verbal mechanisms for providing access to knowledge, transmitting information and offering aesthetic enjoyment. The gradual development of the visual order of the page and of the parts of the book highlight the visual evolution of the printed book. Additionally, new parts of the book, such as the title page, as well as the development of front matter and back matter provided further information and visual devices to the reader for using, understanding and interpreting the text.

In incunables, we can observe guide letters in the position of the initials that indicate the initial letter to the illuminator/artist, and to the reader as well (picture 3). These guide letters were soon to be abandoned, at the end of the incunable period; even though we can find them even in the first decades of the 16th century, as in the edition of the work of Ovidius by Aldus Manutius, Venice 1502 (picture 5). The use of woodcut initials was gradually established.

Woodcuts and engravings were used as to illustrate and decorate printed books for all readers leading in this way to the democratization of taste apart from the democratization of knowledge (Banou, 2017: 24−26). As discussed in the second chapter, these woodcuts were colored usually by professionals; furthermore, some of them were stamped and not printed. Susy Marcon (1986, 2003) enlightens these examples of "xilo-miniatura" in her work whereas McKitterick synopsizes (2008: 101): "In parts of Northern Italy (and especially in Venice), woodcuts were for some years stamped in as the basis of marginal decoration, and were either left as they were, or were worked up with color." Marcon (2020: 67−70) focuses on case studies of colored woodcuts bringing to light aspects and interaction related to this particular method of copies' embellishment. Armstrong (2010: 779) writes in regard to the Venetian incunables that "the early 1470 s was also a period of intense experimentation as printers and miniaturists sought to "finish" the massive onslaught of newly printed books. One technique that was probably intended to speed the process of decoration was to enhance the margins of in dividual copies of a given edition with wood-cut borders stamped by hand." This reminds us of the coloring books of our Age for which we will discuss below.

The quest for the personalized book (for one copy) and/or for personalized publishing services (for a number of copies) derived and still derives from a number of reasons that include patterns of vanity, consumption, power, self-esteem, sense of uniqueness, family relations, friendships, fame, loyalty, prestige as well as taste and luxury. The uniqueness of the copy and its artistic value constitutes an object with strong symbolic capital representing virtues that the owner would like to be attributed to him/her. Nowadays, these virtues and issues vary according to the person and the kind of provided publishing services. The book is often a trophy exhibiting recognition, success, devotion; it might be a memory device, a dedicatory object of symbolic value or a gift. The origins of the nowadays personalized copies can thus be traced back to the invention of printing, when hand decorated/illuminated copies, often with unique binding, were offered as gifts or commissioned by book collectors of the era. The book as luxurious commodity was also emerging in that hybrid form.

During the Renaissance, the printer/publisher offered personalized copies in order to satisfy the needs and meet the expectations of powerful and wealthy readers/collectors. In the 15th century and during the first decades of the 16th century, collectors, booksellers, bibliophiles, editors and printers-publishers collaborated with miniaturists, illuminators, binders for illustrating, decorating and binding specific number of copies; a few of these copies (of classical editions mostly) might be printed on vellum or even parchment or on better quality paper, as discussed below. This was to be gradually abandoned during the late 16th century although luxury editions diachronically have been produced so as to meet the expectations of specific audiences. In that context, numbered copies and specific illustration and ornamentation have always been used in terms of embellishment, promotion, marketing, innovation, competition, prestige, interpretation; thus they developed the visual identity of the book in often complex environments.

In that framework, a categorization proposed and enriched for the early printed book (during the incunable period and the first decades of the 16th century) may be as follows (Banou, 2017: 57–58).

1. Methods used to unique copies (also called "luxury" copies):
   - Hand illumination (decoration and illustration)
   - Unique Binding
   - Painted emblems/coat of arms
   - Handwritten dedications (Richardson, 1999: 54–55)
   - Colored prints

- Rubrication (initials, headings, titles etc.)
- Cut-and-paste books
- Painted fore-edge
- Hand dedications
- Rubrication
- Copies printed on vellum or parchment (very few copies of classic editions or of bibles or of collectable editions) Copies printed on paper of better quality or on colored paper
- Colored woodcuts by professionals

2. Methods used to a usually very small or small number of copies of the edition:
- Rubrication
- Copies printed on vellum or parchment (very few copies of classic editions or of bibles or of collectable editions) Copies printed on paper of better quality or on colored paper
- Colored woodcuts by professionals

The use of vellum or different quality of paper or even parchment implies that the printed book was still be considered inferior to the manuscript one by some collectors. Thus, the material for the copies destined for gifts or for receiving hand-illumination was supposed to be of better quality. Very few copies of specific editions (such as classical texts or works of devotion) were printed on vellum or parchment. Werner (2018: 9) writes that "although hand-press books were overwhelmingly printed on paper, some early books were printed on parchment (sheep skin) or vellum (calf skin). But the cost of procuring enough skin to print even small print runs of books was expensive. And vellum, which shrunk and expanded depending on humidity, was not ideally suited for working with presses" while according to Howard (2009: 39): "parchment quickly fell out of favor, except in rare cases where it was sought for aesthetic reasons." Richardson (1999: 10–11) writes that vellum was used in the early years of printing for works of devotion due to its durability and due to the "exclusiveness of the material appealed to customers as wealthy as they were pious" recognizing that "thereafter vellum was used only occasionally for a few de luxe copies of an edition, destined to be presented as gifts or collected by bibliophiles." Armstrong (2020: 783–784) focuses on the significant number of the copies of the editions of da Spira and Jenson in Venice printed on vellum. This method would be abandoned during the 16th century.

More specifically, in regard to the first category, hand illustration and decoration (in initials, headpieces, tailpieces, margins, first page of the text, borders etc.) created a unique copy of great artistic value; in some cases these illuminations are considered masterpieces and are studied exhaustively nowadays. Hand-illuminated copies were often accompanied by painted or gilded edges of the book (top-bottom-fore edges) as in the

130   3. Converged aesthetics: Personalized publishing services

manuscript precedent whereas they were specifically and luxuriously bound. Unique bindings are the common feature between the manuscript and the printed books which were sold sewn and not bound till the industrial cover prevailed. Emblems of the noble and wealthy owners were painted at the first page after the book was bought or ordered. Hand-decorated borders with floral patterns framed printed text. Gold leaf or shell gold as well as sepia ink were used as well. It was not uncommon for the booksellers to have already hand-painted copies in their shop, in which only the space for the emblem was left blank so as the buyer's to be inserted after the acquisition. Moreover, as already mentioned at the second chapter, rubrication was a method of decorating a number of copies exhibiting thus the coexistence of mechanical printing methods and hand-decoration which was applied in a massive way, ordered by the publishers (Fuessel, 2005: 19, 56). Due to the augmented demand for hand-illuminated incunables, numerous "foreign" artists were active in Venice (Armstrong, 2020: 791). It was not unusual the same artists to illustrate and decorate both printed books and manuscripts. The publishing value chain at its beginning was thus enlarged with miniaturists and artists whose work was of augmented demand after the invention of printing.

The first mentioned above category includes methods and strategies which are implied and used to unique copies, for books that were intended to recall the manuscript tradition and be a work of art. Methods used to a certain number of copies of the same edition define the second category shedding light on the influence of the manuscript on the printed book, on the hybrid books produced during the incunable period as well as on the publishers' methods and strategies. For instance, rubrication was used to a number of copies (in titles, initial letters, head chapters, heading and elsewhere in the page), as discussed in the second chapter; it was ordered by the printer/publisher during the first decades after the invention of printing. Richardson (1999: 20) uses the term "hand-finishing." In this case, the method applies to many copies and obviously is more affordable for the reading audience. Armstrong (2020: 782) defines "hand illumination to include decoration in gold and coloured paints, or figural and architectural designs drawn in pen and ink, usually enhanced with watercolour tints" distinguishing from the "rubrication, red and blue initials, or initials flourished in contrasting colours of ink." McKitterick (2008: 101) commented that "standardized illustrations or decorations were also a means to achieve (and to suggest to readers in different places) formal coherence among different copies of the same text. Stencils were occasionally employed to make easier the decoration of initial letters, or the colouring of illustrations, for example."

Some of the methods referred above may adjust to both categories such as the coloring of woodcuts and rubrication, which could be used

The Visual Identity of the Book

3.1 Converged aesthetics: The evolution of "luxury" copies and deluxe editions **131**

to a number of copies and might be ordered by the printer/publisher, being thus a more affordable method aimed to a wider reading audience. Actually, the coloring of prints, mainly of woodcuts, by professionals had been another method for embellishing the printed book and recalling the manuscript tradition. It is though not unusual to find copies colored by the readers. Rubrication, as discussed in the second chapter of this book, was applied to initials, headings, titles, subtitles, specific words, during the first decades of printing when printing in red had been rather time-consuming and expensive. Richardson (1999: 20) uses the term "hand-finishing." The expectation of the color was strong enough at the beginning of the printed book. "Colour was an important formal element in printmaking almost from the start, since we can reasonably assume that the earliest woodcuts were often if not usually made with the expectation that they would be coloured by hand" (Parshall, 2015: xii).

We may find hand illumination in printed books during the first decades of the 16th century, even in portable (*libri portatiles*) and more affordable books such as the one published by Aldus Manutius in Renaissance Venice. For example, at the copy in picture 7 of the work of Ovidius, published in 1502 by Aldus Manutius, which is printed in small, portable size, the first page of the text, after the title-page (*Ovidii Nasonis Metamorphoseon liber primus*) is hand-decorated (picture 7) at the bottom of the page and at the initial letter, which is gold-colored in blue background. The floral patterns at the bottom margin and the extended use of the bright blue color characterize the decoration of the copy. Apart from in foglio editions, printed on vellum or on high quality paper, "pocket" editions of the classics were also hand decorated and illuminated.

Hand illumination was in some cases expected in incunables. At the *Psalterium* published in Milan by Bonus Accursius in 1481, the text was printed in two columns, in Greek (left) and in Latin (right); at the copy in pictures 1 and 2, the initial letters were added by hand with blue ink and they appeared in such a manner in all the book (picture 2). The first page of the text, which is also the first page of the book, is hand-illuminated (picture 1). The letter M in the Greek text is hand decorated in gold and the background is blue whereas the initial B in the Latin Text is designed in a simple, plain manner colored in blue. The bottom of the page is embellished with floral patterns. Bright blue and gold are used extendedly. The coat-of-arms, the emblem of the owner, is hand-illuminated in its green framework. The left upper margin of the book near the initial M is also hand-decorated with the same floral patterns in which blue, gold, bordeaux prevail. This is a copy that might be called typical of hand-illuminated incunables. It is not lavishly illustrated, the decoration and illustration are restricted to the first page of

The Visual Identity of the Book

the text/edition, and initial letters are rubricated in all the pages of the copy. The colophon is very simple without and decoration.

Thus, in that kind of hybrid, "luxury" book there is a continuity from the manuscript precedent form; furthermore, considering these copies from the point of view of a reader or collector of the incunable era, we can assume that this was the copy expected, similar to the books used for centuries. Meanwhile, the printed book with the guide letters in the space for the initials, with the emerging title-page and the ongoing changes, which was sold unbound (with no cover, and the sheets shewed together), was the form of the book—affordable, portable, accessible, friendly, massively produced—that reached the gradually expanding reading audience. The printed book as mass information medium had success and spread throughout Europe thriving.

During the first decades of printing, personalized luxury copies were strongly related to patronage. It has to be pointed out that luxury copies were intended not only to be read but also to be shown and exhibited, as well as to enrich the collection adding thus value to an already famous library. From this point of view, competition between collectors and noblemen has also to be considered. The printed book in these terms is a material object of artistic value and a symbol of power, wealth, fame, prestige, taste, cultivation, taste, probably family tradition. On the other hand, the wide reading audience constituted by students, scholars and the popular reading audience, focused on the printed book as produced by the printing presses. This was due not only to financial reasons but also due to aesthetic and practical ones; the printed book was gradually maturing as information and visual device, gaining thus its specific identity as discussed in the second chapter. It was gradually becoming more friendly, convenient, affordable, accessible as well as desirable and aesthetically admirable. Woodcut and later engraved ornaments and illustrations, title-pages, frontispieces, together with the use of red ink, embellished the printed book which was thriving. Thus, the book as content and object satisfied the differentiated needs of each kind of reading audience.

Although the transition from manuscript to the printed book was gradual for the collectors and bibliophiles of the upper class, we have to recognize that the printed book—as developed towards the end of the 15th century—was spread widely to the augmenting reading audience taking the key role both as visual information device, and as a desirable object. The visual identity of the printed book, as discussed in the second chapter, prevailed and led to the democratization of both knowledge and taste. The memory of the manuscript book seemed to fade during the 16th century (even though, specific features had been embodied to the printed book) to the wide reading audience; the printed book was the protagonist by being friendly, affordable and nice.

3.2 The systemization of deluxe and limited editions from the Renaissance to nowadays

The maturing of the printed book and the development of its visual identity during the first centuries of printing, the widening of the reading audience, changes in the publishing chain, as well as social, economic and cultural issues led to the rearrangement and redevelopment of luxury editions and unique copies created for collectors, bibliophiles, eclectic readers who could afford to pay for them. From the late 16th century, we might observe that there is a systemization in the production of deluxe, limited, exclusive, collectable editions.

In this chapter, we will look at the evolution and features, on the one hand, of luxury or limited editions and, on the other, of customized, unique copies, studying the ideology and reasons for their creation and production. We will try to highlight the consumer, reading and collectable behavior of the reading audience, the publishing policies and strategies, the complex relationships of the stakeholders and the transformation in the publishing value chain, the audience's expectations, the making of these editions, the impact of technology and the ongoing issues. We will point out that "collectable" does not always mean expensive whereas unique copies were not always orders or gifts to wealthy patrons. "Books formed part of the physical environment that conditioned the physical environment of their users" (Knight Todd, 2009: 51).

Additionally, as we will discuss thereafter, personalized publishing services and customized copies are nowadays in some cases affordable and produced in a number of copies. In that framework, we will trace the features and parameters of such publishing services nowadays, as well as the impact of technologies, whereas the term "collectable" behavior will be discussed. Furthermore, the chapter will look at the complex relationships and ongoing issues developed in the publishing chain of luxury editions and customized copies since the past centuries with the aim to explain their use and impact as well as to interpret ongoing changes nowadays.

3.2.1 Deluxe, limited, collectable, exclusive editions

Terms like deluxe, limited, collector's (collectable), exclusive editions were and are still used; these terms express and exhibit the other face of the publishing industry, that of luxury publications for collectors, bibliophiles and eclectic readers who can afford to acquire them. The copies were and are in some cases numbered. Among the features of these editions, we may recognize special bindings (leather or cloth bound editions or copies), slipcases, boxes, high quality illustration and decoration, high quality paper or vellum, ribbons as bookmarks, illustrated end-papers, colored or gilded fore-edges. It must though be considered that the design and the visual order of such editions was the choice, decision, strategy and policy of the publishing company, and not the work of the artist or the desire-order-expectation of the wealthy reader-customer-patron. Thus, from the 17th century, deluxe, luxury editions were produced and promoted; on the other hand, we always find unique copies due to personalized, specific features such as binding. Hand-illumination was almost abandoned whereas new methods for luxury editions prevailed.

These expensive editions might be limited to a specific number of copies (sometimes numbered) and their visual identity plays the key role. The materiality of the book is the cornerstone of their "luxury," collectable, admirable, "extraordinary" identity. The design of the book, with emphasis on features such as the quality of paper, the illustration and decoration, the binding, the fine printing, is exhibited to potential users, readers, collectors, customers. In our digital era, collectable, deluxe, limited editions are of success to specific audiences and some publishing companies focus on them.

Certainly, the systemization in the production of deluxe, limited, exclusive, collectable editions has to be studied and insfractured in the social, economic and cultural conditions of the era alongside with the success and maturing in printing and illustration techniques. These editions were promoted and advertised through the popular channels of each era exhibiting their advantages and meeting the expectations of a gradually augmenting reading audience (which was upgrading economically and socially) for which the printed book was not only an information and knowledge transmission medium but also a medium of prestige, taste, social status, power, and wealth. The deluxe, limited, even numbered editions added value to their library being an object of recognition and of taste; this was demonstrated in the making of the books.

Additionally, these deluxe editions were obviously of value to bibliophiles and collectors. McKitterick (2005: 93) writes that "the early seventeenth century was, for the engraving trade, one of consolidation and of expansion. The increasing use of rolling press in the second half of the sixteenth century meant that plates could be printed on a larger size and more easily that had been feasible hitherto and, the engraving trade grew rapidly." Fine printing, and what was and is considered as such, was and still is the fundamental issue and main element of the editions discussed.

The features of deluxe, limited, collectable and obviously expensive editions nowadays may include illustration and/or decoration by famous artists specifically created for the edition, slipcases or

3.2 The systemization of deluxe and limited editions from the Renaissance to nowadays 135

boxes, hand-numbered copies, ribbon page markers, painted−decorated−marbled−gilded−painted (top-bottom-fore) edges,[1] marbled or decorated end-papers,[2] deckle page,[3] sewn pages,[4] specific binding (cloth binding and in most cases leather binding or even to use gold "deeply inlaid in the "hubbed" spine"[5]). Marbled paper may also be used and end-leaves or end-papers might be decorated; in the 17th century, marbled paper was used as well as other "kinds of patterned or coloured paper, or (in luxury bindings) watered silk" (Oxford Companion to the Book, 2010: 700). Modern deluxe editions recall that kind of end-papers by developing or redeveloping elements that are recognizable and established as indispensable part of fine printing.

In that framework, deluxe, limited, excluded, numbered editions nowadays set a specific category for a targeted audience of collectors, bibliophiles and for those who want to offer a privileged gift or enrich their library or even exhibit their taste and social status; they are also offered as gifts in many cases. The visual identity of these editions is their significant and most important asset; it is obvious that they aspire to recall or imitate the visual identity of the first editions of classic works or more generally of the deluxe book as known for centuries. It must be pointed out that new technologies are used as in the case of colored and printed edges of the book. Apart from illustration and decoration, all the parts of the book and the elements of the page have been given special concern and are designed and produced in detail so as to be part of a limited printed edition. Copies are sometimes numbered. Thus, every copy is different and collectable.

These editions are advertised to be signed by the author or by the illustrator, or by other stakeholder/contributor such as the translator or the author of the introduction/foreword. Most of the books published in deluxe and limited editions are classic works of literature so as to be

---

1 Marbled edges: usually the top, bottom and fore-edge of a book with a multicolored, swirled design, somewhat resembling the coloration pattern of marble stone, https://www.abaa.org/glossary/entry/marbled-edges (date of last access 5/6/2024).

2 "End paper: paper often of coated stock or marbled paper or otherwise "fancy" paper, with one half pasted to the cover; used primarily to give a finished appearance to the binding." ABAA Glossary of terms (date of last access 5/6/2024).

3 Deckle edge natural or sometimes artificial rough edge of page, left uncut; see also cut edges, uncut, and unopened, ABAA Glossary of terms https://www.abaa.org/glossary/entry/deckle-edge (date of last access 5/6/2024).

4 For example https://www.eastonpress.com/deluxe-editions/mark-twains-the-adventures-of-tom-sawyer-3536.html (date of last access 7/6/2024).

5 For example https://www.eastonpress.com/deluxe-editions/don-quixote-3774.html (date of last access 7/6/2024).

The Visual Identity of the Book

136 3. Converged aesthetics: Personalized publishing services

recognizable and respected by the users−customers−readers. Thus, the author obviously cannot sign the copies which are signed by other contributors who may be famous and well known as the authors of the introduction, epilogue etc. It is though noteworthy that these publishing companies insist on the signing of copies, an element that obviously adds value to the edition or copy recalling the hand dedications of the past. That explains the effort for being all the copies signed whether by other contributors than the author or the illustrator.

Furthermore, these editions are chosen and trusted for being offered as gifts. The features of the book exhibited are mostly visual (apart from introductions or epilogues and signed copies) recalling what is considered to be part of fine printing. It is referred that they "are designed to emulate the fine press editions of the early 20th century."[6] Words such as "unique," "hand-made," "high-quality," "limited," "exclusive" underline the difference from ordinary, massive books[7] just like the hand-illuminated books of the Renaissance. Bonus content is also advertised as well as the bound-in author letter whereas the visual identity of the book is highlighted; obviously, it is the most significant aspect of promotion.

Undeniably, these editions reveal that the book as physical, material object is desirable and that patterns of luxury and uniqueness not only survive but are thriving nowadays. By studying the luxury, expensive, large-sized volumes in a slipcase, that presuppose a specific management of time and space, we can also trace the reasons for their demand and success, reasons that probably go beyond the need for luxury and extend to recalling and redeveloping print and media cultures which bring to light relationships and ideologies.

On the other hand, special and signed editions can be provided by large trade publishers which also promote slipcases/boxed sets with the complete or the major works of well-known authors or of works in specific book series. The slipcases or the clothbound editions are affordable, accessible and collectable for a wider reading audience. For example, Penguin (PRH) advertises its special editions[8] or the "Little Black Classics Box Set" that contains all 80 titles of the little "Black Classics."[9] Penguin, being famous for the high quality paperbacks, provides the

---

6 For example https://www.foliosociety.com/uk/edward-thomas-selected-poems.html. (date of last access 8/6/2024)

7 For example https://www.eastonpress.com/deluxe-editions/mark-twains-the-adventures-of-tom-sawyer-3536.html (date of last access 7/6/2024).

8 For example https://shop.penguin.co.uk/collections/special-editions (date of last access 23/6/2024).

9 For example https://shop.penguin.co.uk/products/little-black-classics-box-set (date of last access 23/6/2024).

The Visual Identity of the Book

opportunity of affordable luxury as the Festive Puffin Clothbound Classics Collection[10] and the "Penguin Clothbound Classics" which are advertised as "bound in cloth and each individually designed by Coralie Bickford-Smith."[11]

As referred in the second chapter, boxes or slipcases bring together works of a trilogy or tetralogy, of a book series or of the same author or of the same theme. Furthermore, they are successful as marketing and promotion methods constituting another aspect of bundling. Collectable or bibliophilic editions can be more affordable, massively produced and accessible. These boxes or slipcases offer to the reader —apart from the visual, collectable, bibliophilic aspect— access to the editions, a rearrangement of the personal libraries and a possible reevaluation of the works. From this point of view, a recommendation is made by the publishing companies for the books as both content and object; works that are chosen and offered together may suggest an approach to classic works.

Thus, we may categorize the users/customers/readers into two categories: the collectors, on the one hand, who give emphasis to the book as a work of art, as a unique material object with specific typographic features and, on the other hand, the wide reading audience who desires and has access to affordable collectable books. In that framework, we have to consider that the book as visual, recognizable object of complex interest (such as bibliophilic) is diachronically one of the aims and scopes of the publishing houses.

3.2.2 Commemorative editions

Commemorative editions for celebrations, coronations, births, victories and other special events (Levarie, 1995: 218) formed a specific category of deluxe books in Europe that were lavishly illustrated and decorated, often of large size and on best quality paper or even vellum, with expensive bindings and sometimes slipcases. They were printed usually to a limited number of copies whereas they were given as a gift or memoir; they were usually not found at bookstores. For example, the luxury volume *Description du Sacre et du Couronnement de leurs Majestés Impériales l'Empereur de toutes les Russies Alexandre III et l'Imperatrice Marie Féodorovna en l'année*, published in 1883 at St. Petersburg, for celebrating the coronation of Alexander III was printed in foglio (66x51 cm) in 200 copies in French and 300 copies in Russian (picture 19).

---

10 For example https://shop.penguin.co.uk/products/festive-puffin-clothbound-collection.

11 For example https://shop.penguin.co.uk/collections/penguin-clothbound-classics. (date of last access 22/6/2024).

138
3. Converged aesthetics: Personalized publishing services

Chromolithography was used at the title-page and at the 27 illustrations whereas headpieces and initials printed in red embellish the text. Black, red, and blue ink was used for the printing of the text. Blue ink was applied to headlines, titles, and words in the text. The book was offered to members of the Imperial family, to the aristocracy and to foreign dignitaries who attended the coronation and celebrations on 15 May 1883. Dedications to these copies are also of value.

This kind of text is survived nowadays in limited or/and deluxe editions produced and distributed sometimes outside the usual channels of the publishing chain; for example, hard bound, large sized volumes, lavishly illustrated, occasionally with slipcases or boxes, are offered as gifts to conferences and anniversaries, and they might be used for various reasons such as to promote, to celebrate a specific occasion, to encourage, to commemorate specific events, features, people, achievements, periods of history. They may be produced by associations, societies, municipalities, companies, banks, etc. Sometimes they belong to gray literature. Dedicatory volumes in numbered copies or limited "luxury" editions provide uniqueness and promote.

3.2.3 Signed books—dedications

Hand dedications were used widely in printed books (Richardson, 1999: 51−52). The invention of printing and the subsequent rise of the authorship, the communication between author-patron and author-reader and the book as prestigious gift and object during the first decades of printing enabled the author to further communicate massively with the readers and establish his/her fame. In that context, hand dedications can be observed in printed books to friends, colleagues, patrons or readers. Since the 19th century, hand dedications were further systemized and used by publishers as part of their promotion strategies (meetings with the author, book presentations and discussions) whereas signed books by the author appeared on the bookshelves of bookstores; moreover, specific occasions were organized so as the reader to meet in person the author who signed the copies.

Meanwhile, printed dedications appeared being part of the front matter. It is though noteworthy that during the 15th century, printed dedicatory letters and texts to patrons of the editions as well as to wealthy and powerful noblemen can be found in incunables. Printed dedicatory letters or poems or texts were among the methods for recognition and for acknowledging the wealthy patrons whose name and contribution was mentioned and praised in the book whether after the text (back matter) or before (front matter). These remains of patronage in the printed book have an exceptional significance pointing out issues of prestige and of complicated relations that influenced book publishing. This is the case of the dedicatory letter to Pietro Medici by Janus Lascaris that appears in the Anthologia Greaca Planudea, published in Florence in 1494 by Janus Lascaris and printed by Lorenzo de Alopa. The 13-page dedicatory text is printed in Latin at the back matter in capital letters just like the Greek text. In this long text, Lascaris refers also to the Greek alphabet. This led to the censorship of the remaining copies when the French took over Florence; the pages with the dedication to Pietro Medici were removed.

The Greek scholar Janus Lascaris (1445–1535), in his long life and career as a librarian, an editor, a teacher, a scholar and diplomat, traveled, discovered books and met men of letters and of power around Europe. Apart from a librarian to Lorenzo dei Medici, Lascaris designed and edited six editions of ancient Greek texts in Renaissance Florence (1494–1496). As a French ambassador in Venice in 1503, he collaborated with Aldus Manutius for the edition of *Rhetores Graeci*. He was also a friend of the famous French publisher Guillaume Budé. Lascaris combined text and notes at the same page, as in other editions, and used the majuscule letters for the text probably aspiring to recall the ancient Greek scripture and inscriptions offering thus to the visual order of the page. The six editions published in Florence are of interest because they are typical of the incunable typology. Furthermore, the relationship with the Medici family is exhibited whereas luxury hand-illuminated copies, printed in vellum, survive that were given as a gift to the Medici. Apart from the unique copies, the printed dedicatory letters highlighted and praised the offer and role of the Medici in the publishing activity.

Nowadays, signed copies by the author, affordable and easily found at bookstores, have their origin in hand dedications of the past. Signed books are the precedent of these dedications. They are also used to limited, expensive and deluxe editions. Signed trade editions recall uniqueness, taste, collectability, while issues of communication, commitment, participation, prestige have also to be considered. They demonstrate the needs and expectations of the readers for uniqueness and in this way the book is redefined and redeveloped as a unique, material object with collectable and personal value. Dedications may reveal a "personal" relationship and appreciation, and obviously are of bibliographical value.

It is noteworthy that in deluxe and limited editions nowadays, copies are signed not only by the author or illustrator but also by the translator or the author of the introduction/foreword. This can be attributed to the fact that as the author and the illustrator in most cases (since these kind of publications give emphasis to classic books) are not in life, the need and expectation for signed copies (or even for dedications) is satisfied by another stakeholder, such as the translator, the illustrator, and

140
3. Converged aesthetics: Personalized publishing services

other stakeholders such as the editor of the text or of the author of the introduction/epilogues etc. (who are also authors, researchers, academics). The expectations and defined elements develop and sometimes create the need. This is more than obvious nowadays that technology often runs faster than our needs.

3.2.4 Facsimiles

Facsimiles are usually expensive and high-quality reproductions, defined as "exact copies," of older and famous—often lavishly illustrated—editions, intended to satisfy the needs of the bibliophiles. The original edition is reproduced in an accurate manner in every detail. The visual identity and the materiality of facsimiles is of significance. It is though noteworthy that reproductions of first editions or of significant and valuable (as content and as object) editions are reproduced by publishing companies, not as facsimiles but as more affordable reproductions that recall the older editions of classic, famous and beloved works.

3.2.5 (Numbered) prints that accompany the edition

Numbered prints by famous artists, who have illustrated or decorated the book, are offered as a gift together with the book. The book is accompanied by a print, often numbered, that adds value to the edition. This is not unusual and certainly not new. According to the subscription model, which was used for centuries since the decades of 1640–1660 and flourished during the 19th century (Barnard, 2001), the subscriber who had paid for the copy or the copies in advance had several privileges among which the offer of a print as a gift. This subscription model was the ancestor of the preorders, a method that has been redeveloped and rediscovered nowadays with great success (Banou, 2017: 90–93).

3.3 The post-luxury copy: Customized copies, personalized publishing services and reader engagement

The term "post-luxury" copy is introduced in this book so as to describe and investigate unique and/or customized copies nowadays; these copies seem to go beyond luxury since customers/users/readers can order and acquire such personalized and often unique copies in a more affordable and systemized manner in comparison to previous centuries. The chapter will enlighten issues and trends of personalized, customized books nowadays studying the reasons and parameters of such strategies. It is though noteworthy that in our digital era the printed book maintains its status of prestige and luxury. The book is still a symbol of power, taste, wealth, prestige, cultivation, status quo; deluxe and limited editions, signed copies, copies with dedication, customized copies are used as valuable multifunctional objects that demonstrate taste, prestige and fame. Even mass ordered books (books in which the only differentiation from other copies is the name, the place and the photo of the person who ordered or wo will receive the gift) offer to their owners the delight of exhibiting them to visitors, colleagues, or the family. Somewhere between family albums and coffee-table books, these customized copies are used as to offer prestige and fame. These books, on the one hand, continue the long tradition that goes back to the invention of printing, and, on the other, alter the scene as they led to the democratization of customization. After the democratization of knowledge and of taste, the book has revolutionized luxury books developing new patterns for a systemized customization of books and of publishing services.

Thereafter we will look initially at the development, systemization, and evolution of customized books since the early centuries of printing; then we will explore current issues, methods and strategies so as to understand ongoing issues, to trace patterns of continuity, to identify the uses of the copies, to recognize the relationships and changes in the publishing industry, to interpret and to introduce strategies.

3.3.1 Cut-and-paste books

A cut-and-paste book is a hybrid book, a unique book, specifically designed, organized, and created by the reader/creator in terms of cutting and pasting fragments and excerpts from printed books which in some cases were ordered for this purpose. Smyth (2024: 76−115) enlightens the procedure, methods and aspects related to this particular kind of books which reveal an engagement of the reader/producer who is the creator of the unique book. This cut-and-paste book was often exhibited and even became famous as in the case studied by Smyth (2024). Reasons for creating a book like that may include personal participation and engagement, the need for contributing to the dialogue and to the political, financial, social, religious, cultural conditions of the era, the desire to participate or to have an activity.

Obviously this method and technique reminds of the manuscript book in terms of the uniqueness and creativity but at the same time goes beyond that as it is related with the need for participation, intervention, opinion making and expression, dialogue and creativity. It may remind to us nowadays of the albums and diaries in which teenagers—before the advent of the internet and the information technologies—used (and probably use) to paste photographs and extracts deriving from the Press. But

142
3. Converged aesthetics: Personalized publishing services

during the past centuries, apart from personal or family use, this cut-and-paste books were in some cases a public intervention, a proposal and a suggestion that was reminded, discussed and memorized in other texts or circumstances as in the case of the "Whole Law of God" created by Mary and Anna Collett in the middle of the 17th century (Smyth, 2024: 76–115). "This was a handmade book—a unique object—but it was composed of print," writes Smyth (2024: 79). The cut-and-paste book was a complex procedure of organizing, re-reorganizing, cutting, gluing, combining, pasting, suggesting; they thus created a unique book which provided the creator's point of view. It is noteworthy that the two sisters ordered books even from abroad so as to have the material required and to decide on the text and images included. "To this cut-up text, they glued in images: pictures removed from prints or sometimes other books, many of them imported from abroad (English Bibles rarely included illustrations), trimmed and reworked and sometimes conflated to produce something that would later be called collage" (Smyth, 2024: 83).

We may distinguish such cut-and-paste books in two categories: those for personal use and those for public use, although these two options are often converged and not easily defined. Furthermore, the word "creator" instead of "reader" may seem more appropriate as these books extend from reading into creating, suggesting, proposing, introducing, exhibiting. As we will discuss below in regard to the various and complex uses of the book, the cut-and-paste books (later in some cases called collages) express the need for creation, redefine creativity and go beyond reading and pure enjoyment.

The virtual descendant of the "cut-and-paste" books (and of the teenager albums) may nowadays be virtual publications, with the use of multimedia. New technologies enable the users/ readers to augment publications, to add, combine, modify, explain, interact. Furthermore, social media -where the user can upload, show, combine, merge, exhibit, thus "cut-and-paste" in a virtual environment- recall these techniques of the past. Meanwhile, the physical descendant may be observed, apart from children's activity books, to printed books of activities that combine materials whereas collage may be a good example of the echo of the cut-and-paste books. In that framework, reader engagement and thereafter reader creativity are upgraded constituting an aspect of nowadays consumer, reading, and book cultures. The publishing industry exploits these opportunities.

3.3.2 Extra-illustration and reader engagement

According to the Oxford Companion to the Book (2010: 710): "A popular practice of the 18th and 19th centuries, extra-illustration, or grangerization, is the addition of material to a book by someone other than the publisher." Or "usually a volume made into a unique copy with additional illustrations, autographs, or manuscripts added by carefully gluing or tipping-in this extra material."[12] As Adam Smyth (2024: 188) has written, it is a "radical book modification." It is thus a unique printed copy, in which illustrations, autographs, prints and portraits are added and bound together; from this point of view, it is an augmented copy, mainly with illustrative material, that expresses and exhibits the taste and ideas of the creator on the themes of the book. The added material interacts with the printed text and image, thus adding, interpreting, enlightening, commenting, suggesting, redefining, interpreting. Peltz (2018) writes that "it is a process whereby published texts were customized by the cutting and pasting of thematically linked prints and watercolours" Undoubtedly, it may seem a "curious" and rather expensive way to interact. Certainly, extra-illustrated volumes are of high value for the study of book history, book culture, collection culture, communication, reader engagement and participation. Like cut-and-paste books, they are a unique creation of the reader-collector-creator that presupposes organization of the material. Furthermore, extra-illustration or grangerization was an expensive activity since it presupposed not only the acquisition of the prints but also the rebinding and arrangement of the book. The "Biographical History of England" by James Granger is a famous work which was embellished with portraits (Smyth, 2024: 191–192) and is considered as the basis for extra-illustration which was thus named after Granger.[13] It was a method and practice used mainly from the 18th to early 20th century.

Extra-illustration is a method, an activity, a hobby that extends the boundaries of the book, exhibits the pleasures of reader engagement, and promotes interaction, participation, and intervention to the book as material object. They are unique copies but not hand-decorated or illustrated; they are developed and constructed by the addition of printed, illustrated material according to the taste, selections, decisions and ideology of the creator. The extra-illustrated copies were often leather hand-bound.

In that framework, extra illustration may be recognized among the ancestors of reader engagement and participation. The word

12 ABAA Glossary of Terms, "Extra-illustration," https://www.abaa.org/glossary/entry/extra-illustrated (date of last access 10/6/2024).

13 Extra-illustration (or "Grangerizing") was a practice among book collectors from the late 18th to early 20th centuries. Collectors disbound printed works, inserted additional material related to the work's content, and then rebound the whole—thus providing "extra" illustration to the original work. Added material of interest to theater historians can include portrait prints, manuscripts, and playbills." https://guides.library.harvard.edu/c. php?g = 1294023&p = 9509232 (date of last access 10/6/2024).

"augmented" for the unique copy produced further exhibits reader/ user engagement and uniqueness of the single copy, which is been "augmented" in regard to the copy massively produced by the publisher. Nowadays, this specific augmentation can be obtained by the new technologies and might be offered as an option for readers in the line of reader participation; the reader might have the opportunity to add visual material, to use multimedia, to combine different forms of the book whereas, even in printed copies, it is easier—in regard to the past—to "augment," to alter the book by adding visual material. New technologies have altered patterns of production and introduced new printing and publishing models and opportunities, as well as new networks and method of communication (Scolari, 2019).

Thus, extra-illustration means differentiation from the edition as published by the publisher; it is a proposal for the visual identity of the book and it is also a medium of explanation and interpretation of the text as well as of intervention to the literary, political, cultural, social scene of the era. In that context, the reader participated and suggested, decided and commented. Furthermore, these copies were unique and added value to the owner's collection whereas at the same time exhibited the taste, ideas, creativity of the creator. In this way, the reader-owner was a creator and an energetic, dynamic member of the publishing chain who could transform the book, propose explanations on the text and participate in the dialog between stakeholders, sometimes even intervening and influencing.

Peltz (2017) discusses the role of extra-illustration in Britain's social and cultural context highlighting concepts of collection, print and antiquarian culture; she also enlightens extra illustration as an antiquarian practice. Smyth (2024: 190) writes that "extra-illustration was a way of remaking the book that returned to 16th- and 17th-century ideas of the book as incomplete and in flux object... or the unbound sheets bought by readers from bookseller stalls in St. Paul's Churchyard, to be marked, revised, augmented, and even physically dismantled." Certainly, extra-illustration continues, in other ways and by different media, the abitudine of the unique copies of the Renaissance. It is though noteworthy that the reader can create the augmented volume by choosing, deciding, acquiring and organizing the material and does not just order to an expert (such as the illuminator) or the bookseller the illustrated and specifically bound copy as in the Renaissance. In the case of extra-illustration, only the binding is obviously ordered and made by the experts.

Furthermore, the book has been a medium, a device that, on the one hand, expresses and demonstrates user's/creator's ideas and opinions and, on the other, develops, reorganizes, embellishes and recreates the copy as a unique, physical, material object according to the taste and ideas of the owner. This transformation, this metamorphosis of the book obviously aspired not only to embellish but also to redevelop and redesign the book mainly as material object but also as information and ideological device. The reader/user/owner added visual information so as to comment, exhibit, propose and upgrade the reading experience and the interpreting of text.

Nowadays it is obviously more affordable and not as time-consuming to create such customized copies. Smyth (2024: 190−191, 213−215) refers to the connection and relationship of "extra-illustration" with the present and more specifically to artists' books. Moreover, this "extra" method undeniably suits our era in which information sharing, communication, access are among the key values. What we call "extra illustration" could be nowadays applied to both printed and electronic books as well as virtual material and multimedia.

Beyond that, "extra-illustration" can be traced in our digital era and further be developed and used as a method in customized books and personalized publishing services either in hand-made, handicraft books in which readers/users/creators develop their copy recalling thus the tradition of hand-illuminated and extra-illustrated copies or in virtual publications in which multimedia material can be added. The books are thus been augmented, redesigned and reconstructed. In the case of printed material, this augmentation and extra-illustration can be traced not as such in coloring books but in handicraft activities much popular in our era. Coloring books express this aspect of book culture but readers/users are obviously to be limited to the boundaries, borders and instructions provided; even though, these coloring books might be enriched and augmented by added material offered by a range of choices, as we will discuss at the fourth chapter. Meanwhile, social media in which users upload visual material and comments might be a parameter that encourages the augmented copies and the redevelopment of "extra-illustration" nowadays in other environments. In that context, the book is a vivid, dynamic object due to transformation and customization, expressing the creator's ideas and aspects and intervening to the ongoing themes. Moreover, this might be a leisure activity, a hobby that relates creativity with communication, taste with information sharing. In that context, the use of new information and communication technologies is obviously significant.

We thus may refer not only to "post-luxury" but also to augmented copies of our hybrid era. We have as well to consider that unique copies have not been reduced; they have been and still are created due not only to aesthetic but also to ideological reasons that have to be explained and studied in their social, political, economic and cultural framework.

3.3.3 Customized copies

Customized, personalized copies not only survive nowadays but indeed form a specific feature and method. We may distinguish these copies in three categories. Firstly, we have to refer to books/copies that are massively and affordably produced by specific publishing services; in that case, the text, illustration, design, cover, dust jacket have been designed and can be ordered: the only feature of customization is the insertion of the photograph and name of the person as well as a few personal details required. Secondly, customized copies are created by the owner, collector, reader often combining the printing techniques and elements with the new technologies. In that case, the copy is unique, often for personal use and of personal value, often exhibited at home or in social media, and sometimes even being famous. The origins of those copies can be traced at the cut-and-paste books and at extra-illustration that created unique, augmented copies during the 18th and 19th centuries. Thirdly, artists' books, works of high aesthetic value that are a work of art.

The uses of these copies can point out the common features in the publishing activity, exhibit ongoing trends and interpret customer/reader/collector behavior. In that framework, the printed book will be studied as gift, as symbol of taste, prestige and power, as an object of desire, as collectable material. It is obvious that unique, luxury copies are defined by the book as material, visual and desirable object. The visual identity of the book and its specific characteristics are the advantages that define this category. Even though, this unique book, characterized by its materiality, is also defined in some cases as an information device and a medium for the transmission of knowledge. Personalized, customized copies are also created so as to contribute to the text, to add comments, to note and even amend, to add portraits or illustrations. Sherman describes them as "radically customized copies—copies, that is, where the text is not just annotated but physically altered, sometimes even cut up and combined with other texts" (9). This can be found in classical and religious texts. Inserting text, diagrams, illustrations, maps from other books was supposed not just to annotate but also to offer another point of view or summarize or amend or synopsize or propose.

As discussed, extra-illustration and cut-and-paste books (Smyth, 2024: 76−105; 188−215) created and offered a different point of view, a new aspect, a contribution to the social, political, cultural, religious and economic conditions of their era. The reason may be attributed to the need for a new book, a new proposal, a new point of view, a new inter-pretation of the text or even combination and discussion of different texts. This augmented and differentiated copy was "limited" to a few people who could have access; sometimes these books were famous due to their visual identity or innovated context or due to the famous people who admired or even used them, as in the case described by Smyth (2024) when King Charles I visited in 1641 Little Gidding and took in his hands, in the manor house, the heavy, big, unique, handmade book titled *The Whole Law of God*, composed by Mary and Anna Collett (Smyth, 2024: 76–80). Obviously, this was "the book" on which the creators and owners had spent a lot of time and money. Nowadays, the creation of these books may be a hobby, an activity offering satisfaction and delight to the creator. This need and expectation for a unique copy and for the introduction and expression of messages as well as of interpretations is not any more limited nor difficult but it can be fulfilled and at the same time be accessible due to a number of reasons including information technologies and social media.

Even though, we have to wonder, in the case of the first category of customized books (copies that are massively and affordably produced by specific providers), what we mean by saying that the text is personalized, and to which extent or in which ways a novel, a classic work, such as "Pride and Prejudice" or "War and Peace," can be personalized. From this point of view, this is a stereotyped, systemized service that is already designed and is reproduced massively to a large number of customers, offered by specific companies/providers. Obviously, we cannot refer to traditional publishing companies, which develop their publishing policy and decide on the titles to publish, but to companies which provide specific publishing services.

As stated above, these copies have the function of a family album, a beloved book or a coffee-table book which can be shown to visitors. Among the advantages of this specific kind of personalized books we have to consider the love for books and the possible encouragement for reading. For example, when a fairy tale is customized with the name and photo of the child, its use might encourage reading and the love for books.

According to McKitterick (2018: 85) "in countries and circles where the fashion developed for gilt decorated spines on books, the appearance of shelves and of libraries was transformed. For some people, fine bindings, large- and fine-paper copies, illustrations and a careful choice of editions were all to be emulated to a greater or lesser extent." These elements nowadays go beyond as to exhibit, demonstrate and create collection and reading habits, behaviors and cultures as well as the social status quo. Unique copies develop a culture not only of collection but also of exhibition and sharing.

3.3.4 Personalized publishing services nowadays

Specialized, personalized publishing services are offered nowadays; these services are affordable and easy to be ordered and completed. On the one hand, they certainly continue the tradition of unique copies and satisfy the needs and expectations of the readers/owners for a personalized book, different from the others; on the other hand, they are a mass

148 3. Converged aesthetics: Personalized publishing services

medium, designed and offered via the internet and a centralized system. Copies are only personalized in specific details that are required during the order.

Personalized publishing services are offered by a number of enterprises and often from start-ups (not from traditional publishers) as well as from some bookstores. Readers—commissioners are informed via the webpages and special platforms so as to take advantage of these services; guidelines are provided as to facilitate the commissioners to proceed to the personalization. The steps usually require the child's/the person's name and photo, as well as the dedication that will appear. Other information is required according to the kind of text and the services offered (such as the date of birth). Thus, both visual and verbal material is requested and used. The edition is already designed and illustrated; the reader/user/commissioner can choose from a variety of titles, taking into consideration the theme, the author, the plot/story, the quality of illustration, the mise en page, the cover and other features. The demand and success of personalized copies regards both the visual identity of the book and the content.

Initially, the commissioner has to choose, from the catalog provided, the work in which the information, verbal and visual, will be in a stereotyped way inserted. Options may be categorized according to the kind of text, the age and the sex of the person, the occasion for creating and offering this book. Gifts are thus no longer offered to the wealthy, powerful people (such as the noble patrons in Renaissance) but to members of the family or friends or colleagues, through personalized copies and/or even through specifically written context enriched with visual and multimedia material that has been provided by the commissioner. From this point of view, these editions continue in a democratized framework the tradition of luxury copies of the first centuries of printing. Furthermore, these personalized publishing services might develop a new framework for reader/user engagement and new marketing tools.

It is noteworthy that in the case of personalized copies or even editions, we can obviously recognize the dominance of the printed material, which can be explained by practical, emotional, psychological, functional, visual and other parameters. Even though, digital publications offer numerous opportunities for convergence, interactivity, participation and reader engagement. In some cases, personalized, customized copies (that incorporate personal information) are intended to play the role of a family album or diary having even the function of a memory device or a memoir of special occasions. Furthermore, they are often offered as gifts in celebrations (whether family or professional) for anniversaries, weddings, birthday, graduation, retirement and other important events. These books are considered a successful way for celebrating and for satisfying the beloved ones.

The Visual Identity of the Book

The personalized creation of a book, that has the function of a family memoir and/or of a dedicatory edition, brings to light the emotional and psychological attachment of the reading audience to the printed book as well as the cultural and ideological concepts related to the print culture. These specific publishing services—by combining storytelling, ghostwriting, crowdsourcing with editorial services and multimedia technologies—might been thought to revive the interest of the readers and create added value to the printed books although questions are set. By enabling readers to decide and intervening in the creation of a novel, short text, memoir, poem, reader engagement is enforced in the publishing process. Readers—customers—users decide both on the content and on the artistic identity, and pay for them. Continuing thus the tradition of the luxury editions that praised important people or their coronations, weddings and other "important" events of powerful families, these platforms democratize the old methods under the magnifying glass of new technologies. It must though be noted that these copies are produced in the quantity decided by the customers for their use only.

In that framework, further questions emerge regarding the exact role of the reader and of the publisher, the limitations of choices and of decisions, the ideological uses of the book, as well as reader engagement. In an era of many and various challenges, boundaries seem to be reset or are thought to be reset, influencing thus the publishing activity and the publishing chain—circle—circuit as a whole. The book, whether printed or not, seems to confirm its status and prestige. Being a powerful information and communication medium, the book is still an object of desire and of aesthetic value that brings prestige and recognition to its owner, continuing thus its complex visual and ideological role, even in hard times. And according to Calasso (2015: 13) "times are always hard in publishing."

Nowadays, personalized publishing services take advantage of new technologies and techniques so as to insert personal information (both visual and verbal, such as the name of the person, date of birth and place) and visual material (such as photos) to specific number of ordered copies (personalized copies). They can also add and use specific features such as colored edges of the book, ribbons as bookmarks, recognizable illustrations and ornaments. The reproduction of such personalized copies is affordable, systemized and merchandised. The visual identity of the book is obviously more important as it is due to it that the user is attracted and convinced to order the personalized copies. In that context, the reader-user-customer does not participate neither co-creates the book which is already designed and offered as an option. The copies produced are similar to each other; the inserted name, personal information and photo of the person is of significance.

The model that was applied to Renaissance and Baroque books (Banou, 2017: 31—33) can as well be used for nowadays personalized

150   3. Converged aesthetics: Personalized publishing services

publishing services. We use the term "customer" instead of "reader" since the symbolic capital of these books is mainly situated in their visual identity and unique characteristics; the added value mainly, but not exclusively, derives from customization. The story is usually a classic work or a fairy tale. Obviously, the model is, on the one hand, publisher-centered since the publisher decides, designs, organizes, provides and promotes the already selected options of the books. The reader is called to choose and decide among the online options already prepared and offered. At the same time, the model is obviously customer−reader centered since their needs and expectations, as well as feedback, are taken into consideration carefully. Customers, who order personalized copies through websites and platforms, are aware of the kind of services provided. The choice is made from a wide range of books (stories, tales, fairy tales, classic works etc.) in which illustration, cover, dust jackets, book decoration, binding are essential. Moreover, the decision and choice might be artistcentered. This could be a more expensive, unique, "luxury" option if the artist illustrates the book specifically for the person intended. In most cases, a combination of the above might be observed with the role of the publisher and the author prevailing.

Personalized publishing services have been rediscovered nowadays being rather affordable, accessible and convenient for the wide reading audience. Questions include the grade of personalization, the participation of the reader, the role of the publisher, the ideological and aesthetic uses of the book. Personalized publishing services might encourage the reader/ user to participate to the making of the visual identity of the book by coloring (as in the case of coloring books), inserting further personal information (verbal and visual), choosing decorative patterns, updating, combining. In that case, the user could combine, continue, finish, redesign, select, complete the already designed, choose from the offered ornaments.

Thus, personalization in publishing can be distinguished according to the kind of text, the visual identity of the book, the uniqueness of the copy, the purpose of the order. One of the criteria might be the kind and extent of personalization.

According to the kind of text, personalized books may be categorized in children's books, fiction, coloring books, manuals, bibles, pet books, erotic, anniversary/celebration books; additionally, there are titles for family relations. Children's picture books probably are among the most known and celebrated personalized books; it is a gift of high value offered from parents and relatives with multiple symbolisms and psychological uses exhibiting family relationships. A number of options are offered to the customer-reader according to the event/occasion/celebration (there are books ready to be personalized for birthday, new baby, mother's day, father's day as well for Christmas or other holidays). Additionally, there are editions that focus on family relations shedding light to roles such as grandfather, grandmother, parents etc.[14] Pets are included in that category: "dog books" or "cat books" are good examples.[15]

In regard to fiction books, long sellers—classic works (usually in the public domain) are offered to readers (such as *Pride and Prejudice, Romeo and Juliet, Alice's Adventures in Wonderland, Emma*[16] etc.). It is obviously a successful category since the works are recognizable, long-established, much appreciated. Questions raised include the extent of personalization and of participation, the uses of the book, the reception of the work, the relation and commitment to the text, the way the names of the characters might be changed. Everyone can be a hero/heroine if some copies are ordered. The crucial question is if these books are read or just shown and used as objects. Personalized coloring books form a specific category. It is noteworthy that personalized newspaper books for specific dates are offered as an option (for example, the headlines of the day of the birthday). In regard to Bibles,[17] customization is limited to the name of the user-customer on the cover. Coloring books,[18] as we will discuss below, presuppose reader engagement and participation.

Printed dedications take a key role in all personalized editions. The customer can also choose poems, quotes or write a few lines so as to be inserted in the book. Thus, the user—customer has a wide range of options upon to decide. Parameters that may influence the decision include aspects of the visual identity of the book, the kind of text, the extent of customization. Regarding customization, the reader might decide on specific elements of the visual identity of the book, as already discussed. Obviously, higher grade of participation and engagement by the reader implies different services and options, and higher price.

Personalized services go back to the hand-illuminated incunables and early printed books, and derive from the desire for prestige, power, self-promotion, fame, and communication. Inevitably questions emerge in regard to the nature, function and purpose of customized books

---

14 For example https://www.wonderbly.com/pages/books-for-grandparents https://www.putmeinthestory.com/personalized-books/why-i-love-grandma.html date of last access 24/6/2024 (site was closed on 14/4/2024).

15 For example, https://www.wonderbly.com/personalized-products/dog-save-the-day-book, https://petventuresbook.com/ (date of last access 24/6/2024).

16 For example https://imthestory.com/ (date of last access 24/6/2024).

17 For example https://personalizedbibles.com (date of last access 23/6/2024).

18 For example https://www.putmeinthestory.com/personalized-adult-coloring-books (date of last access 24/6/2024).

The Visual Identity of the Book

nowadays. Initially, we may wonder if they are really unique copies taking into consideration that they are already designed and produced on demand; personalization means to insert just the information provided, the photo and the dedication. Obviously, they are not luxury copies as in the past. Furthermore, these books are not mainly intended to be read but rather to be exhibited whereas the boundaries between a family or personal album/diary and a story or novel are not strictly defined. Sometimes, they form part of everyday life. Coffee-table books are probably been replaced in some cases by personalized copies and editions which demonstrate the happiness and success of the owner. This vaguely reminds of the almanacs and calendars during the first centuries of printing that were used as memory devices and personal notebooks.

It is noteworthy that the printed book dominates in such publishing services. The books ordered, offered, desired are mainly printed. This apotheosis of the printed material enlightens not only the use but the ideologies, aspects and expectations which seems to maintain its status quo as a symbol of power, taste, wealth, and knowledge. The printed book is still of use for exhibiting the social status as well as for demonstrating devotion and love in the family. The public and the private are been served by the book which has been adapted to new audiences and thus to new needs and expectations. In an era in which the boundaries between the public and the private are not always defined (as in the case of social media), the book as a massive medium is used also in a private mode, as centuries ago. At the same time, it can become public if the owner decides to exhibit it using social media and enlarged online communities.

In the case of massively personalized copies, the role of the reader is not dynamic and obviously there is no engagement. The orderer just provides the information requested, the photos and the dedication, choosing from an online catalog the work to be personalized and probably offered as a gift. Another question concerns the reading–consumer behavior and habits related to personalized books and if they further encourage reading. Do they manage to cultivate an everyday culture of the book? Do they encourage further reading introducing people into the world of books? Personalized coloring books might go a step beyond as they imply the active participation of the reader.[19]

In that context, potential audiences have to be redefined due to new information and communication technologies, to users' needs and expectations, to experimentation in the publishing activity, to interactivity, to current trends and issues. The rewards seem to be many for the customers–users. Obviously personalized books go beyond luxury to

19 For example https://publishingperspectives.com/2016/03/adult-coloring-books-and-publishing-light-dark/. (date of last access 3/4/2024).

aspects related to social, economic, cultural, ideological, psychological issues. Everyone can be a literary hero/heroine—this is already a reward for the customer. The above have to be studied in a broader framework that incorporates publishing, literature, history of reading, psychology, book history, media etc. On the one hand, readers often identify themselves in the plot, in the heroes and heroines of fiction. The success of the novel in the 19th century brought about, among other factors, identical changes in the publishing industry transforming the typology of the books and the role of the stakeholders in the publishing value chain as well. In our digital age, as technology further enforces the emerging role of the reader and gives the opportunity of a more dynamic presence, it is more than expected that the reader will be offered a variety of opportunities and services. Rewards differ according to the kind of text, the audience and the stakeholders, the time, the aim of the order. Rewards may include communication, membership, strengthening of the family ties, interaction, self-esteem, recognition.

3.3.5 Reader creativity. The case of coloring books

One significant aspect that has to be considered is the success of coloring books nowadays. The explosion in the production of coloring books in our hybrid, digital era demonstrates the coexistence of different media, as well as the need for creativity, participation and reader engagement in a handicraft and creative manner that goes back in time. The user/reader colors and creates, combines and suggests to the printed material. Questions have raised about the nature and function of these books, about their role and place. One of the main questions may be "are they books?" Synopsizing, it may seem curious that in our virtual Age, coloring books have such a great success which can be attributed to the need of the reader for creation, handicraft expression, participation, engagement. That kind of books is also regarded to have antistress results. Thus, coloring books may be considered a step forward and an exploration to creativity as the reader/user not only colors but also combines and creates; reader creativity, participation and satisfaction may be the key points that explain their success. Additionally, coloring books might be designed so as to further encourage readers to continue, to finish, redesign, complete the already designed or even propose and introduce new borders, decorative patterns, ornaments, even designs.

Furthermore, readers can use the colored by themselves prints for embellishing and decorating as well as for exhibiting and showing their "work." Cut-and-paste techniques may also be included bearing in mind habits and methods of past centuries, as discussed above. Moreover, we are obviously reminded of the coloring of prints during the Renaissance. The origins of coloring books can thus be traced in the Renaissance print coloring, as discussed in the second chapter, when the hand-coloring of the printed or stamped by hand framework/design (illustrations, ornaments, decorative borders) was mainly work of an expert; additionally we can find copies in which readers have colored the woodcuts or engravings.

In conclusion, coloring books nowadays exhibit the different uses of the book demonstrating the need of the reader for the printed material, which is related to user engagement and to the importance of the physical participation. Not being a work of an expert, coloring books may be a leisure activity, a hobby, a communication medium, an antistress or relaxation method; the latter is often advertised and demonstrated. Furthermore, these coloring books take the reader back to the childhood by reminding of coloring and creative attempts with the children's activity books, creating thus a connection with previous experiences and desires. This connection is significant since it builds a relationship with the memory of creativity and gives the sense of continuity. Additionally, we may assume that in our virtual Age of automation, in which we do not even write with a pencil or pen, coloring books offer the experience of the paper and the pencils, thus of something "different" from our daily habits, which is creative, handcrafted and obviously much enjoyable. From this point of view, that kind of books reveal the needs of the users for physical activity as well as for creativity. It is also noteworthy that sometimes coloring books narrate a story or often they are based on popular, classical novels. Apart from being recognizable, these coloring books may introduce the readers to the text and to the author. Moreover, this participation and creativity may exceed the printed book and explore the digital opportunities. Reader participation and engagement is obvious; even though coloring books go a step forward into creativity. The reader does not only participate but creates.

3.4 The uses of the book

The book has been and still is a symbol of power, taste, knowledge, fame, cultivation, prestige, wealth, self-esteem, self-confidence. It is true that "the material form given to a book has a great deal to do with the symbolic value that is ascribed to it" (Cummings, 2010: 63). Thus, the visual identity of the book had and has a significant role beyond reading. In that framework, the book is a symbol, an everyday object, a collectable and desirable object, a device of personal memory, a notebook, an information medium, a communication medium, a storage device. It is also part of the reader's life and of the culture of the era.

Considered a valuable, respectable and useful object, the book was and is often offered as gift.

In numerous portraits, scholars and aristocrats of Renaissance or of the Enlightenment appear with a book in hand. Nowadays, the background at tele-conferences, online courses, and meetings is often a library; books are shown at the background continuing the visual tradition of the exhibition of books so as to highlight the taste, knowledge and cultivation of the person speaking. As McKitterick (2018: 28) writes: "Such uses do not always require that the books in question are regularly read. Presence and external appearance are as important as content."

Additionally, apart from the professional success and the social status quo, the book nowadays might be a demonstration of family happiness, family tights, good relationships, self-esteem. In the place of coffee-table books and of the "old-fashioned" photograph albums, there exist the personalized copies ordered from the readers/users/customers. Specific publishing services are offered by publishing enterprises that provide users—orderers with family stories and material for personal myths. The hero in the story may be one of the members of the family or of the colleagues. Furthermore, self-publishing provides the opportunity to authors to publish their work, and gain fame and communication; the rise of self-publishing worldwide (Thompson, 2021: 216—282) declares the need for people to be published, the struggle to often manage it outside the traditional channels of the publishing houses, the options for self-publishing.

From the Renaissance patron who ordered or received as gifts personalized, customized copies till the democratization of the personalized copies nowadays, many issues and aspects of this continuing tradition have to be studied. The book is a private and also a public object that is exhibited and informs about the taste and state of the owner-reader-user. The private becomes public with the aim not only to demonstrate but also to initiate a dialog, to share information, to exhibit the status quo, even to communicate ideas. At the same time, books are domestic devices adding value to the family relations and stories. They may serve as manuals and memory books, as domestic treasuries that narrate and reproduce the story of the family, obviously not always as it is but as it is aspired to be. It reminds of the early modern readers: "the use of books in ways not prescribed by their texts seems to have been something of an everyday imperative" (Knight Todd, 2009: 42). Books, especially large-sized printed volumes, were used as storage devices, as notepads. Flyleafs and front matter were used for the readers' comments, thoughts and notes on the text and sometimes for recording facts and dates that do not have any relation to the work. Additionally, as discussed in the second chapter, marginalia -apart from printed- may be manuscript (notes and comments of the reader on the text). Knight Todd (2009: 43—51) investigates these spaces and functions of the book.

In that framework, the book is undeniably an object of desire and of high personal value, importance and significance. Probably this explains why books are always offered as gifts; since the book is not only useful but also beautifully structured, illustrated, bound, colored, etc., it is a proper gift, being as affordable as wanted. For example, children's picture books are offered, promoted and advertised as gifts. Complex relationships and visual expectations, that go back in time, prevail.

Knight Todd (2009: 41) focus on "books that furnish space and furnishings that like books have the capacity to fill minds with information" and Smyth (2014) refers to the different uses of the book. As discussed just above, hybrid books, customized copies and personalized publishing services constitute a rather bibliophilic, visual and aesthetic use of the book which goes beyond reading and extends to private and public uses of the book. Phillips and Bhaskar (2019: 5−6) write: "they [people a hundred years ago who bought fake bookshelves] wanted not real books but just the patina of learning, the cultural capital associated with them. It indicated that the place of the book was, in this more competitive environment, shifting; that the role of books, maybe even of text, was, in some areas, becoming ornamental rather than structural."

The printed books serve also as notepads storing the personal use and reading of the copy. Flyleaves are also used for noting. Books have also another function described by Thomas Tusser in his book published in 1570: "these texts might be copied out, but they might also have been cut out and pinned or glued to the walls" (quoted in Smyth, 2018: 23). Books are living with their users and take part in everyday life. Book collecting, book showing, book sharing, book discovering are parts of our culture. We also note, comment, dedicate, even draw or paint on books. Cut-and-paste, collages, and coloring books shed light to the book as viable, handicraft object. Books may also be rare (McKitterick, 2018), old, collectible, of aesthetic and economic value, part of libraries (public and private), indispensable part of our culture and civilization. Renata Ago (2013: 189) writes that "if, like paintings, books were also collectible objects, 'ornamental and useful' for houses and palaces, it was natural to pass them on to children...." Furthermore, readers-users could always compose and create their own anthologies and miscellanies whereas they could intervene in their own copy as material object. From this point of view, reader participation and engagement is obviously not something new; it goes back to the invention of printing. As we have discussed, readers interact not only with the text but with the book as object. Furthermore, in certain cases, readers go beyond participation and exceed to the making of the book as unique copy or as privileged edition. In that framework, reader engagement is combined with creativity and interactivity.

The "post-luxury" copy, term introduced and used in this chapter, has a number of functions that often go beyond luxury and have to do with self-esteem, communication, membership, success, prestige, acceptance. Publishers have new opportunities to exploit, new issues to consider, new challenges to manage; they do know though that these challenges and opportunities derive form the past being in most cases the ancestors of already used, developed and tested method and strategies. The book is thus redefined as visual object recalling the past by its innovation. Publishers in a changing world explore, exploit and extend their role. As the quest for distinguished books and roles in the publishing industry prevails, they decide on the strategies and publishing policies.

In that context, the visual identity of the book through the design and structure of its page and of its parts is called to play a multifunctioned role exhibiting patterns of consumption, communication, information sharing, reading and writing. So, the past explains the present and the present offers the tools for understanding/interpreting the past; both are developing the strategies for the future.

CHAPTER

4

Conclusions: Challenges and opportunities

4.1 Reframing the world: Visual structures, strategies, and uses of the book

The publisher must be much more of an opportunist than the editor; at any rate to begin with. In order to get going at all one may have to publish books which one would send elsewhere later on. At any rate I do set this standard that whatever we publish shall have some virtue in it, even though it may not be of the very first class. **Geoffrey Faber to T.S. Eliot (Toby Faber, 2021: 10).**

4.1.1 Books as desirable, complex devices

The printed book reframed, redeveloped and restructured the world, and it keeps on doing so. As we have discussed, themes such as discoverability, globalization, convergence of media, communication, reader engagement, reader creativity, interaction are more than significant nowadays. One of the main questions might be the following "Will the book survive"? No answer and prediction for the future can obviously be done. Certainly, the book has survived and continues so in complex globalized environments, in various forms and in constant challenges. In that framework, the visual identity of the book takes a key role in the publishing activity as well as in consumer behavior; additionally, it could further encourage reader engagement and participation, cultivate reader creativity, promote books and create cultures of the book. The visual identity of the book, defined traditionally as the materiality of the printed book, extends nowadays to new forms of the book (electronic book, virtual publications) in which convergence and interaction are among the main features. Thus, the visual identity can be synopsized

The Visual Identity of the Book
DOI: https://doi.org/10.1016/B978-0-443-19167-1.00004-8
Copyright © 2025 Christina Banou. Published by Elsevier Ltd. All rights are reserved, including those for text and data mining, AI training, and similar technologies.

160
4. Conclusions: Challenges and opportunities

also as the aesthetic capital which has to be recognized as one of the capitals of the publishing industry playing an important role in book promotion, in reader and consumer behavior, in the reception of the text, in communication and information sharing as well as in the publishing policy and strategies of the publishing companies.

In this book, we tried to investigate the evolution of the visual identity of the printed book since the invention of printing, exhibiting the decisions, policies, aspects, and strategies mainly of the publishers, as well as of other stakeholders of the publishing chain. From this point of view, we also looked at the development of the publishing value chain. The book focused initially on the creation of the visual order of the printed page and on the development of the book as an information and visual device that matured in complex and often different environments and had multifunctioned roles in information sharing, in communication, in the cultivation of taste. The impact of new printing and illustration techniques during the Renaissance, as well as of information and communication technologies nowadays was also highlighted; additionally, the relationship of the printed book with the manuscript precedent was investigated in order not only to exhibit the continuity between the two forms but also to explore continuities and challenges nowadays. At the same time, the materiality of the book was studied in regard to the promotion strategies of the book, to the needs and expectations of the readers, whereas issues of reader engagement were looked at. The visual expectations of the reading audience were discussed in the broader framework of the democratization of taste.

Emphasis was given on the long period of the maturing of the book during the first centuries of printing and on the hybrid forms of the book that enlighten issues and trends of the nowadays publishing industry and of the transformations of the book as well. By studying the evolution of the book and through this of the publishing industry, not only we can further and better interpret current aspects and changes but we can also evaluate and exploit new opportunities, take advantage of the "new" challenges, suggest methods and introduce strategies. Moreover, we better understand that "new" may often be a rather traditional word which does not express the potential, background and provenance of various methods, aspects, trends, decisions, strategies. The complex transition from the manuscript to the printed book not only sheds light to the understanding of ongoing trends, such as the coexistence and convergence of media, but may offer to the better exploitation of current opportunities and to the introduction of new features. For example, luxury editions and copies of the first centuries of printing may explain and interpret nowadays personalized publishing services, hybrid forms of the book, customized copies and reader engagement highlighting as well the reasons, relationships, strategies and procedures related to them. Thus, by exhibiting the multifunctioned methods and policies, we commented on reader engagement and reader creativity explaining at the same time strategies and changes in the publishing value chain.

Furthermore, the creation and maturing of the visual identity of the printed book as known and trusted for centuries enlightens various aspects of augmented value for us nowadays. The visual mechanisms were developed in such a way by the publishers, printers, editors and other stakeholders as to serve the readers' needs alongside with the promotion of books; publishers aspired to exploit on the one hand the opportunities of the new medium and on the other to continue the established tradition. The ways by which the publishers and other stakeholders, including the readers, explored and took advantage of the new opportunities inevitably have much in common with the ongoing changes and opportunities of our digital era. Issues of innovation, experimentation, success, imitation, repetition, collaboration have also to be examined. In this book, new terms were introduced such as converged aesthetics or post-luxury copy.

Visual structures of the book were investigated and led us to the exploration of the visual strategies decided by the publishers, authors, editors, artists, readers and other stakeholders; thereafter the visual uses of the book were outlined. We conclude that books nowadays not only survive but thrive since their value, meaning, offer and role are defined not only in regard to the content but in regard also to the visual identity and visual meanings as well as to the different roles and uses of the book. As discussed, the uses of the book are many and complex, not only reduced to reading but extended to creating, participating, engaging, communicating, sharing, "One of the reasons why books will endure is that they don't merely or straightforwardly convey text to readers. They are not only messengers, although they are that too. Books are themselves incredible objects whose beauty and complexity enriched the text being read" (Smyth, 2024: 338).

Books are desirable, complex devices that go beyond reading; they are an object of memory, thought, delight, concerns, ideas synopsizing also the personal story of the reader-owner. Every book can be customized by its reader in a personal manner, in everyday life. The book is a visual object, whether printed or not, that in its long journey, as described in this book, was developed so as to serve the needs, create and then satisfy expectations, reach the thoughts of the reader, share information, disseminate knowledge and inspire dialog. At the same time the book had to promote itself. The visual order of the printed page as described above was created during the first centuries of printing, so as to be the visual expression and device not only of the content of the book but of the quests and feelings of the reader. The story and evolution of the book is

162
4. Conclusions: Challenges and opportunities

made by the stakeholders in the publishing value chain; publishers had a key role in the making and maturing of the book, as well as in the organization and systemization of the publishing activity. The elements of the page were investigated so as to exhibit its visual order; by deconstructing the page and the book, we can understand the mechanisms, ideologies, needs and strategies of the medium and of the stakeholders.

Coming to the conclusions of the book, we will comment on the visual structures, uses, strategies and issues. In an era of ongoing challenges and opportunities, as nowadays, the visual identity might show the way to strategies and policies redefining the nature of the book and offering privileged visions in regard not only to the identity but also to the structure and function of the book that extends beyond the traditional borders. The evolution of the book as visual object has been investigated in this book with emphasis on particular aspects so as to enlighten the opportunities in relation to the nature of the book and to the framework in which it has been designed, created, produced, distributed, promoted, discussed, read, bought, converged.

Readers collect books; the love for books constitutes one more factor and element not only for the "survival" but for the continuity of the printed book in a changing world and its transformations into other kinds of books such as the ebook and the virtual publications. The visual order of the page as highlighted in the second chapter, alongside the analysis of book parts as information mechanisms, provides the framework for explaining the impact of the printed book on other media; at the same time the development of the visual identity might not only interpret current changes but also introduce new aspects for visual strategies and publishing policies.

4.1.2 From reader engagement to reader creativity

Books are designed, edited, published, illustrated, promoted, distributed, sold, managed, advertised, discussed, acquired, shown, exhibited, collected, shown. They are also converged, innovated, altered in new ways due to new technologies and mainly due to the nature of the publishing industry—an industry of innovations and revolutions, as already discussed (Phillips and Bhaskar, 2019: 3—4). Books have a lot of uses, roles and functions, ranging from reading, delighting, informing, communicating, sharing, learning, exchanging, entertaining, being shown and exhibited; books may go beyond the identity of the common copy produced by the publisher into augmented forms of visual exploration and delight of the reader. The visual order of the page and the of the parts of the book, as investigated in the second chapter, and the aesthetics of the book still matter and still play a significant role in new forms and types of the book as

The Visual Identity of the Book

well as in new publishing and business models. Challenges and opportunities for both the book and the publishing industry are undeniably many and several; the publishing industry seems to be at a constant turning point—and so seems to be the book, which, as commented, is being redefined every day.

Unique, hand-illuminated copies and limited, collectable editions of the past are the precedents of customized books and personalized publishing services nowadays which extend the boundaries of the book and redefine older methods and aspects. The book as unique object still takes a leading role. Additionally, cultures of the book are developed due to the book as a visual, beloved, unique object of personal value and memory. Each printed book records the time and place and conditions of reading as well as the comments and notes on the text and on the reception of the text, being thus a device and a notebook of personal study, time, aspect, memory. Private libraries save, store, remind, and express the history and evolution of the owner's taste, research, studies, culture, being thus a synopsis of his quests and life in books.

The visual identity of the book as developed since the invention of printing still defines and frames the identity of the book, which is inevitably altered, augmented and expanded due to the new opportunities. Even though, it is more than interesting and fascinating to study and explore the convergence of media, as well as to suggest methods. As highlighted in the third chapter, the need and expectation of the reader to actively interfere and participate in the book production and design, to intervene and furthermore to customize the copy are among the bedrocks of the contemporary publishing activity. As argued, coloring books nowadays continue and incorporate the cut-and-paste as well as the extra-illustration tradition, demonstrating that creativity and intervention are trends and features of value that can be further expanded and extended to books, whether printed or electronic. Coloring books, as well as other forms of the book can further encourage reader creativity which is a step ahead reader participation.

Reader engagement is a term used widely nowadays exhibiting the emerging and dynamic role of the reader in the publishing chain and publishing activity, the various and often complex ways of reader participation, the impact of interactivity and the significance of the emerging reading communities. Even though, as it was pointed out in the second and mainly in the third chapter, reader participation and engagement has always been a feature of the publishing activity. Especially, during the first decades of printing, the reader had sometimes a protagonist role in deciding on book illumination and binding since illustration, decoration and binding were sometimes left to the reader so as to order them according to his/her taste and economic affordance. Hand illumination and specific binding were ordered by illustrious patrons of political and/or

164 4. Conclusions: Challenges and opportunities

religious power; sometimes printers/publishers, as we have discussed, offered unique (hand illuminated and bound) luxury copies as gifts so as to acknowledge and recognize the wealthy and powerful patrons' contribution to the edition. Renaissance booksellers bought copies printed on better paper or vellum or even parchment so as to sell them to important readers, having the hand decoration and illustration already commissioned; only the emblem remained to be added.

Cut-and-paste books and extra illustration constitute good examples of reader engagement; readers planned, organized and selected both the content and the images for the book they had in mind. The case studies provided by Adam Smyth in *Book Makers* (2024) are a very good example. Meanwhile, various examples of intervention and reader engagement may be observed from the Renaissance to nowadays. Readers sometimes colored their copies or bound them uniquely or bound together texts creating their miscellany; they might add their initials to the spine of the copy. Furthermore, different jackets from the publishers' ones were sometimes used so as to protect the text whereas ex libris always demonstrate the taste of the reader. The reader comments, notes, underlines, writes the name or/and the place and date of acquisition, sketches, dedicates, even colors, adds, highlights; this copy is one of those produced by the publisher with no extra or specific characteristics but it is personalized by its use saving the personal story of itself and of its reader being thus a notebook or a treasury of the times and conditions of reading, rereading, using, showing, existing, collecting, thinking and rethinking. The above define the history of the copy and of the personal library exhibiting that these unique copies create a visual-print culture as well as a culture of reader participation and contribution.

Books were and are also used as notepads and as devices for the readers' personal memory, being "memory devices" (Reid 2019: 63). From this point of view, books seem to have their own contribution and significance to the "times" of the reader being a thesaurus of memories related not only to the reading, gifting, acquiring of the book but also to the everyday life of the owner expressing sometimes the thoughts and participation of the reader in social, cultural, political conditions of the era. The uses of the book provide a privileged point of view for the understanding of the ongoing trends of the publishing industry as well as for proposing and developing methods and strategies based on the visual identity of the book. Back pages at the end of the book created a space for noting, being thus a means of understanding, briefing and commenting on the text. During the 19th-century blank pages usually served for advertisements of other works of the same author, or of the series or of similar titles of the publishing house. Even though, there was always space for the reader to note and comment.

Nowadays, the intervention, introduction, suggestion, commission, selection, design and "creative" contribution of the reader is often homogenized and commercialized since the customer/reader fills in a form with the required fields so as to order the desired book in the number of copies wanted. Thus, the Renaissance patron has nowadays become customer who orders the customization, personalization of the product already provided or decides on the unique book to acquire. Even though, customization can go beyond that so as to encourage a more active role of the reader and to incorporate the decisions and choices of the reader/user.

One significant aspect that has to be considered is the success of coloring books nowadays. As pointed out, the explosion in book production of the coloring books in our hybrid, digital era demonstrates the coexistence of different media, as well as the need for creativity, participation and reader engagement in a handicraft and creative manner that goes back in time. The user/reader colors and creates, combines and suggests to the printed material. Questions have raised about the nature and function of these books, about their role and place. In the third chapter, we investigated the features of that kind of books. Synopsizing, it may seem curious that in our virtual Age, coloring books have such a great success which can be attributed to the need of the reader for creation, handicraft expression, participation. They are also expected to have antistress results. Thus, coloring books may be considered as a step toward creativity since the reader not only colors but also combines and creates. Additionally, coloring books might be designed so as to further encourage readers to continue, finish, redesign, complete the already designed or even propose and introduce new borders, decorative patterns, ornaments, drawings.

Furthermore, readers can use the colored prints for decorating and mainly for exhibiting and showing their "work." Coloring books nowadays, reminding the coloring of prints in Renaissance, exhibit the different uses of the book demonstrating the need of the reader for the printed material; this need is related to user engagement and it can be extended to other electronic and virtual forms of publications.

4.1.3 The customized book and personalized publishing services

One of the challenges and possible opportunities for the publishing industry are the customized books or the production of copies that might be customized. The move from product to service is also recognized among the experiments and options of the publishing industry (Phillips and Bhaskar, 2019: 419). Nowadays, there are publishing services, as already discussed, that focus on customization. Furthermore, as mentioned just above, in the case of coloring books, the reader often desires and aspires to

166 4. Conclusions: Challenges and opportunities

cocreate, to participate in the making of the visual identity of the book. The success of coloring books together with the rise of handicraft hobbies demonstrate the quest for creation. In that framework, personalized publishing services may provide to the readers—users the option to cocreate, to decide, to choose and to be personally involved in the making of the visual identity of the book. New technologies provide these opportunities and options either to the printed book or to the new forms of the book (electronic books, virtual publications) with the use of multimedia. The reader—user can insert visual, verbal, audio, multimedia material or might decide among the options provided (for example, the frontispiece, the decoration or the title page can be decided and chosen among a range of suggestions). This method obviously recalls the augmented copies of extra-illustration and cut-and-paste books. Technology, apart from making it easier to participate in the creation of a customized book, provides new opportunities. Furthermore, the reader—customer—user—owner can create a unique book of value not only in the personal but also in public sphere. Nowadays, via social media as well as due to communication and information technologies, the book can be promoted and exhibited. In a digital, globalized world, uniqueness and customization might constitute the other face of Janus. The rise of self-publishing has also to be considered (Thompson, 2021: 216−282).

Thus, one may wonder: "is this the end of the publisher?." Obviously not. As argued in many parts of this book, the publishing industry is characterized by innovation, experiment, and adaptability. It has the charisma and the privilege to use technologies, techniques, applications, theories, movements, trends, theories in favor of itself and of the books produced. Neither the radio nor the cinema nor the telephone nor the television nor the internet have succeeded in disappearing the books and the publishers (as well as other stakeholders of the publishing chain). This is due to the products and services they provide; although changes and redevelopments are many and significant, the corner stone of the publishing house is as old as typography: new authors and books are introduced, books are designed and have their visual identity, and every link of the publishing chain has added value to the book.

The book, as complex product, with great symbolic value, has many, different uses as described above. The invention of printing led to the democratization of knowledge and of taste; we can further comment that printing techniques as well as new technologies nowadays have brought about the democratization through participation and customization.

4.1.4 The complex uses and the "future" of the book

The book is not supposed and is not intended only to be read. The book can be read, reread, discussed, shown, exhibited, recommended, seen, shared, exchanged, bound, rebound, enjoyed, noted, shown, dedicated, offered as a gift, used as a symbol, sold and bought, transformed, combined with other media, introduced, spread, approached, cut and pasted, collected, transmitted, customized, painted, decorated. It can be influenced and influence; it can be a mirror of its Age and at the same time innovate. It is used for teaching, learning, information sharing, enjoining, discovering, transmitting knowledge and information, giving fame, entertaining, introducing, creating celebrities and revealing. It is a visual information device. It is also a memory device and can be used as even a personal diary and reader's notebook reminding of past periods of our lives. It is an object of desire and a (potential) work of art. It may be a luxury product or a unique creation due to its use by the reader. It may revolutionize or relate to specific traditions or recall past methods. It may be a living book—a book that lives with us, and will probably continue to live after us. And it is the product of the publishing company and the publishing activity of each time declaring the relations and roles in the publishing value chain.

Furthermore, as McCleery (2019: 21) writes: "Publishing houses are vain institutions: they trace, if at all plausible, their pedigrees as far back as possible, and they issue histories of themselves in a manner few other sectors dare." These pedigrees look at the future and show the way to ongoing and further opportunities and challenges. Undeniably the "histories of themselves" constitute the high symbolic and cultural value of the publishing industry.

Nowadays, it is easy for the reader to order, acquire and customize books as well as to communicate, express opinion, recommend and share information. Maybe in the future it will be easier to have access to titles, to intervene in the publishing activity, to further customize books, to take a more active role in the publishing process. Information and communication technologies, social media, Artificial Intelligence, multimedia, new business models, new publishing models, online communities of readers may provide more choices, challenges and opportunities as well as questions to be answered and problems to be solved. But in the core of the publishing industry and activity, there is the need to discover books, authors, works, content and the strong desire to enjoy a desirable book which is friendly, convenient and nice.

We cannot speak of the future and certainly we cannot predict. The estimations and thoughts of the "death of the printed book" or of the publisher have obviously failed. To the question if the printed book would be just an object of research for historians, researchers and students, admirable and maybe stored and exhibited in museums and libraries, we may think of the success of multipaged novels and multivolumed works, of personalized books nowadays and of the success of coloring books. Moreover, we have to discuss and think of the aesthetics

168   4. Conclusions: Challenges and opportunities

of the book in complex environments that tend to become more and more complicated. Even though, in concluding this book, it is exhibited that the book as visual object, whether tangible or intangible, whether printed or not, is of constant added value, desirable by the readers, indispensable for the transmission of the content and for information sharing. The visual order of the page and the parts of the book work on explaining and providing the keys for understanding and interpreting. The visual identity of the book in all forms has a multifunctional role on the one hand in understanding, sharing, exhibiting, communicating, interpreting the text and on the other in creating the aesthetic identity of the publishing house, codeveloping the publishing policy and exhibiting the publishing history. As for promotion, the book per se has always been the best promotion method and the best advertisement of itself.

4.1.5 The printed word and the virtual word. Convergence of media

The printed word and the virtual word. The former is permanent and the latter not? In social media and online communities, the visual framework, the visual environment is the recognizable element and key issue. Even if the text, the message, the photo, the video is deleted, the visual framework is still the recognizable, permanent evidence that refers to the use and function of the medium. Even if readers tend to think that the content is something we currently consume and use, and maybe will be of no value tomorrow, the value lies in the technological and visual framework. In an "in-permanent" world, the visual information is important and the publishing company guarantees the value of the content and of the services provided.

In that context, the visual identity of the book can be characterized as an element of visual "permanency"; the visual structure of the book in all its forms creates and defines a friendly, accessible, updated and convenient medium that develops and further encourages its use. Convergence of media and reader engagement are basic elements. Since changes and innovations are relied upon the previous forms of the book, there is nowadays a sense of continuity and coexistence, although technologies seem to revolutionize. Actually, old issues, aims and scopes are defined and fulfilled by new opportunities.

By deconstructing, understanding and explaining the page, as investigated in the second chapter, we can further and better explore and exploit the new opportunities. The introduction of features, elements, and issues of older forms of the book to the "newest" ones may on the one hand shed light and interpret current needs and expectations, and on the other lead to the introduction, adaptation and redevelopment of these visual features and strategies nowadays. The metamorphosis of luxury copies nowadays has also to be studied as a continuity and as a transition from precedent forms to most recent; the technological, social, educational, cultural and economic framework is obviously of great importance. Convergence of media takes the leading role in nowadays publishing industry (Phillips, 2014: 116−128); this is not new but recalls previous experiences, strategies and forms of the book. Coexistence of media, interaction, combination, convergence seem to redefine the book as well as the publishing industry and the publishing value chain. Printed, digital, electronic, audio, visual and verbal, multimedia, augmented, traditional coexist. Convergence expands into public and private.

Scolari (2019: 142) highlights the changes and aspects of content distribution and content consumption in the new media economy, in the framework of networks and new textualities: "The emergence of novel actors—like booktubers, maybe the most powerful book prescribers in the second-decade of the twenty-first century together with Amazon top reviewers—has introduced new conflicts and tensions into the publishing niche." New stakeholders and new roles emerge: the role of the reader/user is altered and upgraded due to social media, online reading communities, social networks, new publishing models. Darnton (2009: 67−77) has discussed the structural changes and the features of the books and "old books." Scolari (2019:141) writes that "new readers have gone beyond that practice: they write and edit, either by cutting, moving, changing the order, or just introducing their own text." In that context, the question that raises is how the visual identity of the book is to be determined and restructured in that framework. The role of reader engagement and creativity might be significant.

Although technology nowadays seems to alter dramatically our lives and thoughts, we have to bear in mind that—as investigated in this book—the needs, expectations, methods, thought, values, and aims are to a great degree common. Values such as convergence of media, globalization, access, information sharing, transmission of knowledge, communication are diachronic. Additionally, diachronic are the publishers' policies and needs for feedback from the readers/customers, for communication with the reading audience, for successful marketing strategies, for cooperations, and sufficient promotion methods, for catalog building and for the creation of a recognizable identity. "There are always hard times in publishing" (Calasso, 2015) and innovative times as well—this has also to be considered. From this point of view, the development and evolution of the visual identity of the early printed book demonstrates the ways and procedures by which the precedent forms and issues were adapted, altered, and served as substantial elements in the most recent forms of the book.

170
4. Conclusions: Challenges and opportunities

When the printed book was the "new" medium and printing was the revolutionary technology, hybrid books synopsized and exhibited the maturing of the printed book, the convergence of media and the transition from the manuscript to the printed book. Furthermore, the development of the visual identity of the printed book was based initially on the manuscript precedent with which coexisted. Methods such as hand illumination, rubrication, hand coloring of prints were often applied to incunables and early printed books through a complex system of relationships. Obviously, new elements and parts were introduced, such as the title-page, whereas the printed page gained its visual identity as described in the second chapter. Publishers/printers explored and exploited the opportunities of the new medium combining them with the used, tested, and expected elements. The book as a visual and information medium had to satisfy the readers' expectation and needs, which were though changing and upgrading rapidly due to the new environment.

The transition from the manuscript to the printed book explains not only the coexistence of the printed book with the new forms but also the strategies, working methods and techniques of the publishers exhibiting at the same time their policies, aims and attitudes toward experimentation and innovation. In an era of continuous changes and challenges, it is noteworthy to wonder what "innovation" means. Even from the invention of printing, a few publishers innovated and introduced elements (which sometimes were not new but derived from the older forms of the book or from other media). On the other hand, most publishers repeated, imitated, and adopted the new features; even though, the word "imitated" does not express clearly their working methods and aims since it as not just an imitation but rather an adaptation of the introduced elements so as to be harmonized with their identity or to help them develop their recognizable identity. Regarding the visual identity of the book, publishers innovated, experimented, introduced, imitated, followed, suggested, developed and redeveloped, altered, repeated, enhanced.

The visual order of the page as developed in early printed books, during the first centuries of printing, is still the framework and the basis for the visual order of new forms of the book and of publications. The printed book, known and trusted for years, creates thus in a changing world a "certainty" of provenance and the basis for further explanations, extensions, redefinitions.

4.1.6 Waiting for the unexpected: Visual expectations and adventures

Readers have expectations for the visual identity of the book as they have for the content. These visual expectations are based often on the known, tested, familiar, successful, identified elements, patterns and design. Visual elements that have already added value to the book are recognizable; this is the case of series, for example. Apart from the thematic selection of works, the recognizable visual identity is an advantage, a strong issue for the publisher that cultivates a stable relationship with the reader. Woodcut illustrations at the first printed books or title-pages in the 16th century or the illustration of novels in the 19th century were expected from the reader; sometimes they embellished the book in a tested manner: they appeared where they were expected, they were designed as expected. Even though, every time the decoration or illustration or other part of the book or element of the page was revolutionized in a successful manner, and new patterns, issues, techniques, thematics were introduced; this innovation—whether praised or not—was discussed, imitated, repeated.

Thus, the expected and the unexpected in the publishing industry are the two faces of Janus: the reader expects the familiar but at the same time is waiting for the new and innovative. That is what happens with the content of books. Most people recognize that they visit a bookstore (physical or electronic) so as to search for a specific work but they discover other books that did not know they existed or had been translated or republished. The unexpected, the element of surprise is significant and strong in the publishing industry (Calasso 2015: 31) and leads to the desire for exploring and establishing the new so as to discuss, comment, note, praise, recommend, promote, advertise, inform, share, contribute, compete. Innovation and experimentation in publishing go hand in hand with tradition.

In that context, the desire for new books is related to the visual identity; there are books, which attract, delight and promise to the reader. Reading and customer experience implies not only reading the text but also enjoying, using and exploring the book as material object. This is a book experience, that goes beyond and incorporates reading experience, bibliophilic attitudes, customer expectations, collection cultures. The book is an adventure in which the visual material is presupposed for a number of functions such as guiding the reader, introducing to the text, facilitating the use of the book, delighting, interpreting, informing, giving clues for the explanation. These "unexpected" innovative books create a tradition in their turn by establishing specific features. In most cases, the reading audience seems ready to receive, adopt, enjoy, recommend them.

The visual identity of the book, as highlighted and investigated in this book, had diachronically an impact on the publishing value chain, which was enlarged due to new stakeholders and roles.

4.1.7 Discoverability, promotion, and visual identity

It is of importance to investigate the role of the visual identity not only in book promotion but—in a wider context—in discoverability, which is among the key issues of our times (Phillips, 2014: xix) related to information seeking behavior and to book promotion. Reading networks have been developed since the invention of printing as information sharing and communication took a leading role. "Word of mouth" seemed to be the most important channel for book promotion, alongside with printed catalogs, bookmarks, posters and written recommendations. Thereafter, the almost "revolutionary" role of the Press not only in book promotion but in communication and information sharing is undoubtable. The telegraph, the telephone, the better post services further facilitated the access to books; it was easier for the reader to order, find, buy a book as well as to be informed and inform about it. Newspapers and magazines offered book reviews, book presentations, news on the publishing industry and the opportunity to share opinion and to contribute to discussions and dialog. Additionally, printed catalogs by publishers of bookstores shaped an important information tool for readers and bibliophiles. There was abundance of information and plenty of new media for being informed and sometimes engaged. It was the Age that the book clubs or reading clubs were introduced at the same time that reading rooms, circulating libraries and reading societies were founded. Public libraries started, since the middle of the 19th century in Britain, to be "Free to All, Open to All" (Lyons, 1999).

Nowadays, new technologies, social media, and social networks have brought about significant changes and at the same time strategies and aspects in regard to book promotion, consumption and use. Obviously, writing, communication, editing have been changing. Baron (2009) provides a panorama of the changes in writing. This is not unfamiliar with the evolution of the book. The way we communicate and read influences and defines the way we write. This is more than obvious in our era of short messages, emails, abbreviations at the social media and at other platforms. In that framework, visual information and communication is important. The publisher as an entity is always forced to confront markets directly, even when it pretends such influences have no bearing (Phillips & Bhaskar, 2019: 235).

The visual identity nowadays can offer options, suggestions, participation, cocreation, interaction, interactivity by adopting features from the past and exploring the new opportunities provided by technologies. Thus, the publishing policy of the companies is developed according on the one hand to the tradition and knowledge of the past, of previous forms of the book, of past strategies and methods, and on the other with new opportunities, tools, media and issues. Publishers have always invested in tested and used methods and strategies and at the same time they were extremely adaptable to changes and to trends introduced; sometimes this was a matter of survival, sometimes a matter of innovation and experimentation. Certainly, a few publishers took the

4.1 Reframing the world: Visual structures, strategies, and uses of the book **173**

leading role in innovating and experimenting in regard to the visual identity (Aldus Manutius, Anton Koberger, Christoph Plantin, Elzevirs, L. Hachette, Allen Lane, and others); it must though be pointed out that the whole industry has been adaptable and ready to create and use.

4.1.8 Short forms, multipaged books and the reintroduction of classics

Short forms and multipaged books nowadays are the two faces of Janus. They go hand-in-hand. Short forms, which are recognized as a feature of our era are harmonized with the coexistence and competiveness of media; moreover, they offer to the reader a viable and convenient reading form because lack of time is often recognized as the main factor that prevents people from reading. "Already we can see a return to shorter forms of writing, such as short stories and novellas, and serialized fiction which responds almost in real time to the market" (Phillips, 2014: xiv). Short forms can be easily read everywhere and on every device accompanying the reader in various activities; furthermore, they may encourage reading creating thus new readers, even inspiring people who otherwise would not read. The device on which we read, the kind of text, the serialization and the visual identity of the book define the reading experiences of short forms; additionally, visual experiences of the book are significant for the understanding and interpreting the text but also for the creation of a consumer culture. Even though, visual experiences related to short forms are not a feature only of our digital era. These short forms recall chapbooks or printed short forms (tales, fairy tales, lives of saints etc.) in the vernacular, which were very popular, familiar, affordable and thus successful during the first centuries of printing. They were targeted mainly to the wide reading audience; illustration was supposed not only to embellish, decorate, and promote the book, but also to help readers—who often could hardly read—to understand and interpret the text, to share information, to communicate. Thus, illustration offered a visual textual experience which developed a reading and customer behavior. The visual identity of these books was of significance for their promotion and success.

On the other hand, multipaged volumes are of great success, especially to young readers; the success of the Harry Potter books is a very good example as well as the long sellers by Tolkien. Additionally, serialized fiction responds to the readers' needs and expectations creating devotion to the books and anxiety for the next work; at the same time, communities of readers are further encouraged, the word of mouth being thus among the successful promotion methods. There is a visual continuity on these works; from one book to the other the design often reproduces and at the same time upgrades and enriches the trusted

174   4. Conclusions: Challenges and opportunities

visual elements; the visual order of the page and the organization of the book (front matter and back matter) often recall the first books and editions of the series although new elements may be introduced. In that context, collection culture is created in regard to series or books by the same author. Sometimes collectible or anniversary or limited editions or books in slipcases are produced alongside with other products (not only for reading but also for everyday life such as mugs, pencils, cloths etc.) creating thus a culture of collecting, of consuming, of gifting as well as of reading. Readers are not only consumers or users but also the interlocutors of the book often expressing visual cultures.

One of the main issues and challenges of the nowadays publishing industry is the redesign and publishing of the classics for younger generations of readers as well as the reintroduction of these works to existing readers and researchers. These long sellers are introduced to reading generations in multiple visual ways and methods. Apart from the use of the first or of older editions' visual identity, a new design is more often proposed; apart from verbal paratext (introductions, epilogues, forewords, timelines, sources from archives or correspondence etc.) the visual identity of such works and series has been carefully proclaimed according to the strategies and publishing policy of the publisher. We may talk of a second (or third or fourth etc.) life of these classic works. Publishers usually have to decide not on whether or not to recall the tradition but the way and the grade to which that visual tradition will be explored, reviewed, enriched, and innovated. The visual tradition is indispensable, is the starting point, which will be enriched, modified, altered or denied but not ignored. Some publishers may go beyond that tradition and innovate altering thus the traditional visual perceptions, introducing new modes of visual information and creating new visual expectations; others may recall clearly the visual tradition on which modifications are few.

New information technologies enable even small and recently established publishers to create their own specific identity by redeveloping and reusing elements and visual patterns in a new framework adopting and adapting trends and issues from the past of the book. From this point of view, innovation sometimes comes through the tradition.

4.1.9 Publishing industry and democracy

The publishing industry respects and fights for the diachronic values of our civilization: freedom, democracy, equality, inclusion, diversity, citizenship. Freedom to write, freedom to publish, freedom to talk about books, freedom to communicate. Associations and federations of publishers, whether international (International Publishers Asoociation), European

(Federation of European Publishers) or national, in collaboration with associations of booksellers/librarians–information scientists, such as IFLA, ILA, IBA, organize and take action so as to promote books and reading, organize reading policy, encourage information literacy, to fight for the freedom to publish, to defend copyright, to help communities, to plan reading policy, to defend the rights of the publishers and of the publishing chain, to promote diversity. The printed book was always created and promoted to multilingual different markets reaching readers all over the world. Globalization was a main feature since the Renaissance. Libraries, free to all, open to all, as well as bookstores were the places of dialog and communication.

Publishing organizations, associations, federations provide data for the above whereas conferences, meetings, actions, and researches are organized. The corner stone is freedom and Democracy. The printed book was, since its birth, a massive medium that transmitted knowledge and information. At the book fairs, there is also the great opportunity of round table discussions, seminars and meetings. The promotion of literacy and reading, of digital citizenship are among the priorities of the publishers.

The World Book Capital is a good example. "The World Book Capital Network (WBCN) acknowledges the power of books and reading as cornerstones to more inclusive, peaceful and sustainable societies. The WBCN strengthens the World Book Capital programme's existing commitment to literacy, lifelong learning, copyright, and freedom of expression after its relaunch as a Network".[1] Madrid was the first World Book Capital in 2001. The advisory committee is composed of UNESCO, the International Publishers Association (IPA), the International Federation of Library Associations and Institutions (IFLA), the International Authors Forum (IAF) and the European and International Booksellers Federation (EIBF).

A lot of discussions takes place in regard to diversity in the publishing industry and the publishing value chain as well as for the Environment. "Development in the industry have led to a reduction in waste" (Phillips, 2019: 152). In a globalized world, in which information, access, communication and participation are key issues, the book and the publishing industry not only remind and transmit but also cultivate to the readers the values of our civilization: freedom, equity, democracy, equality, diversity, respect. The book is a medium of freedom.

Publishing was always an activity of multilanguaged and globalized worlds. In that context, the visual identity of the book, and more specifically the illustration, the image, the picture goes beyond the word and the

---

1 Source: https://www.unesco.org/en/world-book-capital-network (date of last access 16/7/2024).

176   4. Conclusions: Challenges and opportunities

text. For example, silent books or picture books are aimed to approach different audiences (such as refugees) constituting a cultural diversity.

4.2 Constant challenges for the book and the publishing industry. Future research

Many questions have been raised and many discussions have been done in regard to the future of the book which obviously no one can predict. Hayes (2022) in his work on the images of reading in the American Utopian novel, highlights the graphic design in Utopia and the book of the future in regard to illustration and visual appearance. It is noteworthy to outline how the book of the future was imagined and which was the role of its visual appearance. Hayes (2022: 157) writes that "Book illustration also approached perfection in Utopia." Taking as starting point that certain American 19th century authors "foresaw ways to make the printed page easy on the eye, both aesthetically pleasing and physically soothing" (154), he investigates images and functions of the book of the future in different works and authors. It is interesting and more than useful to know how the book was imagined in a promising future in which technology would provide the opportunities, technologies, and tools for complex suggestions. For example, we read about multicolored ink "which could be used to suit the mood and subject of the written word" (156), about techniques in illustration, photographs printed in natural colors, inexpensive illustrations, about books that would be issued with "multicolored pages," about gorgeous books and the aesthetic experience in reading. All the authors of the utopian novel referred in Hayes (2022: 154–160) imagined and reimagined the physical, visual appearance of the book as a tool and device that leads to the development of the aesthetic experience in reading and to understanding the text.

Undeniably, new technologies and changes in the publishing industry during the last decades of the 20th century and the 21st century have exceeded these imaginary approaches. New information and communication technologies (extending to social media and the much discussed AI) alongside with the social, economic and cultural conditions have developed—as we have commented—the framework and provided the tools for new publishing and business models, for changes in the structure of the industry and in the publishing value chain, for the upgraded role of reading communities, for new promotion strategies, and for other forms of the book which lead to convergence of media. We have thus to consider the coexistence of older forms of the book with the new ones, hybrid books, reader engagement, interactivity, alongside with changes in the production–design–distribution–promotion of books. We have

The Visual Identity of the Book

also to take for granted that "the book remains the bastion of both deep and immersive reading" (Phillips & Kovac, 2022: 67).

In that context, the role of the visual identity of the book is more than significant in a world of visual information and visual communication. "New" forms of the book and new opportunities that derive mainly—but not only—from technologies offer a privileged field for innovation and experiment. Though, as tradition and innovation in publishing go hand in hand, we have to investigate not only the origins but also the redevelopment and reconstruction of previous and even diachronic strategies, trends, features, and methods. The transition from the manuscript to the printed book, and the long development and maturing of the printed book, as discussed in the second chapter, not only is recalled when we study our hybrid era of convergence and coexistence of media but also it offers to us the tools and the keys for interpreting ongoing changes and aspects. Bearing in mind that "a new medium is never an addition to an old one, nor does it leave the old one in peace. It never ceases to oppress the older media until it finds new shapes and positions for them" (McLuhan: 174), new and old forms of the book interact and create book cultures. Activities, forms, and materials are combined in complex environments in which engagement and thereafter reader creativity are upgraded, constituting thus an aspect of nowadays consumer, reading and book cultures. Furthermore, personalized publishing services and customized copies, investigated at the third chapter, enlighten another point of view of the publishing activity and of convergence of media.

As highlighted in this book, the methods, strategies, decisions of the printers/publishers during Renaissance in regard to the exploitation of the opportunities and to specific development and adaptation of the introduced "new" patterns and issues resembles our era. The publishing business is successful, adaptable and always promising since the invention of printing. Levarie wrote that (1995: 82), "Johan Fust and Peter Schoeffer, printers, were the men who first made it [printing] a successful enterprise."

Additionally, the development of the printed page and of the book were studied so as to exhibit the common features and trends with the publishing industry and the book nowadays as well as to enlighten the transition from older to different forms of the book and approach their coexistence. The changes, whether major or not, took place since the invention of printing; it was argued that the abundance of books during the Renaissance and the opportunities provided by the printing and illustration techniques as well as from the nature and function of the printed book led to the need for managing information and for exploring and gradually transforming the medium just as nowadays. Thus, we can point out to an abundance of changes and challenges since the incunable period. Among the purposes of this book is to explore these challenges and opportunities and to study the strategies, policies and

178   4. Conclusions: Challenges and opportunities

decisions of the stakeholders arguing that innovation and adaptivity is a constant challenge of the publishing industry and activity.

In our hybrid world of coexistence and convergence of different media, questions for the publishing industry and the book raise regarding their development, function, and nature. These questions often extend to the changes and developments in the publishing value chain exploring the relationships and collaborations, the emerging role of specific stakeholders, the introduction of new strategies and policies. At the same time, questions are set in regard to the boundaries between the printed and other, "new" forms of the book, between traditional and innovative, between the traditional publishers and new publishing models. The printed book survives, even thrives in specific audiences and kind of texts, and coexists with other forms of the book (such as the electronic and audio book) and with competitive media. In that framework, the visual identity of the book in a changing era—in which diachronic values prevail—is evolving in a complex environment of emerging challenges, roles, technologies, combinations, collaborations, strategies and policies. Being a mirror of our Age, the visual identity of the book in all its forms aspires and manages to epitomize current trends, ideas and issues on the one hand and on the other to further innovate and revolutionize its uses and functions. Visual expectations and customer behavior, publishing policies and strategies have to be studied in regard to new ways of reading, enjoying, sharing, informing and understanding which in turns create new cultures of the book.

Questions are also set in regard to the boundaries not only between verbal and visual, between traditional and innovated, printed and other but also between private and public, globalized and localized, expected and unexpected. In the third chapter, the boundaries between the mass copy and customized publishing services, between the publishing policy of the publisher and personalized publishing services, between the traditional role of the publisher and self-publishing were highlighted.

In that context, relationships between text and image, text and paratext, between front matter and back matter emerge and shape the visual identity of the book. The role of the reader and of communities of readers is to better and further been studied in regard not only to interactivity but also to discoverability, information sharing and to the shaping of the "public opinion" for books. Social media and recommendation technologies take a leading role in the development of public taste in books, in promotion, in communication and information sharing and thus in determining information behavior and discoverability. Furthermore, as discussed in the third chapter, customized copies and personalized publishing services nowadays constitute an issue, a habit, a trend that has to be investigated in complex relationships and obviously goes back in time. Such publishing services, by being more affordable and massive,

4.2 Constant challenges for the book and the publishing industry. Future research

can exhibit the uses of the book, the customer and consumer behavior, the redevelopment of the publishing chain; additionally, they can enlighten issues of taste and prestige that go back to Renaissance. The evolution of patronage and reader engagement are also issues that have to considered in regard to personalized publishing services.

For the above reasons, the book is constantly redeveloping and evolving. By studying the development of the visual order of the page and of the parts of the book as information-visual mechanisms, the book was approached in this monograph as a multifunctional visual, information and memory device that exceeds the boundaries of personal and public, of old and new, of traditional and innovative. Visual expectations and dialogs are created whereas books have a lot or roles and functions. Books can be read, shown, exhibited, shared, noted, recommended, exhibited, stored. And probably due to the above, we may explain the existence and continuity of the book in turning points and in hard times, in times of innovation and convergence of media. This book, by deconstructing the page and the book, and discussing the evolution of every element and part of the page and the book, tried to trace and study the patterns, relations and mechanisms of the evolution of the visual identity of the book so as to exhibit the transition and coexistence of aspects, media, strategies and trends. In that context, the role of the publisher and printer has been exhibited and has to be further exploited.

Noone obviously can predict what the future of the book will be. Concluding this book and synopsizing, we can though assume that the above issues and trends will continue to be of research value and through their approach will offer a method, a privileged point of view and an aspect on the study of the book and of the publishing industry.

Future research on the visual identity of the book could focus on the publishing value chain, on the production–design–distribution–bookselling–reception of the book in regard both to the past and to the present of the publishing industry. Issues of reader participation– engagement–creativity, of convergence of media, of the complex and symbolic uses of the book in societies, of the design of books, of interactivity and collaborations have also to studied in accordance to new information and communication technologies, to social media, to Artificial Intelligence, the impact of which has to be explored, defined and investigated. In that context, "new" publishing and business models, "new" forms of the book, as well as changes in the publishing value chain are of specific interest constituting a privileged research field. On the one hand, the researcher has to look back, to the past of the publishing industry and of the book so as to reapproach, to explore (for example, copies and editions which are "discovered" in libraries and collections, and have to be studied in regard to theories and aspects), to rediscover, to analyze, to combine, to redevelop, to enlighten specific issues and at

180   4. Conclusions: Challenges and opportunities

the same time to introduce, to suggest, to propose theories, approaches, methods.

Additionally, the investigation of the work and contribution of specific stakeholders and of specific people in publishing contributes to the study of the above mentioned themes from another point of view going deep in time through case studies. Furthermore, the recognizable visual identity of the series since their origins can provide a tool not only for the investigation of nowadays ongoing issues but also for the introduction of visual strategies and publishing policies.

In a globalized publishing world, the introduction, development and reception of new publishing and business models as well as of new trends, opportunities, strategies and issues in small or smaller publishing markets is of research interest. The investigation of the unique features and trends of each industry alongside with its publishing history and identity will enlighten the visual identity of the book in regard to the development of the publishing chain. Globalized and localized, innovative and traditional can be thus studied so as to shed light not only to publishing strategies but to the role of the book in specific societies. In that context, the visual identity of the book in different markets and industries will exhibit the issues discussed above such as the evolving taste and expectations of the readers, the relationship of tradition with innovation, the role of the publisher and the redevelopment of the publishing chain, the impact of technologies, the convergence of media. Numerous works have already been conducted for specific publishing industries, and obviously this is a research field of augmented interest.

The impact of new information technologies, including AI, on the publishing industry and more specifically on the visual identity of the book is one of the main research fields. On the other hand, research on the transformations and transitions of the book in the past provide to us the tools and methodology not only for understanding and interpreting but also for exploiting current opportunities, for introducing strategies and innovating. Research on the past of the publishing industry and activity will always offer to reframing and investigating the complex relationships, changes, and mechanisms in publishing. The identity of the publishing company is diachronically based on the twofold: recognizable visual/aesthetic identity and choice of titles according to declared aims and policies. The former has to be further studied and enlightened in the framework of multidisciplinary publishing studies, which implies methods from book history, art history, literature, print culture, graphic design, media studies, marketing. Additionally, publishing is not only one of the creative industries with great economic impact but also a corner stone for the values of our civilization: access to information and knowledge, communication, equality, democracy, information sharing, equity, cultivation of taste. In that context, the book will keep going, evolving, transforming; and its typology will (try to) serve the above.

Books are the spine of societies and civilizations, and probably they will continue to be in any material, form, and typology. By exploring the visual order of the page, by investigating the visual identity and typology of the book, by studying it as information−visual−memory device, we can discover and exploit the fascinating and exciting history of the book. Furthermore, by deconstructing the page as to understand its verbal and visual mechanisms, we can offer a valuable point of view and a tool for future navigations.

Bibliography

References

Ago, R., 2013. Gusto for Things: A History of Objects in Seventeenth Century Rome. University of Chicago Press (first edition *Gusto delle cose*, Donzelli Editore, 2006).

Armstrong, L., 2020. The decoration and illustration of Venetian Incunabula. From hand illumination to the design of woodcuts. In: Dondi, C. (Ed.), Printing R-Evolution and Society 1450–1500. Fifty Years that Changed Europe. Edizioni Ca Foscari, Venice, pp. 773–816.

Armstong, L. (1991). The Impact of Printing on Miniaturists in Venice after 1469. In Hindman, S. (Ed.), *Printing the Written Word. The Social History of Books. circa 1450–1520*. New York–London: 174–202.

Ash, T., Page, R., Ginty, M., 2012. Landing Page Optimization. The Definite Guide to Testing and Tuning for Conversions, second edition John Wiley and Sons, Indianapolis.

Baines, P., 2005. Penguin by Design. A Cover Story 1935–2005. Allen Lane, London, An imprint of Penguin Book.

Baldacchini, L., 1995–1996. Dal manoscritto al incunabolo. Continuita' o rottura? Note su qualche studio recente. In: Scarsella, A. (Ed.), Metodologia Bibliografica e Storia Del Libro. Atti del Seminario sul libro Antico Offerti a Dennis E. Rhodes, X-XI. pp. 105–119. (1995–1996), σ.

Baldacchini, L., 2009. Aspettando il Frontespizio. Pagine Bianche, Occhietti a Colophon nel Libro Antico. Edizioni Sylvestre Bonnard, Milano.

Baldacchini, L., 2019. Il libro Antico: Storia, Diffusione e Descrizione, 1st edition terza edizione, Roma: Carocci, 1982.

Banou, C., 2017. Re-inventing the Book. Challenges from the Past for the Publishing Industry. Elsevier—Chandos Publishing, Cambridge–Oxford, Foreword by Angus Phillips.

Barberi, F., 1969. Il Frontespizio Nel Libro Italiano del Quattrocento e del Cinquecento. Edizioni Il Poliphilo, Milano, 2 volumes.

Barberi, F., 1983. Il frontespizio nel libro italiano del Seicento. La Bibliofilia LXXXV, 49–72.

Barbier, F., 2001. Histoire du Livre. Armand Colin, Paris.

Barker, N., 1985. Aldus Manutius and the Development of Greek Script and Type in the Fifteenth Century. Chiswick Book Shop Inc, Sandy Hook-Connecticut.

Barnard, J., 2001. London Publishing, 1640–1660: Crisis, Continuity and Innovation. Book History 4, 1–16.

Baron, D., 2009. A Better Pencil. Readers, Writers and the Digital Revolution. Oxford University Press, Oxford.

Baverstock, A., 1993. AreBooks Different? Marketing in the Book Trade. Kogan Page, London.

Baverstock, A., 2004. *How to Market Books*. Kogan Press, London.

Berg, K., 2007. Contesting the page: the author and the illustrator in France, 1830–1848. Book History 10, 69–101.

Berger, S., 2016. The Dictionary of the Book. A Glossary for Book Collectors, Booksellers, Librarians and Others. Rowman & Littlefield, Lanham–London.

184

Bertram, G., Buettner, N., Zittel, C., 2021. Gateways to the books. early modern frontispieces — introduction. In: Bertram, G., Buettner, N., Zittel, C. (Eds.), Gateways to the Book. Frontispieces and Title-Pages in Early Modern Europe. Brill, Leiden—Boston.

Bhaskar, M., 2013. The Content Machine. Towards a Theory of Publishing from the Printing Press to the Digital Netwrok. Anthem Press, London & New York.

Blair, A., 2010. Too much to Know: Managing Scholarly Information before the Modern Age. Yale University Press.

Blocklehusrt, H., Watson, K., 2015. The Printmaker's Art. A Guide to the Processes used by the Artists from the Renaissance to the Present Day. National Galleries of Scotland, Edinburgh.

Boardley, J., 2019. Typographic First. Adventures in Early Publishing. Bodleian Library, University of Oxford, Oxford.

Borsuk, A., 2018. The Book. MIT Press, Cambridge, MA—London.

Bourne, C.M.L., 2019. In: Dunkan, D., Smyth, A. (Eds.), Book Parts. Oxford University Press, Oxford, pp. 191—208.

Braida, L., 1999. Stampa e Cultura in Europa tra XV e XVI secolo. Laterza, Roma - Bari.

Briggs, A., Burke, P., 2005. A Social History of the Media from Gutenberg to the Internet, second edition Polity Press, Oxford.

Calasso, R., 2015. The Art of the Publisher. Penguin, London, trans. Richard Dixon.

Cale, L., 2019. Frontispieces. In: Dunkan, D., Smyth, A. (Eds.), Book Parts. Oxford University Press, Oxford, pp. 25—37.

Carter, V., Hellinga, L., Parker, T., 1983. Printing with gold in the fifteenth century. The British Library Journal 9 (1), 1—13.

Chartier, R., 1994. The Order of Books. Readers, Authors and Libraries in Europe between the 15nth and 18nth centuries. Polity Press, Cambridge (first edition in French: 1992).

Chartier, R., 2014. The Culture of Print. Power and the Uses of Print in Early Modern Europe. Princeton university Press.

Clark, G., Phillips, A., 2014. Inside Book Publishing, fifth edition Routledge, London and New York.

Classen, A., 2014. The survival of medieval manuscript culture in the early modern age: the other side of a universal paradigm shift. Publishing Research Quarterly 40, 30—47.

Cock-Starkey, C., 2017. The Booklovers; Miscellany. Bodleian Library, University of Oxford, Oxford.

Cummings, B., 2010. The book as symbol. The Oxford Companion to the Book. Oxford University Press, Oxford, pp. 63—65.

Da Costa, A., 2020. Marketing English Books, 1476—1550. How Printers Changed Reading. Oxford University Press, Oxford.

Dackermann, S. (Ed.), 2002. Painted Prints. The revelation of Color in Northern Renaissance and Baroque Engravings, Etchings and Woodcuts. Pennsylvania State University Press, Pennsylvania.

Dames, N., 2019. Chapter Heads. In: Duncan, D., Smyth, A. (Eds.), Book Parts. Oxford University Press, Oxford, pp. 151—164.

Darnton, R., 2009. What is the history of books? The Case for Books. Past, Present and Future. Public Affairs, New York, pp. 175—206.

Darnton, R., 1996. The Forbidden Bestsellers of Pre-Revolutionary France. Norton, New York & London.

Day, M., 2011. *Intended to Offenders*. The running titles of the early printed books. In: Smith, H., Wilson, L. (Eds.), Renaissance Paratexts. Cambridge University Press, Cambridge, pp. 34—46.

Donati, L., 1953. Iniziali con la Corona. Gutenberg Jahrbuch 9—10.

Dondi, C., 2010. The European Printing Revolution. The Oxford Companion to the Book. OUP, Oxford, pp. 52—61.

Dondi, C., Dutta, A., Malaspina, M., Zisserman, A., 2020. The use and reuse of printed illustrations in 15th-century Venetian editions. In: Dondi, C. (Ed.), Printing R-Evolution and Society 1450–1500. Fifty Years that Changed Europe. Edizioni Ca Foscari, Venice, pp. 841–872.

Dunkan, D., Smyth, A. (Eds.), 2019. Book Parts. Oxford University Press, Oxford.

Eisenstein, E., 1983. The Printing Revolution in Early Modern Europe. Cambridge University Press, Cambridge.

Espie, J., Gillispie, A., 2024. Authorizing the canon: chaucer in the world of print. In: Turner, M. (Ed.), Chaucer Here and Now. Bodleian Library Publishing, Oxford, pp. 49–71.

Faber, T., 2021. Faber & Faber. The Untold Story. Faber, London [first published 2019].

Farkas, D., Geier, R., 2024. Strategic Content Marketing. Creating Effective Content in Practice. Routledge, Abington–New York, chapter 9.

Feather, J., 2006. A History of British Publishing, second edition Routledge, London & New York.

Febvre, L., Martin, H.-J., 1990. The Coming of the Book. The Impact of Printing. 1450–1800. Verso, London–New York.

Field, H., 2019. Playing with the Book. Victorian Movable Picture Books and the Child Reader. University of Minessota Press.

Fleming, J., 2011. Changed opinion as to flowers. In: Smith, H., Wilson, L. (Eds.), Renaissance Paratexts. Cambridge University Press, Cambridge, pp. 48–62.

Franklin, A., 2019. Woodcuts. In: Dunkan, D., Smyth, A. (Eds.), Book Parts. Oxford University Press, Oxford, pp. 209–222.

Gaskell, P., 1972. A New Introduction to Bibliography. Oxford University Press, Oxford.

Genette, G., 1997. Paratexts. Thresholds of Interpretation. Cambridge University Press, Cambridge [ed. pr. Editions du Seuil, Paris 1987.

Goldman, P., 2010. The history of illustration and its technologies. The Oxford Companion to the Book. Oxford University Press, Oxford, pp. 137–145.

Greco, A., Rodriguez, C., Wharton, R., 2007. *The Culture and Commerce of Publishing in the 21st century*. Stanford Business Books (Stanford University Press), Stanford.

Greco, A., Milliot, J., Wharton, R., 2013. The Book Publishing Industry, third edition Routledge, New York & London.

Gutjahr, P., Benton, M., 2010. Illuminating Letters. Typography and Literary Interpretation. University of Massachusetts Press.

Hayes, K.J., 2022. The Future of the Book. Images of Readership in the American Utopian Novel. Oxford University Press, Oxford.

Houston, K., 2013. Shady Characters. The secret Life of Punctuation, Symbols, and Other Typographic Marks. W.W. Norton.

Howard, N., 2009. The Book. The Life Story of a Technology. The John Hopkins University Press, Baltimore.

Immel, A., 2010. Children's Books. The Oxford Companion to the Book. Oxford University Press, Oxford, pp. 130–136.

Jecmen, G., Spira, F., 2012. Imperial Augsburg. Renaissance Prints and Drawings, 1475–1540. National Gallery of Art, Washington, p. 72.

Jennett, S., 1951. The Making of Books. Faber & Faber, London.

Johns, A., 1998. The Nature of the Book. Print and Knowledge in the Making. The University of Chicago Press, Chicago and London.

Kemp, M., 1996. Temples of the body and temples of cosmos: vision and visualization in the vesalian and copernican revolutions. Picturing Knowledge: Historical and Philosophical Problems Concerning the Use of Art in Science. University of Toronto Press, pp. 40–85.

Knight Todd, J., 2009. "Furnished" for action: renaissance books as furniture. Book History 12, 37–73.

186 Bibliography

Kwapisz, J., 2019. The paradigm of Simias, 2019. De Gruyter, Berlin–Boston.

Layron, E., 1994. *The Sixteenth Century Greek Book in Italy. Printers and Publishers for the Greek World*, Venice: Library of the Helllenic Institute of Byzantine and Post-Byzantine Studies.

Leitch, S., 2024. Early Modern Print Media and the Art of Observation: Training the Literate Eye. Cambridge University Press, Cambridge.

Lewis, J., 2005. Penguin Special. The Life and Times of Allen Lane. Viking (Penguin), London.

Lowry, M., 1979. The World of Aldus Manutius. Business and Scholarship in Renaissance Venice. Blackwell's, Oxford.

Luna, P., 2019. Book Design. In: Phillips, A., Bhaskar, M. (Eds.), The Oxford Handbook of Publishing. Oxford University Press, Oxford, pp. 291–310.

Lyons, M., 1999. I nuovi lettori del XIX secolo: donne, fanciuli, operai. In: Cavallo, G., Chartier, R. (Eds.), Storia Della Lettura nel Mondo Occidentale. Edizioni Laterza, Roma–Bari, pp. 371–410.

Lyons, M., 2008. Reading Culture and Writing Practices in Nineteenth Century France. University of Toronto Press, Toronto.

Madej, K., 2016. Interactivity, Collaboration, and Authoring in Social Media. Springer.

Marcon, S., 1986. Esempi di xilominiatura nella Biblioteca di San Marco. Ateneo Veneto: Revista di Scienze, Lettere ed Arti CLXXIII (1986), 173–193.

Marcon, S., 1987. Ornati di penna e di pennelo: appunti su scribi-illuminatori nella Venezia del maturo umanesimo. La Bibliofilia 89, 121–144.

Marcon, S., 2003. Figure, tra penelli e legni. In: Zorzi, M. (Ed.), La vita nei libri. Edizioni illustrate a stampa del Quattro e Cinquecento dalla Fonnazione Giorgio Cini. Edizioni della Laguna, Venezia, pp. 55–80.

Martin, H.J., 1995. *The History and Power of Writing*, trans. Lydia Cochrane. The University of Chicago Press, Chicago & London.

Matthews, N., Moody, N. (Eds.), 2007. Judging a Book by Its Cover. Fans, Publishers, Designers, and the Marketing of Fiction. Ashgate Publications, London.

McCleery, A., 2019. Publihing History. In: Phillips, A., Bhaskar, M. (Eds.), The Oxford Handbook of Publishing. Oxford University Press, Oxford, pp. 21–38.

McKitterick, D., 2005. Print, Manuscript and the Search for Order. 1450–1830. Cambridge University Press, Cambridge.

McKitterick, D., 2018. The Invention of Rare Books: Private Interest and Public Memory, 1600–1840. Cambridge University Press.

McLuhan, M., 1997. Understanding Media. The Extensions of Man. MIT Press, Cambridge Massachusetts–London [ed. pr. 1964].

Miglio, M., 1983. Dalla pagina manoscritta alla forma a stamapa. La Bibliofilia LXXXV, 249–256.

Morison, S., 1949. Four Centuries of Fine Printing. Two Hundred and Seventy-Two Examples of the Work of Presses established between 1465 and 1924. Ernest Benn Limited, London.

Murray, S., 2007. publishing studies critically mapping research in search of a discipline. Publishing Research Quarterly 23, 3–25.

Parshall, P., 2015. Preface. In: Stijnman, A., Savage, E. (Eds.), Printing Colour 1400–1700. History, Techniques, Functions and Receptions. Brill, pp. xii–xvi.

Partington, G., 2019. In: Dunkan, D., Smyth, A. (Eds.), Book Parts. Oxford University Press, Oxford, pp. 11–24.

Peltz, L., 2017. Facing the Text. Extra-illustration, Print Culture, and Society in Britain, 1769–1840. Huntington Library Press, San Marino.

Peltz, L., 2018. The Extra-Illustration of London.: the gendered spaces and practices of anti-quarianismin the late eighteenth century. In: Myrone, M., Peltz, L. (Eds.), Producing the Past. Aspects of Antiquarian Culture and Practice. 1700–1850. Routledge (ed. pr. Ashgate Publishing 1998).

Bibliography

Phillips, A., 2014. Turning the Page. The Evolution of the Book. Routledge, Abington. Oxon & New York.

Phillips, A. (Ed.), 2015. The Cottage by the Highway and Other Essays on Publishing. 25 Years of Logos. Brill, Leiden–Boston.

Phillips, A., 2019. Publishing and Corporate Social Responsibility. In: Phillips, A., Bhaskar, M. (Eds.), The Oxford Handbook of Publishing. Oxford University Press, Oxford, pp. 147–161.

Phillips, A., Bhaskar, M., 2019. The Oxford Handbook of Publishing. OUP, Oxford.

Phillips, A., Kovac, M., 2022. Is this a Book? Cambridge University Press, Cambridge.

Reid, P., 2019. Reading by Design. The Visual Interfaces of the English Renaissance Book. The Toronto University Press, Toronto, Buffalo, London.

Reid-Walsh, J., 2017. Interactive Books. Playful Media Before Pop-Ups. Routledge, New York–Abington OX.

Rhodes, N., Sadway, J. (Eds.), 2000. The Renaissance Computer. Knowledge Technology in the First Age of Print. Routledge, London & New York.

Richardson, B., 1994. Print culture in renaissance Italy. The Editor and the Vernacular Text, 1470–1600. Cambridge University Press, Cambridge.

Richardson, B., 1999. Typography, Writers and Readers in Renaissance Italy. Cambridge University Press, Cambridge.

Scolari, C.A., 2019. Networks: from text to hypertext, from publishing to sharing, from single author to collaborative production. In: Phillips, A., Bhaskar, M. (Eds.), The Oxford Handbook of Publishing. Oxford University Press, Oxford, pp. 127–146.

Sherman, W.H., 2005. Toward a history of the manicule. In: Myers, R., Harris, M., Mandelbrote, G. (Eds.), Owners, Annotators, and the Signs of Reading. Oak Knoll Press, pp. 19–48. http://www.livesandletters.ac.uk/papers/FOR_2005_04_001.pdf.

Sherman, W.H., 2010. Used Books. Marking Readers in Renaissance England. University of Pennsylvania Press.

Sherman, W.H., 2011. The Beginning of *The End*. Terminal paratext and the birth of print culture. In: Smith, H., Wilson, L. (Eds.), Renaissance Paratexts. Cambridge University Press, Cambridge, pp. 65–83.

Smith, M.M., 2000a. The Title-Page. Its Early Development. 1460–1510. Oak Knoll Press.

Smith, M., 2000b. Medieval roots of the Renaissance printed book: An essay in design history. In: Tucker, G.H. (Ed.), Forms of the "Medieval" in the "Renaissance": A Multidisciplinary Exploration of a Cultural Continuum. Rookwood Press, Charlottesville, pp. 143–153.

Smith, H., Wilson, L. (Eds.), 2011. Renaissance Paratexts. Cambridge university Press, Cambridge.

Smyth, A., 2018. Material Texts in Early Modern England. Cambridge University Press, Cambridge.

Smyth, A., 2024. The Book Makers. A History of the Book in 18 Remarkable Lives. The Bodley Head, London.

Squires, C., 2007. Marketing Literature. The Making of Contemporary Writing in Britain. Palgrave Macmillan, New York.

Stijnman, A., Savage, E., 2015. Printing Colour 1400–1700. History, Techniques, Functions and Receptions. Brill.

Striphas, T., 2009. The Late Age of Print. Everyday Book Culture from Consumerism to Control. University of Columbia Press, New York, Chichester, West Sussex.

Thompson, J.B., 2010. Merchants of Culture. The Publishing Business in the Twenty-First Century. Polity Press, Cambridge.

Thompson, J.B., 2021. Book Wars. The Digital Revolution in Publishing. Polity Press, Cambridge.

Werner, S., 2019. *Studying Early Printed Books, 1450–1800. A Practical Guide*. Wiley–Blackwell.

188 Bibliography

Williams, H., 2021. *Laurence Sterne and the Eighteenth Century Book*, Cambridge. Cambridge University Pres.

Wolff, K., 1991. Kurt Wolff. A Portrait in Essays & Letters. The University of Chicago Press, Chicago & London.

Zappella, G., 1988a. Il ritratto nel libro italiano del Cinquecento. Editrice Bibliografica, Milano, 2 volumes.

Zappella, G., 1988b. Iniziali "parlanti" nel libro italiano del Rinascimento. Grafica 6 (1988), 56–77.

Zappella, G., 1989. Incisione, illustrazione, figura. (L' iniziale). Miscellanea Marciana di Studi Bessarionei II-IV (1987–1989), 221–260.

Zappella, G., 1998. Le marche dei tipografi e degli editori italiani del '500. Editrice Bibliografica, Milano, 2 volumes.

Zappella, G., 2004. Il libro antico a stampa. Struttura, techniche, tipologia, evoluzione. Editrice bibliografica, Milano.

Zappella, G., 2013. L' Iniziale. Vecchiarelli, Manziana.

Further reading

Banou, C., 2011. Backlist and frontlist, bestsellers and longsellers in a small publishing market: the case of the Greek Publishing Industry at a turning point. International Journal of the Book 8 (2), 139–154.

Barchas, J., 2013. Graphic Design, Print Culture and the Eighteenth Century Novel. Cambridge University Press, Cambridge.

Baverstock, A., 2012. Are publishers born or made? Logos 23 (1), 30–37.

Bhaskar, M., 2015. Towards paracontent. marketing, publishing and cultural form in a digital environment. In: Phillips, A. (Ed.), The *Cottage by the Highway and Other Essays on Publishing. 25 Years of Logos*. Brill, Leiden–Boston, pp. 275–291.

Bornstein, G., 2006. Material Modernism. The Politics of the Page. Cambridge University Press, Cambridge.

Cavallo, G., Chartier, R. (Eds.), 1999. Storia Della Lettura Nel Mondo Occidentale. Edizioni Laterza, Roma–Bari.

Cerf, B., 1977. At Random. The Reminiscences of Bennett Cerf. Random House Trade Paperbacks, New York, with an introduction by Christopher Cerf.

Donati, L. (1967). "Le iniziali iconografiche del XVI secolo," στο *Studi Bibliografici. Atti del Convegno dedicato alla storia del libro italiano nel V centenario dell' introduzione dell' arte tipografica in Italia* (Bolzano, 7–8/10/1965), Firenze, 219–239.

Epstein, J., 2001. Book Business. Publishing. Past, Present and Future. W. W. Norton & Company, New York–London.

Finkelstein, D., McCleery, A. (Eds.), 2001. The Book History Reader. Routledge, New York & London.

Finkelstein, D., McCleery, A., 2012. An Introduction to Book History, second edition Routledge, New York & London.

Gillies, M.A., 2007. The Professional Literary Agent in Britain. 1880–1920. The University of Toronto Press, Toronto–Buffalo–London.

Goldman, P., Cooke, S., 2016. Reading Victorian Illustration, 1855–1875: Spoils of the Lumber Room, second edition Routledge, London & New York.

Grafton, A., 1999. L' umanista come lettore. In: Cavallo, G., Chartier, R. (Eds.), Storia della lettura nel mondo occidentale. Edizioni Laterza, Roma–Bari, pp. 199–242.

Haining, P., 1979. Movable Books: An Illustrated History, 1979. New English Library, London.

Haskell, F., 1980. Patrons and Painters: A Study in the Relations between Italian Art and the Society in the Age of the Baroque, second edition Yale University Press, New Haven & London.

Bibliography

Haynes, C., 2010. Lost Illusions. The Politics of Publishing in Nineteenth Century France. Harvard University Press, Cambridge Massachusetts and London.

Horrocs, J., 2022. Reforming the *Art Preservatve*: nineteenth century British printing manuals and the discourse for design. Book History 25, 351–382.

Ionescu, C., 2011. Book Illustration in the Long Eighteenth Century: Reconfiguring the Visual Periphery of the Text. Cambridge Scholars.

Janzen-Cooistra, L., 2011. Poetry, Pictures and Popular Publishing. The Illustrated Gift Book and Victorian Visual Culture. 1855–1873. Ohio university Press, Athens-Ohio.

Johnson, M., 2019. What is a book? Redefining the book in the digitally social age. Publishing Research Quarterly 35, 68–78.

Kist, J., 2008. New Thinking for 21st Century Publishers. Emerging Patterns and Evolving Stratagems. Chandos Publishing, Oxford.

Kovac, M., Phillips, A., van der Weel, A., Wicshenbart, R., 2019. What is a book? Publishing Research Quarterly 35, 313–326.

Logos, 2005. The Literature of the Book. A Select Bibliography with Critical Essays, of Books By, About and For the Book Professions. Logos, Oxford.

Miller, L.J., 2007. *Reluctant Capitalists. Bookselling and the Culture of* Consumption. The university of Chicago Press, Chicago & London.

Mondadori, M., 1985. Una Tipografia in Paradiso. Mondadori, Milano.

Montanaro, A.R., 1993. Pop-Up and Movable Books: A Bibliography. Scarecrow Press, Metuchen, N.J.

O'Leary, B., 2011. Context first: a unified field theory of publishing. Publishing Research Quarterly 267, 211–219.

Penguin, 1985. Fifty Penguin Years. Penguin, Middlesex.

Penguin, 2007. Seven Hundred Penguin Covers. Penguin, London.

Phillips, A., 2017. Have we passed Peak Book? The uncoupling of book sales from economic growth. Publishing Research Quarterly 33, 310–327.

Primeau, T., 2002. The technology and materials of renaissance and baroque hand-colored prints. In: Dackermann, S. (Ed.), Painted Prints. The revelation of Color in Northern Renaissance and Baroque Engravings, Etchings and Woodcuts. Pennsylvania State University Press, Pennsylvania.

Rickets, R. (Ed.), 2002. Adventurers All. Tales of Blackwellians of Books, Bookmen, And Reading and Writing Folk. Blackwell's, Oxford.

Robertson, F., 2013. Print Culture. From Steam Press to Ebook. Routledge, New York and London.

Rosen, J., 2003. The horizon of a new discipline: inventing book studies. Publishing Research Quarterly 19, 11–19.

Ross, E., 2014. Picturing Experience in the Early Printed Book. Breydenbach's Peregrinatio from Venice to Jerusalem. The Pennsylvania State University Press, Pennsylvania.

Saenger, M., 2006. The Commodification of Textual Engagements in the English Renaissance. Ashgate, London.

Sher, R.B., 2006. The Enlightenment and the Book. Scottish Authors and Their Publishers in Eighteenth Century Britain, Ireland & America. The University of Chicago Press, Chicago & London.

Squires, C., 2010. The history of the book in Britain from 1914. The Oxford Companion to the Book. Oxford University Press, Oxford, pp. 188–193.

Stepanova, M., 2007. Disciplinary duality: the contested terrain of book studies. Publishing Research Quarterly 23, 105–115.

Stoicheff, P., Taylor, A. (Eds.), 2014. The Future of the Page. University of Toronto Press, Toronto.

190 Bibliography

Sutherland, J., 2007. Bestsellers. A Very Short Introduction. Oxford University Press, Oxford.

Trettien, W., 2019. Title pages. In: Dunkan, D., Smyth, A. (Eds.), Book Parts. Oxford University Press, Oxford, pp. 39–49.

Turner, M., 2024. Chaucer in the twenty-first century. In: Turner, M. (Ed.), Chaucer Here and Now. Bodleian Library Publishing, Oxford, pp. 183–203.

Appendix 1
Illustrations

Picture 1

ἀνθρώπων ἐν ζυγοῖς τοῦ ἀδι-
κῆσαι. αὐτοὶ ἐκ ματαιότητος
ἐπιτοαυτό.
μὴ ἐλπίζετε ἐπ'ἀδικίαν καὶ ἐ
πὶ ἁρπαγμα μὴ ἐπιποθεῖτε.
πλοῦτος ἐὰν ῥέῃ μὴ προστί
θεσθε καρδίαν.
Ἅπαξ ἐλάλησεν ὁ θεός δύο
ταῦτα ἤκουσα ὅτι τὸ κρά-
τος τοῦ θεοῦ καὶ σοῦ κύριε
τὸ ἔλεος. ὅτι σὺ ἀποδώσεις
ἑκάστῳ κατὰ τὰ ἔργα αὐτοῦ.

ψαλμὸς τῷ Δαυὶδ ἐν τῷ
ἐναι αὐτὸν ἐν τῇ ἐρήμῳ τῆς
ἰουδαίας. ξβ.

Ὁ θεός ὁ θεός μου·
πρός σε ὀρθρίζω.
ἐδίψησέ σε ἡ ψυχή μου. ποσα
πλῶς σοι ἡ σάρξ μου.
ἐν γῇ ἐρήμῳ καὶ ἀβάτῳ καὶ ἀ
νύδρῳ οὕτως ἐν τῷ ἁγίῳ ὤ-
φθην σοι τοῦ ἰδεῖν τὴν δύνα-
μίν σου καὶ τὴν δόξαν σου.
ὅτι κρεῖσσον τὸ ἔλεός σου ὑ-
πὲρ ζωάς. τὰ χείλη μου ἐπαι
νέσουσί σε.
οὕτως εὐλογήσω σε ἐν τῇ ζωῇ

hominum in libris iniuriam
facere. ipsi ex uanitate
simul.
Non sperate in iniusticiam. &
in rapinam non concupiscite.
diuitiæ si fluant non appo-
nite cor.
Semel locutus est deus. duo
hæc audiui quoniam pote-
stas dei & tui domine
misericordia. quoniam tu reddes
unicuique secundum opera eius.

Psalmus dauid in
esse eum in solitudine
iudææ.lxii.

Deus deus mei
ad te manico.
Sitiuit te anima mei. multipli-
citer tibi caro mei.
In terra deserta & inuia & in a-
quosa sic in sancto appa-
rui tibi uidere uirtu-
tem tui. & gloriam tui.
Quoniã melior misericordia tui su
per uitas. labia mei lauda
bunt te.
Sic benedicam te in uita

I i

Picture 2

Illustrations

Io. Lascaris Rhyndacenvs Petro Medici. S.

C VM graecas litteras qvae per mvltas iam aetates sopitae nõ minvs profvnda qvam latinae dõrmitatione obtorpverant. experrectas sensim qve ab interitv se se recipientes inspice rem. vt eas aliqvando a fedissima barbarie. qva di v iam et iniqvissimé opprimvntvr in pristinvm nitorem et dignitatem remeare posse confiderem. Non alienvm ab officio meo esse existimavi. vt si qvid esset in qvo his opitviari possem. qvicqvid foret id tandem praestare eniterer. atqve adeo mõnitvs Epicteti sententia. qvi nec minima in qvo vis stvdiopraecipit esse despicienda. novam hanc et litterarvm stvdiosis pervtilem imprimendi oc casionem nactvs litterarvm graecarvm elementa a deformi et indecenti admodvm depravatione vendicare cõnstitvi. Cvm qve animadverterem ea rvm notas. qvae inpraesentia svnt in vsv impressio ni adhibitas nec excvdi commode nec apte invicem cohaerere posse. qvod perplexae nimivm et circvm volvtae sint priscas litterarvm figvras iam div obsoletas diligéntivs inqvisivi atqve hvic impri mendi artificio per excvsores atqve idgenvs opi fices accommodatas impressoribvs tradidi. cvravi qve vt his epigrammatvm ante omnia rarissimvm et egregivm opvs in qvampivrima editvm exempla ria litterarvm stvdiosis passim legendvm exhibere tvr. qvo ex hac re librorvm qvoqve penvriae pro

Picture 3

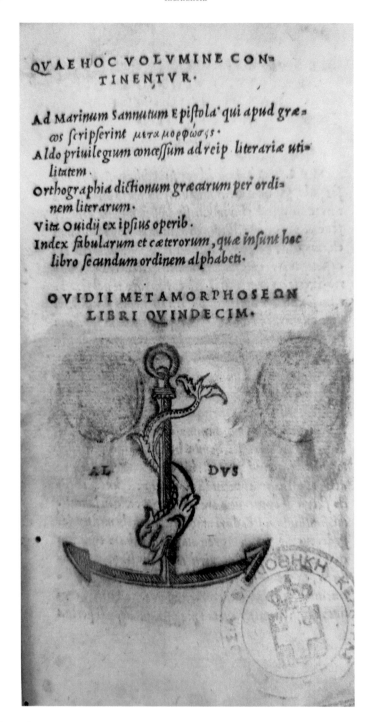

Picture 4

atq; ubi opportunum fuerit fine ulla penitus contra=
dictione publicandam curetis·quemadmodum in ue
stra obedientia maxime confidimus· et de Amicorū be
neuolentia plene speramus· Datæ in nostro ducali pa
latio Die·XIIII·Nouemb· indictione sexta·M·DII·

LAVS DEO·

INDEX *græcolatinus di*
ctionum græcarum in
libris transmutationum
ouidij secundum ordi=
nem Alphabeti· ubi oēs
casus· quos mutuare a
græcis latini cõsueuerūt,
et latine, et græce cum
suis accentibus adnotan
tur·remittitur autem le=
ctor ad semipaginam in
qua dictio est· quæ semi=
paginæ sunt· 404·

  BANTEVS
a   *abantea·aban=*
    teum· ὁ ἀβάν
    τgos ἡ ἀβαντgα
τὸ ἀβάντgον ·380·
A *bantiades·abantiáden·*
ὁ ἀβαντιάδης · ον ἀβαν =
τιάδην· IOI·

A *baris·abaridos· et aba*
rios abarida·et abarin·
ὁ ἄβαρις· τ8 ἀβάριδος· κ̣
ἀβάριος ·ον ἀβάριδα· και
ἄβαριν · III·
A *bas· ábantos· ábanta·*
ὁ ἄβας· τοῦ ἄβαντος· τὸν
ἄβαντα · λυικέως και ὑπερ
μνήσρας ὑός· II2·
A *castus·acaston· ὁ ἄκασος·*
ον ἄκασον· 194·
A *ctiacus·actiaca·actiacū·*
ὁ ἀντιακός· ἡ ἀντιακή·
ον ἀντιακόν· 338·
A *æstes·acesten· ὁ ἀκέσης·*
ον ἀκέσην· 349·
A *chaia·achaian· ἡ ἀχαία*
τὴν ἀχαίαν· 325·
A *carnán·acarnános·acar=*
nána·acarnánes·acarná
num·acarnánas· ὁ ἀκαρ
ναν· τ8 ἀκαρνᾶνος· ον ἀ=

            a iiii

Picture 5

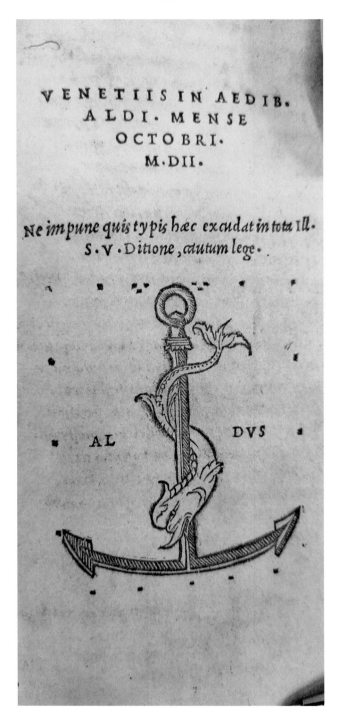

Picture 6

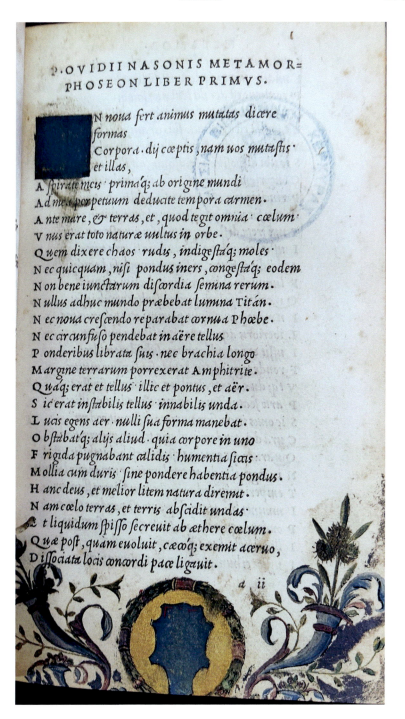

Picture 7

Picture 8

PETRI GYLLII
DE
BOSPORO
THRACIO,

LIBER PRIMVS.

VM Novam Romam Conſtantinopolitanam ſim deſcripturus, mihi priùs deſcribendus videtur Boſporus, princeps creator Byzantii, melior & præſtantior, quàm Byzas hujus Vrbis conditor; (quamvis hic optimus & Deo ſimillimus fuiſſe traditur;) quo Vrbs

Picture 10

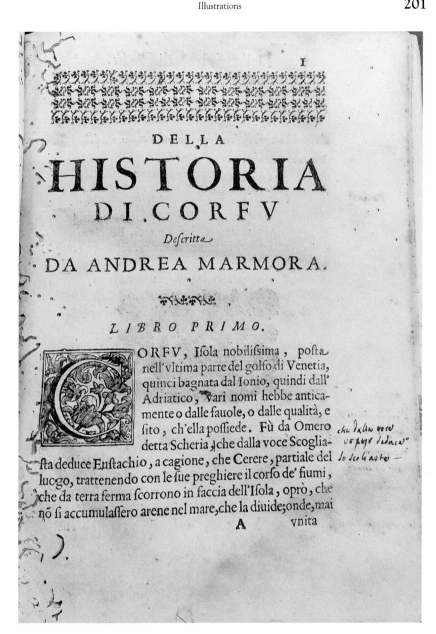

DELLA
HISTORIA
DI CORFV
Descritta
DA ANDREA MARMORA.

LIBRO PRIMO.

ORFV, Ifola nobilifsima, pofta nell'vltima parte del golfo di Venetia, quinci bagnata dal Ionio, quindi dall' Adriatico, vari nomi hebbe anticamente o dalle fauole, o dalle qualità, e fito, ch'ella poffiede. Fù da Omero detta Scheria, che dalla voce Scoglia-fta deduce Euftachio, a cagione, che Cerere, partiale del luogo, trattenendo con le fue preghiere il corfo de' fiumi, che da terra ferma fcorrono in faccia dell'Ifola, oprò, che nō fi accumulaffero arene nel mare, che la diuide; onde, mai
A   vnita

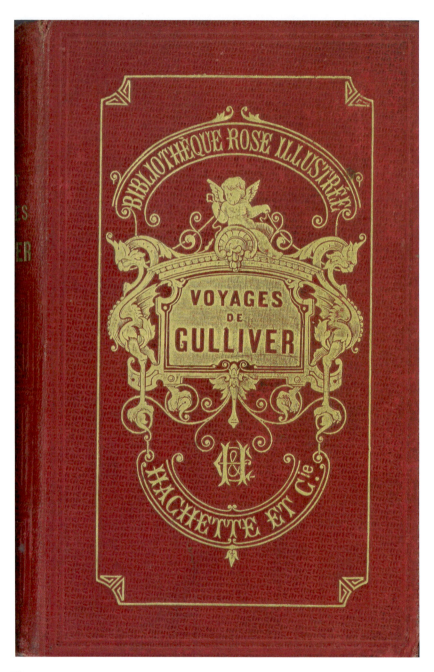

Picture 12

VOYAGES
DE GULLIVER

A LILLIPUT, A BROBDINGNAG

ET AU PAYS DES HOUYHNHNMS

PAR SWIFT

TRADUITS DE L'ANGLAIS
ET ABRÉGÉS A L'USAGE DES ENFANTS

AVEC 57 GRAVURES

NOUVELLE ÉDITION

PARIS

LIBRAIRIE HACHETTE ET Cie

BOULEVARD SAINT-GERMAIN, 79

1872

Tous droits reservés

Picture 13

204

Illustrations

10 VOYAGE

tout à fait en liberté; et à l'égard des habitants, c'était avec raison que je me croyais d'une force égale aux plus puissantes armées qu'ils pourraient mettre sur pied pour m'attaquer, s'ils étaient tous de même taille que ceux que j'avais vus jusquelà. Mais la fortune me réservait un autre sort.

Quand ces gens eurent remarqué que j'étais tranquille, ils cessèrent de me décocher des flèches; mais par le bruit que j'entendis, je connus que leur nombre s'augmentait considérablement; et, environ à deux toises loin de moi, vis-à-vis de mon oreille gauche, j'entendis un bruit pendant plus d'une heure, comme des gens qui travaillaient. Enfin, tournant un peu ma tête de ce côté-là, autant que les chevilles et les cordons me le permettaient, je vis un échafaud élevé de terre d'un pied et demi, où quatre de ces petits hommes pouvaient se placer, et une échelle pour y monter, d'où un d'entre eux, qui me semblait une personne de condition, me fit une harangue assez longue, dont je ne compris pas un mot. Avant de commencer, il s'écria trois fois : *Langro Dehul san*. Ces mots furent répétés ensuite, et expliqués par des signes pour me les faire entendre. Aussitôt cinquante hommes s'avancèrent, et coupèrent les cordons qui attachaient le côté gauche de ma tête, ce qui me donna la liberté de la tourner à droite, et d'observer la mine et l'action de celui qui devait parler. Il me

A LILLIPUT. 11

parut être de moyen âge, et d'une taille plus grande que les trois autres qui l'accompagnaient, dont

Un d'entre eux me fit une harangue. (Page 10.)

l'un, qui avait l'air d'un page, tenait la queue de sa robe, et les deux autres étaient debout de cha-

Picture 14

206 VOYAGE AU PAYS DES HOUYHNHNMS.

son honorable famille et pour tous ses amis, j'osais assurer qu'on ne croirait jamais dans mon pays qu'un Houyhnhnm fût un animal raisonnable, et qu'un Yahou ne fût qu'une bête.

Ils ont des Yahous pour les servir. (Page 208.)

CHAPITRE IV.

Idées des Houyhnhnms sur la vérité et sur le mensonge. Les discours de l'auteur sont censurés par son maître.

Pendant que je prononçais ces dernières paroles, mon maître paraissait inquiet, embarrassé, et comme hors de lui-même. Douter et ne point croire ce qu'on entend dire, est parmi les Houyhnhnms une opération d'esprit à laquelle ils ne sont point accoutumés, et lorsqu'on les y force, leur esprit sort, pour ainsi dire, hors de son assiette naturelle. Je me souviens même que, m'entretenant quelquefois avec mon maître au sujet des propriétés de la nature humaine, telle qu'elle est dans les autres parties du monde, et ayant occasion de lui parler du mensonge et de la tromperie, il avait beaucoup de peine à concevoir ce

Picture 15

10   CES PAUVRES PETITS!

bisaïeule sévère et noble; et la ville basse, son arrière-petite-fille, gaie et marchande. La ville haute a conservé sa physionomie du moyen âge. Elle serre autour de sa basilique romane, comme une poule des poussins, ses maisons démodées, noires, humides, presque désertes, où ne logent plus que quelques chanoines paralytiques et tranquilles. Toutes les rues de la ville basse l'escaladent joyeusement, mais deviennent subitement tristes avec ses paliers en cailloux de la Loire et ses rampes en fer tordu.

Un beau matin, par une de ces rues tortueuses, froides et ennuyées, débouchèrent, comme deux cigales de printemps, le petit Gennaro et sa sœur Maïa.

Gennaro avait un chapeau pointu décoloré, un court manteau de drap bleu, des chiffons autour des jambes, et les jambes, jusques au ventre, dans des bottes démesurément longues, larges, épaisses et lourdes. Un ancien gendarme retraité et compatissant les lui avait données un jour de grosse pluie, je ne sais où. Maïa portait le joli costume italien bariolé; quelques lambeaux de linge retenus par des ficelles lui emmaillotaient les pieds. Un mouchoir en marmotte sur la tête, et, autour des reins, un lé d'étoffe autrefois verte : c'était tout.

« Nous voici près d'un *dôme* voué à la madone,

Gennaro et Maïa.

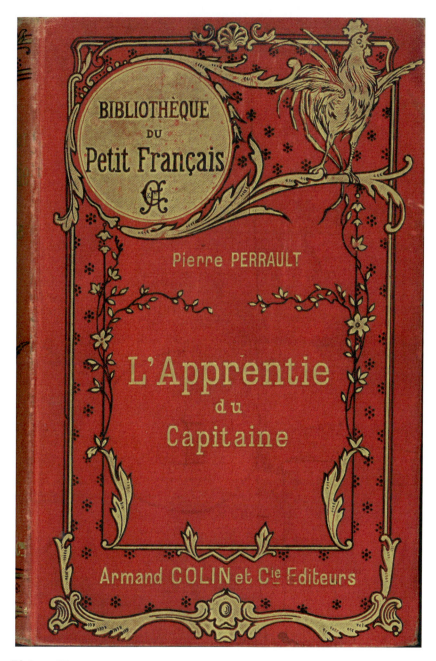

Picture 17

24   L'APPRENTIE DU CAPITAINE

« Tu l'as connu, toi, ce Joseph de ma marraine?
— Non. Les Prussiens l'ont tué pendant la guerre, la grande guerre, tu sais?
— Oui. Il était donc soldat?
— Non. Il paraît qu'il avait un pied déformé : il ne pouvait servir.
— Alors, ils sont venus le tuer chez sa maman, le pauvre!
— Tu n'y es pas; je vais te raconter toute l'histoire. Je l'entends une fois par jour la semaine et deux fois le dimanche, tu peux croire que je la sais.

« Cette pauvre mère Rigot, elle est bonne comme le bon pain, mais elle répète toujours la même chose.

« Elle avait donc ce garçon, rien que lui. Il s'appelait Joseph, comme moi; et le fils du capitaine Rugle...

— Qu'est-ce que c'est que le capitaine?
— Je te l'expliquerai tout à l'heure. Son fils, donc, avait une bonne place; il était ingénieur dans une usine, aux environs de Paris. Il connaissait Joseph Rigot depuis son enfance, ils allaient ensemble à l'école. Alors, il l'avait fait nommer contremaître dans son usine. Ce M. Rugle, l'ingénieur, était marié et il avait un petit garçon.

« Il faut te dire que son père, le capitaine, n'était pas riche, il ne possédait que sa maison et une ferme valant vingt-cinq mille francs, à peu près, de l'avis de la mère Berthon.

FILLEULE ET PARRAIN   25

« Ah! il faut te dire encore qu'il était veuf, le capitaine, et qu'il s'est remarié. De ce second

Jocelyne se prélassait dans la chaudière.

mariage, il y a une fille. Elle s'appelle Édith. On dit qu'elle est bien gentille.

3

Picture 19

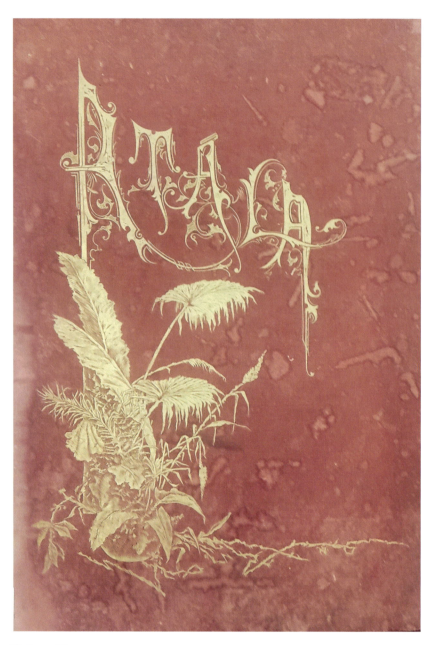

Picture 20

PROLOGO

Una volta la Francia possedeva nell'America settentrionale un vasto dominio che andava dal Labrador alla Florida, dalle rive dell'Atlantico ai laghi più remoti dell'alto Canada.

Quelle immense regioni erano spartite da quattro fiumi che avevano le loro sorgenti nelle stesse montagne: il San Lorenzo, che a mezzodì si perde nel golfo dello stesso nome; il fiume di Ponente, che manda le sue acque a mari sconosciuti; il Borbone, che da mezzogiorno a settentrione si precipita nella baia di Hudson, e il Mississipi, che da nord a mezzodì va a sboccare nel golfo del Messico.

Quest'ultimo fiume per un giro di più che mille leghe bagna una contrada deliziosa che gli abitanti degli Stati Uniti chiamano il nuovo Eden; i Francesi le lasciarono il nome di Luigiana. Molti altri fiumi tributari del Mississipi, quali il Missuri, l'Illinese, l'Akanza, l'Ohio, il Wabash, il Tennessee, la fecondano del loro limo e la fertilizzano di loro acque. Quando per le pioggie stemperate dell'inverno, tutti questi fiumi si sono gonfiati, quando le bufere hanno abbattuto intere distese di foreste, gli alberi sradicati si ammucchiano alle sorgenti e in breve la mota li cementa, le liane li incatenano, e altre piante per ogni parte mettendo radici finiscono di consolidare quei rottami di selve. Così sospinti dai flutti spumanti essi scendono il Mississipi. Il fiume, avuti in suo dominio, li spinge nel golfo messicano e li incaglia sopra banchi di sabbia, moltiplicando così il numero delle sue foci. Di tanto in tanto il fiume ingrossa la sua voce passando sotto le montagne e lancia le sue acque straripanti tra i fusti degli alberi alti come colonne, e d'intorno alle piramidi delle tombe indiane. E come il Nilo di quel deserto. Ma nelle scene della natura alla magnificenza si accoppia sempre la grazia. E mentre la corrente trascina nel mezzo i tronchi morti dei pini e delle quercie, sulle due correnti dei lati si veggono emergere, lungo le spiaggie, delle isole fluttuanti di borraccine e di ninfee, i cui fiori gialli si alzano come piccoli padiglioni. E li verdi serpenti, aironi azzurri, fenicotteri rosati e giovani coccodrilli si imbarcano insieme, passeggeri sullo stesso battello di fiori. E la colonia, spiegate al vento le sue vele d'oro, va ad approdare sonnacchiosa in qualche seno appartato del fiume.

Le due sponde del Mississipi presentano il quadro più meraviglioso. Su quella occidentale le savane si stendono a perdita di vista, le onde di quella verdura, allontanandosi, pare che ascendano verso l'azzurro del cielo, dileguando in esso. Per quelle praterie senza limiti si vedono errare alla ventura degli armenti di fino a tre o quattromila bufali selvaggi. Qualche volta un bisonte decrepito, tagliando le acque a nuoto, viene a straiarsi fra le alte erbe in una delle isolette del fiume. Alla fronte lunata di corna, alla barba antica e fangosa, tu lo piglieresti per il Dio del fiume che gira l'occhio soddisfatto sulla vastità delle sue acque e la selvaggia abbondanza delle sue rive.

Questa vedi sulla sponda occidentale; ma la scena muta sulla sponda opposta e forma un ammirevole contrasto. Sospesi sul corso delle acque, aggruppati sugli scogli e sulle montagne, sparsi qua e là per le vallate, alberi di tutte le forme, di tutti i colori, di tutti gli odori, si mischiano, crescono insieme, spingendo tronchi e rami ad altezze che affaticano lo sguardo. Le viti selvatiche, le bignonie, le coloquintidi s'intrecciano ai piedi degli alberi e su su danno la scalata ai rami, serpeggiano all'estremità delle volte e, lanciandosi dall'acero al tulipano, dal tulipano all'alcea, vengono a formare lunghe fughe di grotte, di volte, di porticati. Talora avviene che quelle liane, svinte d'albero in albero, traversano dei bracci di fiumi e vi gettano sopra dei ponti di fiori. Dal seno di quella foltezza la magnolia eleva il suo cono immobile, e coronata delle sue larghe rose bianche domina tutta la foresta; e non ha rivale che la palma, che vicino a lei leggermente molleggia i suoi ventagli di verdura.

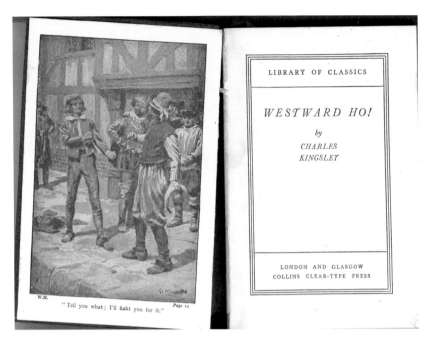

Picture 22

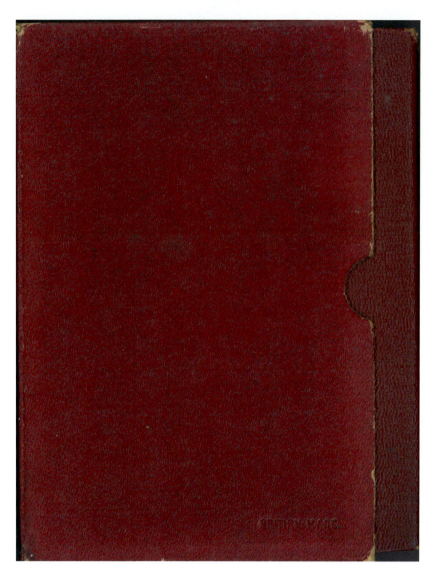

Picture 23

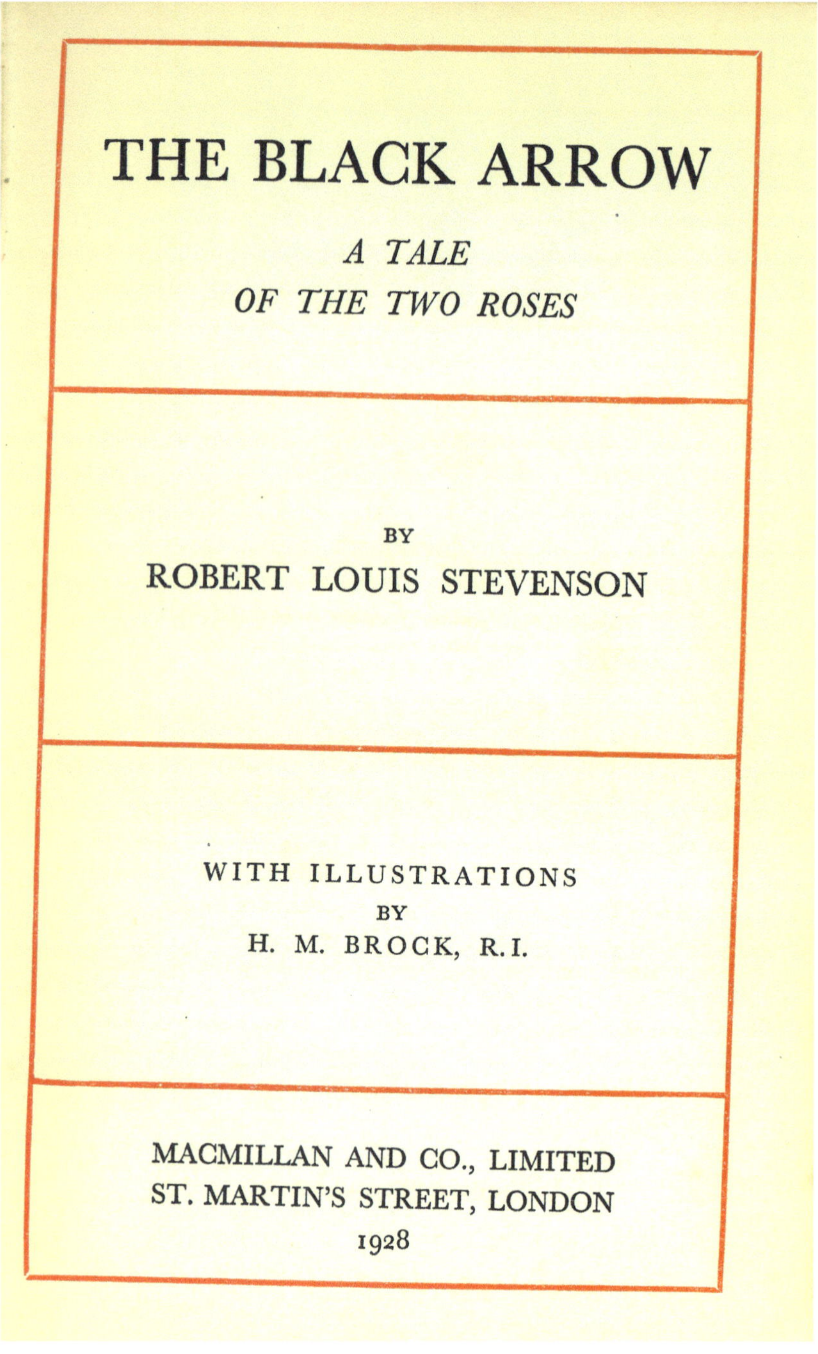

THE BLACK ARROW

A TALE
OF THE TWO ROSES

BY

ROBERT LOUIS STEVENSON

WITH ILLUSTRATIONS
BY
H. M. BROCK, R.I.

MACMILLAN AND CO., LIMITED
ST. MARTIN'S STREET, LONDON
1928

Picture 24

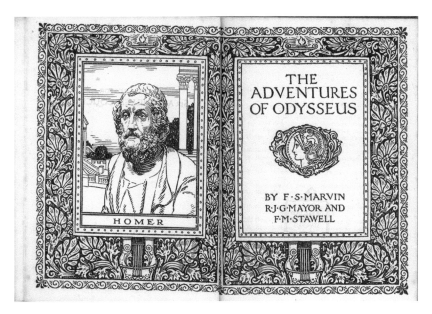

Picture 25

Appendix 2
List of illustrations

1. *Psalterium*, Bonus Accursius, Milano 1481. Hand-illuminated first page of the text.
2. *Psalterium*, Bonus Accursius, Milano 1481, p. Ii. Rubricated initials.
3. *Anthologia Graeca Planudea*, ed. Janus Lascaris, Lorenzo de Alopa [Impressum Florentiae per Laurentiium Francisci de Alopa Venetum], Florence 1494. First page of the dedication to Petro Medici by the scholar Janus Lascaris. Guide letter.
4. Ovidii *Metamorphoseon libri quindeci.*, Aldus Manutius, Venice 1502, title-page, One of the "Libri portatiles."
5. Ovidii *Metamorphoseon libri quindecim.*, Aldus Manutius, Venice 1502, p. aiiii, Guide letter.
6. Ovidii *Metamorphoseon libri quindecim*, Aldus Manutius, Venice 1502, colophon with the printer's mark.
7. Ovidii *Metamorphoseon libri quindecim*, Aldus Manutius, Venice 1502. Hand-illuminated first page of the text "Oviddi Nasonis Metamorphoseon liber primus."
8. P. Gyllii, *De Bosporo, Thracio Lib. III*, Lugduni Batavorum (Leiden), Apud Elsevirios, 1632, title-page.
9. P. Gyllii, *De Bosporo, Thracio Lib. III*, Lugduni Batavorum (Leiden), Apud Elsevirios, 1632, Headpiece and initial letter.
10. Petri Cunaei, *De Repubblica Hebraeorum Libri III*, Ludg. Batavor. (Leiden), Ex Officina Elzeviriana, 1632, title-page. One of the books of the *Republics* series.
11. Andrea Marmora, *Della Historia di Corfu Libri otto*, Presso il Curti, Venice 1672. First page of the text, Headpiece and initial.
12. Jonathan Swift, *Voyages de Gulliver à Lilliput, à Brobdingnag et au pays des houyhnhnms: traduits de l'anglais et abrégés à l'usage des enfant.* Nouvelle éd. Paris: Librerie Hachette et cie, 1872, cover
13. Jonathan Swift, *Voyages de Gulliver à Lilliput, à Brobdingnag et au pays des houyhnhnms: traduits de l'anglais et abrégés à l'usage des enfant.* Nouvelle éd. Paris: Librerie Hachette et cie, 1872, title-page
14. Jonathan Swift, *Voyages de Gulliver à Lilliput, à Brobdingnag et au pays des houyhnhnms: traduits de l'anglais et abrégés à l'usage des enfant.* Nouvelle éd. Paris: Librerie Hachette et cie, 1872, p. 10−11, headlines, pagination, illustration in the text.

218

List of illustrations

15. Jonathan Swift, *Voyages de Gulliver à Lilliput, à Brobdingnag et au pays des houyhnhnms*: traduits de l'anglais et abrégés à l'usage des enfant. Nouvelle éd. Paris: Librerie Hachette et cie, 1872, p. 206−207. Tailpiece and vignette as Headpiece, pagination, head-chapter.
16. Aime Giron, Aime (1882), *Es Pauvres Petits!*, Paris: Librerie Hachette et cie., 1882. p. 10−11.
17. Perrault, Pierre (1898*), L' apprentie du capitaine*, illustrated by Marcel Lecoultre, Paris: Armand Colin et cie, cover
18. Pierre Perrault, *L' apprentie du capitaine*, illustrated by Marcel Lecoultre, Paris: Armand Colin et cie, 1898, p. 24−25
19. *Description du Sacre et du Couronnement de leurs Majestés Impériales l'Empereur de toutes les Russies Alexandre III et l'Imperatrice Marie Féodorovna en l'année 1883*, St. Petersburg 1883.
20. Francesco Renato visconte di Chateaubriand, *Atala*, co' disegni di Gustavo Dore', (12 vignette nel testo e 30 tavole staccato), preface and translation Enrico Panzacchi, Tipografia Lombardi, Milano 1887, [Gift by the newspaper *Corriere della Sera* to its subscribers], Hard cover. Large sized (38,5x27,6 cm; 27 pages). Cover in red.
21. Francesco Renato visconte di Chateaubriand, *Atala*, co' disegni di Gustavo Dore', (12 vignette nel testo e 30 tavole staccato), preface and translation Enrico Panzacchi, Tipografia Lombardi, Milano 1887, [Gift by the newspaper *Corriere della Sera* to its subscribers], illustrations by G. Dore', prologue.
22. Charles Kingsley, *Westward Ho!*, London and Glascow: Collins Clear-Type Press, 1900?, frontispiece and title-page.
23. Charles Kingsley, *Westward Ho!*, London and Glascow: Collins Clear-Type Press, 1900? slipcase.
24. Robert Lewis Stevenson, *The Black Arrow. A Tale of the Two Roses*, with illustrations by H. M. Brock, Macmillan & Co, London 1928, title-page.
25. F. S. Marvin, R. J. Mayor and F.M. Stanwell, *The Adventures of Odysseus*, J. M. Dent & sons, London 1941 [first published in this edition 1920), frontispiece and title-page.

Pictures 1−11, 19−21: Books from the Central Public Library of Corfu, after permission to publish.
Pictures 12−18, 22−25: Books from the author's personal Library.

Index of names

A
Accursius, Bonus, 66, 131–132
Aldus Manutius, 5, 11–12, 30, 33–34, 44, 58–59, 68, 93–96, 101–102, 112–118, 126–127, 131, 139, 172–173
Alopa de, Lorenzo, 138–139
Amman, Jost, 65, 92

B
Bertelli, Pietro, 71–72
(Le) Blon, Jacob Christoff, 67
Budé, Guillaume, 139

C
Caracci, Agostino, 92
Carroll, Lewis, 105
Caxton, William, 23–24, 46
Cervantes (de), Miguel, 119
Chaucer, Geoffrey, 43–44, 48
Colin, Armand, 83, 86–87, 103
Collett, Anna, 141–142, 146–147
Collett, Mary, 141–142, 146–147
Corriere della Sera, 84, 103
Cranach, Lucas, 92

D
Daumier, Honore', 92
Dean, George, 73–74
Dean, Thomas, 73–74
Dent, J. M. & Sons, 78–79, 99
Dore, Gustave, 84, 92
Duerer, Albrecht, 92

E
Elzevir, Abraham, 116
Elzevir, Bonaventure, 116
Elzevirs (Elzeviers), 11–12, 34, 94–95, 97, 116
Euclid, 63

F
Ferdinandus, Alexandre, 83
Fuller. S & J., 72–74
Fust, Johann, 66, 177

G
Galen, 53, 64
Giron, Aime, 83
Granger, James, 142–143
Griffo, Francesco, 113
Grandville, Jan–Jacques, 82–83
Gutenberg, Johannes, 2, 6–7, 23–24, 32–33, 62, 65, 101–102

H
Hachette, Louis, 61, 81–83, 86–87
Holbein, Hans the Younger, 92

K
Kalliergis, Zacharias, 53, 64, 68
Koberger, Anton, 33–34, 102, 172–173

L
Lane, Allen, 112–118, 172–173
Lascaris, Janus, 138–139
Lecoultre, Marcel, 83

M
Macmillan Publishing, 95–96
Marchand, Prosper, 99
Marvin, F. S., 99
Mayor, R. J. G., 99
Medici, Pietro, 138–139
Montemagno, Bonaccursius, 23–24
(de) Monvel, Louis-Maurice Boutet, 83
Moxon, Joseph, 60, 64
Mueller, Johannes - v. Regiomontanus, 70
Musaeus, 114

N
Nister, Ernest, 74–75

220

Index of names

O
Ovidius, 93—94, 114—115, 127, 131

P
Penguin Books, 30, 112—114, 116—117
Perrault, Pierre, 83
Peutinger, Conrad, 63
Plantin, Christoph, 118, 172—173
Poussin, N., 92

R
Ratdolt, Erhard, 63, 70
Regiomontanus (Johannes Mueller), 70
Reni, Guido, 92
Reuwich, Erhard, 86
Richardson, Samuel, 5, 7, 21—22, 33, 39, 44,
    47—49, 79—80, 90, 95, 99—100, 110,
    126—127, 129—130, 138
Rubens, Peter-Paul, 92

S
Sachs, Hans, 65
Sandoz, Adolf Karol, 83
Schoeffer, Peter, 65, 177
Shakespeare, William, 95
Speght, Thomas, 48
Spenser Edmund, 76
Stanwell, F. M, 99
Stern, Laurence, 47—48
Stevenson, Robert Lewis, 95—96
Swift, Jonathan, 81—82

T
Theocritus, 68

V
Vesalius, Andrea, 71

Y
Young, Edward, 116—117

Index of terms

A

Aesthetic capital of publishing industry, 13–15
Almanac, 23–24, 34–36, 75–77, 79–80, 113–114, 151–152
Antiporta, 98–99
Audio books, 3, 6, 10–12, 178

B

Back matter, 17, 97, 100–101, 110–111, 127, 138–139, 173–174, 178–179
Bibliography, 22–27
Bibliotheque du Petit Francais, 83
Blurb, 88, 104–105
Business models, 4–5

C

Calendar/Calender, 34, 70, 75–77, 79–80, 113–114, 151–152
Carmina figurata, v. Technopaignia, 68–69
Catchwords, 17, 49–50
Chapter drop, 42
Chapter heads, 17, 26, 41–43, 53–54
Children's book publishing, 72–75
Chromolithography, 67, 72–74, 137–138
Colophon, 17, 25, 84, 87–89, 100–102, 131–132
Coloring books, 3, 6, 57, 67, 85–86, 145, 151, 153–154, 163, 165
Converged aesthetics, 15
  evolution of luxury copies and deluxe editions, 121–132
    categorization of luxury copies, 126–132
    defining luxury copies and editions, 121–126
  post-luxury copy, 140–154
    customized copies, 145–147
    cut-and-paste books, 141–142
    extra-illustration and reader engagement, 142–145

personalized publishing services nowadays, 147–153
  reader creativity, 153–154
  systemization of deluxe and limited editions from the Renaissance to nowadays, 133–140
  commemorative editions, 137–138
  dedications, 138–140
  deluxe, limited, collectable, exclusive editions, 133–137
  facsimiles, 140
  (numbered) prints that accompany the edition, 140
  uses of, 154–157
Cover, 6, 17, 29, 87–88, 91, 93, 97, 103–105, 132, 148, 151, 171
Crowdfunding, 3–4
Cut-and-paste (techniques), 26, 141–142, 153–154, 156, 164

D

Decoration, 50–51
Dedication, 34–35, 63, 137–139, 148, 151–152
Deluxe edition, 64, 79–80, 105, 134, 138–139
Democratization of taste, 106–107
Discoverability, 109–112
Dust cover, 103–104
Dust jacket, 6, 17, 29, 91–92, 95, 103–105, 111–112, 118–119, 122, 149–151
Dust wrapper, 103–104

E

Edges of the book, 64, 86–87, 129–130, 135, 149
End matter, 30, 35, 100
Endnotes, 34–35, 100–101
Engraving, 26, 55, 65, 80, 92, 107, 125–128, 134, 153–154
Excluded edition, 63
Extra-illustration, 26, 142–147, 163, 165–166

221

222

Index of terms

F

Facsimile, 19, 140
Fist, 45, 48
Flap, 71, 73–74, 104–105
Fleurons, 17, 26, 35, 41, 50, 59–61, 89
Flowers v. fleurons and printer's flowers,
   59–60
Folding Pages, 86
Foliation, 17, 34–35, 46–47, 49–50,
   114–116
Footnotes, 34–35, 50
Fore-edge, 43, 87
Front matter, 30, 35, 87–89, 97–100,
   138–139, 155, 173–174
Frontispiece, 17, 26, 34–35, 78–79, 84,
   88–89, 95, 98–99, 112, 132, 165–166

G

Gold (printing in / printed in), 17, 63–64,
   82–83, 103
Gravure, 61, 81–82, 111

H

Half-page, 53, 93–94
Harlequinade, 72
Hand director, 45
Hand-illumination / Hand-illuminated, 52,
   55, 64–66, 76–77, 108–109, 120, 122,
   124, 126–127, 131–132, 145,
   151–152, 163
Headline (page-headline, section-headline,
   running-headline), 17, 28, 34–41,
   137–138, 151
Headpiece, 17, 28, 40–42, 50–54, 59–61,
   114, 129–130, 137–138
Horseless carriage period, 17, 21–34, 118

I

Illustration, 1–2, 7–8, 14, 17, 25–26, 28,
   34–36, 39–40, 55–56, 61–62, 69–70,
   73–74, 78, 81–86, 94–95, 98, 107,
   117–118, 121–122, 131–132,
   163–164, 175–178
Index, 17, 34–35, 45, 51–52, 84–85, 93–94,
   100–101
Indicationum, 45
Indicator, 45
Indicule, 45
Information mechanisms, 87–106
   colophon, 101–102
   cover and dust jacket, 103–105

end of the book, back matter, 100–101
frontispiece, 98–99
frontmatter, 87–88
portrait of the author and the rise of
   authorship, 99–100
slipcases, 105–106
title-page, 88–98
Initial, 17, 25, 28, 34–35, 52, 54–59, 61–62,
   114–115, 127, 131–132, 164
Italics, 113

J

Jacket, 103–104

L

Libri portatiles, 5, 33–34, 58–59, 113–114,
   131
Limited edition, 6, 31–32, 59, 129, 133,
   139–140, 173–174
Lithography, 67, 73–74, 78–79, 98
Living pictures, 73–74
Luxury copy/ies, 123

M

Manicule, 17, 28, 34–35, 45–49
Maniple, 45
Map, 34–35, 71, 86, 100–101, 146
Margin, 17, 30, 43–44, 46, 48, 124,
   129–130
Marginal heads, 43–44
Marginalia / marginal notes, 17, 25, 32,
   34–35, 43–44, 155
Materiality, 2, 8, 26, 67, 74, 76, 109, 134, 140,
   146, 159–160
Metamorphosis, 72
Movable books, 73–74
Movable parts, 17, 69–75
Mutton fist, 45

N

Notebook, 2, 44, 75–76, 107–108, 154–155,
   164

O

Occhietto, 96–97
Ornament / ornamentation, 14, 16–17, 46

P

Pagination, 17, 30, 32, 34–36, 39–41,
   49–50, 80, 115–116

Index of terms

223

Paper, 7–8, 13–14, 19, 30, 52, 63, 69–70, 72–73, 103–104, 124–125, 129, 154, 163–164
Parchment, 63, 124, 126–129
Personalized publishing services, 147–153
Piccoli ferri tipografici, 59–60
Pilcrow, 45
Printer's flowers, v. fleurons, 102
Printer's mark, 80, 83, 88–89, 92–97, 100–102
Printing revolution, 5
Pointer, 45, 69–70
Pointing hand, 45, 47

R

Reader creativity, 153–154
Reader participation engagement, 11
Reframing, 159–176
  books as desirable, complex devices, 159–162
  complex uses, 166–168
  convergence of media, 168–170
  customized book and personalized publishing services, 165–166
  discoverability, promotion, and visual identity, 171–173
  publishing industry and democracy, 174–176
  from reader engagement to reader creativity, 162–165
  short forms, multipaged books and the reintroduction of classics, 173–174
  visual expectations and adventures, 170–171
Renaissance, 2–6, 15, 19–20, 22, 24, 26, 30, 34–35, 41, 44, 47, 51–53, 64–65, 67–68, 78–79, 88, 93–94, 96–97, 99–100, 110–111, 114–115, 120, 123, 126, 128, 136, 138, 148–150, 153–155, 160, 163–165, 174–175, 177–179
Rubrication /rubricated, 8–9, 14, 35, 39, 52, 54–55, 62, 66, 123–126, 129–132, 170
Rubricator, 49, 66, 125–126
Running titles, 17, 26, 28, 32, 34–41, 60, 82
Running-head, v. Running title(s), 37

S

Self-publishing, 3–4, 8–11, 100, 155, 165–166, 178
Setting, 30–34
Signatures, 17, 34–35, 40, 49–50, 75

Signed books, 138–140
Silent books, 6, 12, 85–86, 175–176
Slipcase, 17, 105–106, 137–138, 173–174
Skeleton of a forme, 40
Stencil(s), 65–67, 130
Subchapter, 42–43, 54–55, 59–60
Subheads, 41–43

T

Tailpiece, 17, 28, 50, 53–54, 61, 129–130
Technopaignia (*Carmina figurata*), 68–69
Title-page, 88–98
  architectural title-pagers, 96–97
  with printed decorative framework/ borde, 95–96
  with the printer' s mark/device, 93–94
  with portrait, 95
  simple title-page, 97
  with vignette/illustrations, 94–95
Toy books, 73–74
Trichromatic printing, 67
Typographic identity, 3

V

Vellum, 8, 19, 33–34, 63, 69, 124, 126–127, 129, 131, 137–139, 163–164
Visual dialogs, 109–112
Visual identity, 3
  aesthetic capital of publishing industry, 13–15
  democratization of taste, 106–107
  establishing everyday book culture from Aldus Manutius to Allen Lane, 112–118
  horseless carriage period, 21–34
    bibliography, 22–27
    scene of books, setting, 30–34
  information, discoverability and visual dialogs, 109–112
  information mechanisms, 87–106
    colophon, 101–102
    cover and dust jacket, 103–105
    end of the book, back matter, 100–101
    frontispiece, 98–99
    frontmatter, 87–88
    portrait of the author and the rise of authorship, 99–100
    slipcases, 105–106
    title-page, 88–98
  redefining, 4–10
  structure of, 15–20

224 Index of terms

Visual identity (*Continued*)
  understanding publishing industry, 10–13
  visual expectations of the readers, 107–109
  visual evolution and information mechanisms of, 1–4
  visual order of the page, 34–87
    almanacs, calendars, manuals, and other practical books, 75–77
    chapter heads and subheads, 41–43
    children's book publishing, 72–75
    decoration, 50–51
    edges of the book, 86–87
    fleurons, 59–61
    folding pages, 86
    foliation, pagination, catchwords, signatures, 49–50
    headlines and running titles, 36–41
    headpieces, 51–54
    illustration, 77–86
    initials, 54–59
    manicule, 45–49
    margins, marginal notes, marginal heads, 43–44
    printing in color and colored prints, 64–67
    printing in gold, 63–64
    printing in red, 61–63
    tailpieces, 61
    Technopaignia (*carmina figurata*), 68–69
    volvelles and movable parts, 69–72
Volvelle, 17, 69–72, 74

W

Woodcut, 26, 55, 57, 65, 68, 77–80, 107, 125–128, 130–132, 170–171

X

Xilo-miniatura, 127–128

Printed in the United States
by Baker & Taylor Publisher Services